CROSSCURRENTS *Modern Critiques*

CROSSCURRENTS *Modern Critiques*
Harry T. Moore, *General Editor*

Contemporary American Novelists

EDITED BY

Harry T. Moore

Carbondale

SOUTHERN ILLINOIS UNIVERSITY PRESS

FIRST PUBLISHED, OCTOBER 1964
SECOND PRINTING, MARCH 1965

Library of Congress Catalog Card Number 64–20254
Printed in the United States of America
Designed by Andor Braun

ACKNOWLEDGMENTS

THE EDITOR AND PUBLISHERS of this volume wish to thank the authors for their contributions. Previously published articles are noted below, and acknowledgment is made to the authors and publishers for their kind permission to reprint the articles here.

"Some Children of the Goddess" by Norman Mailer first appeared in *Esquire*, July, 1963. It is reprinted by permission of Norman Mailer.

"The War Writers Ten Years Later" by John W. Aldridge was published in the *New York Times Book Review*, July 29, 1962, under the title "What Became of Our Postwar Hopes?" It is reprinted by permission of the *New York Times Book Review*.

CONTENTS

INTRODUCTION

Harry T. Moore

THE NOVELISTS DISCUSSED in this book are strictly contemporary, belonging to the newest phase of American writing. A few of them began to publish in the early 1940s,
but the majority of them are postwar.

The present volume is, for the most part, made up of
essays on individual authors, occasionally a pair of writers
in one chapter. The only sections of the book which have
appeared before are the first two. Norman Mailer's "Some
Children of the Goddess" was published in *Esquire* for
July 1963, and John W. Aldridge's "The War Writers Ten
Years Later" was in *The New York Times Book Review*
of July 29, 1962. It seemed best to put these before the essays which give more extended treatment to
many of the writers whom Mr. Mailer and Mr. Aldridge
discuss. The later critiques of these same authors may often
disagree with that of Messrs. Mailer and Aldridge, just as
the various writers of those pieces will occasionally have
different views from one another about certain authors,
as cross reference will show. This is all to the good: de-
mocracy at its finest permits healthy and courteous disagreement.

Not that the criticism in this book is lacking in savor.
The Mailer-Aldridge articles get it off to a lively start, and
they plainly say what they are for and against; but, like the
other contributors, they don't, in expressing disagreement
or disapproval, indulge in insult. And this is all that I am
going to say about the contents of the book, for the authors

represented in it speak for themselves, as I've noted; and indeed an essay of my own appears among these and gives me plenty of chance for self-expression. Later on in this introduction I'll mention a few other books on the newer American novel, and in going over them will indicate a few tendencies which critics of it have discerned. Otherwise my function here is to introduce our contributors.

Norman Mailer least of all needs an introduction, and his own works are discussed specifically in one of the essays and referred to in others. Suffice to say here that, since *The Naked and the Dead* (Putnam, 1948), Mr. Mailer has published some nonfiction, a book of verse, two more novels (with another, *An American Dream*, appearing at this moment as a serial in *Esquire*). In giving permission for the present article to be included here, Mr. Mailer expressed the wish that we might also reprint the piece he had written for *Esquire* a month earlier (June 1963), in which he discussed the idea of contemporaries writing on contemporaries. Regrettably, in trying to keep the books in this series to a set length so that the price of the volumes may be standard, we didn't have room to include that essay and can only refer the reader to it.

John W. Aldridge really invented organized criticism of the postwar novel, in *After the Lost Generation* (McGraw-Hill, 1951). *In Search of Heresy* (McGraw-Hill, 1956) dealt with the subject further, as have various reviews and articles Mr. Aldridge has written for leading periodicals over the years. He has lectured in the Christian Gauss seminars at Princeton, has taught at several leading universities, and has lately held a Fulbright fellowship in Europe.

The book begins with the Mailer-Aldridge articles because they range widely and, in treating so many writers, have to do so with brevity; they are better placed at the start than at the finish, since if used for the latter they might have the effect of suggesting that they summarize the book, which they really don't. The reader can go on from them into the fuller treatment of the authors being considered. This material is generally arranged according to the chronology of those writers: their ages or, some-times, the first publication of their books.

First we have two women novelists, Carson McCullers and Eudora Welty, whose first volumes appeared respec-tively in 1940 and 1941. Marvin Felheim, who discusses these two authors, is Professor of English at the University of Michigan. He was co-editor of *Modern Short Stories* (1952), and his own works include *The Theater of Augus-tin Daly* (Harvard, 1956) and *Comedy: Plays, Criticism, Theory* (Harcourt, 1962).

Paul Schlueter, who writes on Mary McCarthy (whose first book appeared in 1942), teaches at Southern Illinois University and contributes criticism to various American periodicals. Charles Alva Hoyt, author of the chapter on Bernard Malamud, teaches at Bennett College. He is now writing an essay on Muriel Spark for a volume similar to this in the Crosscurrents/Modern Critiques series, on the recent British novel; a book which will follow in the course of time.

Frederick J. Hoffman, who writes on Saul Bellow, is the author of numerous volumes, including *Freudianism and the Literary Mind* (Louisiana, 1945; revised 1957), *The Twenties* (Viking, 1955), and the Crosscurrents book *Samuel Beckett: The Language of Self* (1962, re-printed 1964 as a paperback by Dutton). He is professor of English at the University of California, Riverside. Sir Richard Rees, who has been for a long time praising J. D. Salinger in England, formerly edited *The Adelphi*. He is a painter as well as a writer. For the Crosscurrents series he wrote *George Orwell: Fugitive from the Camp of Victory* (1961), and his other books include *Brave Men* (Southern Illinois University Press, 1961) and A *Theory of My Time* (Secker and Warburg, 1963). For Oxford University Press he has edited *J. Middleton Murry: Se-lected Criticism* (1960), and for the same publishers he is editing the complete works of Simone Weil.

Norman Mailer has his turn to be talked about, along with James Jones, in the chapter by Edmond L. Volpe of the City College of New York who, with his colleague

Leo Hamalian edited *Ten Modern Short Novels* (Putnam, 1958). In 1964 Mr. Volpe brought out *A Reader's Guide to William Faulkner* (Noonday Press) and is preparing a study of Thornton Wilder for Crosscurrents/Modern Critiques. The article on Jack Kerouac, by Professor Howard W. Webb, Jr., of Southern Illinois University, grew out of a number of conversations I held with Mr. Webb a few years ago about the Beatniks. I was just becoming interested in them and discovered that Mr. Webb was far ahead of me on the subject, so that later, when this book was being prepared, I felt that he was precisely the man to write on Kerouac, with some asides about the Beatnik movement in general. Mr. Webb's principal interest is Ring Lardner, on whom he has written in various professional journals, also publishing bibliographical material on Lardner.

In New York City in the summer of 1961 I heard Frederick R. Karl of City College speak with intense interest of Joseph Heller's *Catch-22*, just then coming out (I'd read parts of it, at least of an earlier version, in *New World Writing*, and as a sometime member of the Air Force had found it amusing). Frederick Karl has written two volumes on the modern English novel, one of them in collaboration with Marvin Magalaner, both books published in the Noonday Press's Reader's Guide series. Mr. Karl is now editing *The Complete Letters of Joseph Conrad* for Stanford University Press. Gerald Weales, who writes about James Purdy and J. P. Donleavy in the present book, is the author of a novel, *Tale for a Bluebird* (Harcourt, 1961) and *American Drama Since World War II* (Harcourt, 1962), and has written and edited other books on the drama. He teaches at the University of Pennsylvania.

Kay Boyle, author of *Thirty Stories* (Simon and Schuster, 1946; New Directions paperback since 1957) is the author of numerous novels, the first of which, *Plagued by the Nightingale* (Jonathan Cape and Harrison Smith, 1931), will soon be reprinted by Southern Illinois University Press. Miss Boyle, teaching at Radcliffe for the 1964–65 school year, is a member of the faculty of San

Francisco State College. She has long been interested in the work of James Baldwin, and has permitted us to reprint here her brief introduction of him at Wesleyan College in 1962. James Baldwin is discussed at length in the following essay by Robert F. Sayre, who wrote it at Lund, Sweden, at whose university he was resident lecturer in American literature for 1963–64. Mr. Sayre, author of *The Examined Self: Henry Adams and Henry James and American Autobiography* (Princeton, 1962), teaches at the University of Illinois.

The editor's appearance here as commentator on the work of Herbert Gold is *faute de mieux*. Several critics who were approached with an invitation to write on Mr. Gold were unable to do so in time to meet our deadline, so when we were about to go to press I decided to step in. I wasn't a stranger to Herbert Gold's work, since I had written about two of his volumes for *The New York Times Book Review* and knew all the others, had indeed several times taught *The Man Who Was Not With It* (as *The Wild Life*). Charles Shapiro, who kindly suggested to me two or three of the contributors to this volume, has written about Harvey Swados for it. Mr. Shapiro, author of the Crosscurrents volume, *Theodore Dreiser: Our Bitter Patriot* (1962, paperback 1964), is an old hand at editing collections of literary essays: he collaborated with Alfred Kazin on *The Stature of Theodore Dreiser* (Indiana, 1955), and on his own edited volumes of essays on great American and British novels for Wayne State University Press. He is now preparing the Crosscurrents anthology of criticism on the present-day English novel.

S. K. Oberbeck, of the *St. Louis Post-Dispatch*, writes on John Hawkes, of whose work he has long been a student; Mr. Oberbeck publishes criticism for various magazines, and for the *Post-Dispatch* comments on books and art; he is also a columnist for *Focus/Midwest*. William Van O'Connor, who writes on William Styron and John Updike, is the author of two volumes in the Crosscurrents series: *The Grotesque: An American Genre* (1962) and *The New University Wits* (1963). An extremely versatile critic, Mr. O'Connor is also the author of *The Tangled Fire of William Faulkner* (Minnesota, 1954) as well as several other volumes, and he has edited *Forms of Modern Fiction* (Minnesota, 1948) as well as writing a book of college short stories, *Campus on the River* (Crowell, 1959). William Van O'Connor is head of the English department at the University of California at Davis. Our final contributor, Terry Southern, who writes on John Rechy and Robert Gover, collaborated with Richard Seaver and Alexander Trocchi on the anthology *Writers in Revolt* (Frederick Fell, 1963). He has written two novels, *Flash and Filigree* (Coward-McCann, 1958) and *The Magic Christian* (Random House, 1960), and is co-author of a novel first published by Olympia Press in Paris in 1958, and with its American edition, published by Putnam in 1964, attracting great attention: *Candy*.

I may add that, if Ken Kesey's second novel, *Sometimes a Great Notion*, to be published in July 1964 by Houghton Mifflin, had come in before the present book went to press, I might have added a chapter on Kesey, also author of *One Flew Over the Cuckoo's Nest* (Houghton Mifflin, 1962): he is crude but has great force.

Now, before closing, I'll mention a few books on the recent American novel. John W. Aldridge's *After the Lost Generation* (McGraw-Hill, 1951) has been referred to previously. In this study, Mr. Aldridge contrasts the novelists of the first-war generation (such as Ernest Hemingway, F. Scott Fitzgerald, and John Dos Passos) with those who came after the later world war. He finds the earlier authors superior, but discovers good points in several of the newer writers. Among war books, he praises Norman Mailer's *The Naked and the Dead* (Putnam, 1948) as a combat novel, and speaks highly of two war novels which deal chiefly with behind-the-lines personnel: Vance Bourjaily's *The End of My Life* (Dial, 1947) and John Horne Burns's *The Gallery* (Harper, 1947). Mr. Aldridge also discusses Paul Bowles, Truman Capote, Frederick Buechner, and others, as well as the new themes the newer authors frequently write of, such as the race problem and homosexuality. Mr. Aldridge's next volume, *In Search of Heresy* (McGraw-Hill, 1956), is an appraisal, not always praising, of various older and newer writers, among the latter including J. D. Salinger, William Styron, and Saul Bellow. The book also deals with the literary scene in general and points out the danger with which university teaching threatened writers.

In 1957, Granville Hicks edited *The Living Novel* (Macmillan), a series of essays by ten contemporary writers, including three discussed in the present volume: Saul Bellow, Herbert Gold, and Harvey Swados. They all talk interestingly about the problems of the author in today's world. Among the three novelists just mentioned, Saul Bellow wrote on "Distractions of a Fiction Writer," Herbert Gold on "The Mystery of Personality in the Novel," and Harvey Swados on "The Image in the Mirror." All the contributors present a good case for the novel against what Mr. Hicks calls its enemies, which as he points out are numerous, at low, middle, and highbrow levels. But "the serious novel is needed and, happily for us, it is being written. . . . Whether a genius appears or not, I view the future of the novel without alarm: it is safe in the hands of the men and women who have contributed to this volume [*The Living Novel*] and in the hands of others as talented and devoted as they. . . . Not fewer people but more are likely to become convinced that, whatever else may be expendable in contemporary American life, the serious novel isn't." In Herbert Gold's essay, the reaffirmation of faith in the novel seems almost to re-echo what D. H. Lawrence said a little more than a generation ago. Mr. Gold states, "At its best, the art of the novel tells us more that we can find out elsewhere about love and death."

Leslie Fiedler's *No! In Thunder* (Beacon, 1960) covers a wide range of subjects, occasionally touching upon the younger novelists. His *Love and Death in the American Novel* (Criterion, 1960) mentions Saul Bellow and others, but concerns itself chiefly with background and historical depth. But *Waiting for the End* (Stein and Day, 1964) comes within the scope of our subject and expands upon Saul Bellow, Herbert Gold, Robert Gover, Bernard Malamud, Norman Mailer, and others involved in it. Leslie Fiedler is always pungent, and what he chiefly asks for is a good argument, for which he happily provides all the subject matter.

Ihab Hassan's *Radical Innocence* (Princeton, 1961) is a rather full study of American novelists born since 1910, ranging from Norman Mailer, Saul Bellow, and Carson McCullers to J. D. Salinger, Bernard Malamud, Truman Capote, and others; James Purdy and John Updike are regarded as too "new" to be considered. Mr. Hassan is one of those critics more interested in ideas than technique. Too much literary criticism is entirely conceptual; it could learn from art and music criticism, in which the importance of the technical is emphasized. In literature, both the conceptual and the technical should be considered, as they are by the critics in the present volume. In Mr. Hassan's book, he offers many valuable observations on the thematic side. His "radical innocence," the quality he finds in so many American writers, is a discovery by Mr. Hassan that their innocence ("those simplicities which, rightly or wrongly, have been identified with vision in America") has not given way to experience but rather has become more radical, going to the roots, becoming increasingly anarchic and visionary. The hero in our time, Mr. Hassan points out, has become both victim and rebel, and Mr. Hassan believes that the proper mode of expression for this hero is, then, the middle ground of irony. These ideas are forcefully presented, but the authors involved are discussed as if they all used exactly the same language, the same images, the same cadences, and developed character and plot in precisely the same way.

In Henry Anatole Grunwald's *Salinger* (Harper, 1962), the editor says, "There is a feeling in some quarters that altogether too much fuss is being made about J. D. Salinger"—right! Some of the commentators Mr. Grunwald includes are hardly enthusiastic about Salinger, for example John Updike, Maxwell Geismar, Leslie Fiedler, and Alfred Kazin, the last of whom says he regrettably has to apply the word *cute* to Salinger. *Rocking the Boat*, by Gore Vidal (Little, Brown, 1962), is aimed as much at politics and the theater as at the contemporary novel, but the book contains several pertinent essays on that subject as well as separate chapters on Carson McCullers and Norman Mailer. Similarly, Herbert Gold's collection of essays, *The Age of Happy Problems* (Dial, 1962), is largely concerned with social topics, yet it contains a few chapters on current literature, including one on "Fiction of the Sixties." LeRoi Jones's *The Moderns: An Anthology of New Writing in America* (Corinth Books, 1963), has some valuable introductory comments. The anthology includes work by two of the authors discussed in the present book, Jack Kerouac and John Rechy, and also presents a number of other writers, including William Burroughs, Robert Creeley, and Diane Di Prima; it is good to see several items by Michael Rumaker, author of a fine, sensitive first novel, *The Butterfly* (Scribner's, 1962).

An across-the-board treatment of various present-day novelists characterizes *The Creative Present: Notes on Contemporary American Fiction*, edited by Nona Balakian and Charles Simmons (Doubleday, 1963). The authors discussed include: James Baldwin, Mary McCarthy, Vladimir Nabokov, Norman Mailer, Eudora Welty, and J. D. Salinger, with Saul Bellow and William Styron sharing a chapter, James Jones and Jack Kerouac likewise, and Bernard Malamud, Herbert Gold, and John Updike considered together in a section entitled "Fiction of the Fifties." Harvey Breit, Robert Gorham Davis, Mark Schorer, and Diana Trilling are among the critics looking over these novelists. The evaluations are concise and usually valuable. Alfred Kazin's *Contemporaries* (Atlantic-Little, Brown, 1962) takes up a great deal of its space with European and earlier American authors, but also contains essays on J. D. Salinger, Saul Bellow, Bernard Malamud, Norman Mailer, J. F. Powers, Truman Capote, and others. Mr. Kazin is a critic of great range, humanistic at the center, aware of the expressional power of writing, and able to approach literature from many angles. His comments on these newer writers, as upon the older ones, represent a seasoned vision.

An ambitious attempt to encompass a good many novelists, Chester E. Eisinger's *Fiction of the Forties* (Chicago, 1963) examines various types of the novel—the naturalistic, the liberal, the conservative, and the humanistic, as well as the war novel and the "new" novel. Mr. Eisinger includes some older writers, such as William Faulkner but, among others, also treats Mary McCarthy, Budd Schulberg, Truman Capote, Carson McCullers, Eudora Welty, Paul Bowles, Wright Morris, and Saul Bellow. Again we have a critic who focuses largely upon ideas and pays little attention to authors' effectiveness in expressing them, but he often explores ideas profitably—"In Search of Man and America," and so on. The very comprehensiveness of Mr. Eisinger's examination of such themes gives his book a special value.

The Sense of Life in the Modern Novel, by Arthur Mizener (Houghton Mifflin, 1963) concerns itself generally with authors of the past, beginning with Anthony Trollope and Thomas Hardy, but coming up to present-day writers such as J. D. Salinger and John Updike. *Doings And Undoings,* by Norman Podhoretz (Farrar, Straus, 1964), is a collection of articles by the editor of *Commentary,* many of them literary—William Faulkner, F. Scott Fitzgerald, John O'Hara—coming up to such recent authors as Norman Mailer, Saul Bellow, Philip Roth, Joseph Heller, and James Baldwin; one chapter is entitled "A Dissent on John Updike." Mr. Podhoretz flashes a brilliant rapier, and sometimes his thrusts go deep; one of his famous *Partisan Review* articles is included here, "The Know-Nothing Bohemians," an attack on the Beatniks. In one essay, trying to explain the attractiveness of Joseph Heller's *Catch-22,* Mr. Podhoretz quotes a *Commentary* article by Philip Roth which complained that our world "is a kind of embarrassment to one's own meager imagination" as a novelist. "The actuality is continually outdoing our talents, and the culture tosses up figures almost daily that are the envy of any novelist. Who, for example, could have invented Charles Van Doren? Roy Cohn and David Schine? Sherman Adams and Bernard Goldfine? Dwight David Eisenhower?" As Mr. Podhoretz notes, "Anyone who follows the daily newspaper or watches television with some regularity will understand what Roth is getting at. We do often seem to be inhabiting a gigantic insane asylum, a world that, as Roth puts it, alternately stupefies, sickens, and infuriates. No wonder the American writer has so much difficulty 'in trying to understand, and then describe, and then make *credible* much of the American reality.'" But the novel is far from dead, Mr. Podhoretz suggests, as long as we have novels such as Heller's *Catch-22* and J. P. Donleavy's *The Ginger Man*.

In 1964, the English critic Walter Allen, author of several fine studies of the art of fiction and himself a writer of it, brought out *The Modern Novel In Britain and the United States* (Dutton). This book deals principally with writers who came up during the 1920–60 period, omitting those whose first books appeared after 1955. In an epigrammatic and lively fashion, which doesn't neglect considerations of the technical, Mr. Allen shows some interesting differences between the British and American novel, based chiefly on the former's awareness of class distinctions. Mr. Allen, who knows America from numerous visits and extended residence, suggests that it is both advantageous and otherwise for the writer in this country to work in isolation, frequently outside a tradition: isolation sometimes feeds his originality, sometimes subjects him to the spiritual starvation of parochialism. In the foregoing sentences I have paraphrased a small part of my review of Mr. Allen's book for *The Saturday Review* (June 20, 1964), which, after finding a few faults, ended: "This volume is in the main so good that it would be hard to imagine a better one, just now, on its double subject."

And, as I write this introduction, a new book comes in which is to be published on June 23, 1964: *After Alienation: American Novels in Mid-Century* by Marcus Klein (World). Mr. Klein examines in detail only five authors:

Saul Bellow, Ralph Ellison, James Baldwin, Bernard Malamud, and Wright Morris. His theme is that the heroes of modern American novels move from alienation from society to what Mr. Klein calls accommodation—not gray-flannel-suit or Marjorie Morningstar conformity, by any means, but rather a discovery by these heroes that their destiny lies not in isolation, but rather in joining the social battle in a somewhat existential mode of engagement. A largely conceptual critic, Mr. Klein, by concentrating on a few authors, gives himself a chance to develop his points at length.

Now it's time for our own book, which Norman Mailer begins as follows: "I doubt if there is any book I read in the last few years which I approached with more unnatural passion than . . ."—and, with that hard-punching, *in medias res* sentence, we're off!

Southern Illinois University
June 21, 1964

Contemporary American Novelists

SOME CHILDREN OF THE GODDESS

Norman Mailer

I DOUBT IF there is any book I read in the last few years which I approached with more unnatural passion than *Set This House on Fire*. Styron's first novel, *Lie Down in Darkness*, was published when he was twenty-six, and it was so good (one need today only compare it to *Rabbit, Run* to see how very good it was) that one felt a kind of awe about Styron. He gave promise of becoming a great writer, great not like Hemingway nor even like Faulkner whom he resembled a bit, but great perhaps like Hawthorne. And there were minor echoes of Fitzgerald and Malcolm Lowry. Since his first novel had failed to make him a household word in America, he had a justifiable bitterness about the obscurity in which good young writers were kept. But it poisoned his reaction to everything. One of the traps for a writer of exceptional talent, recognized insufficiently, is the sort of excessive rage which washes out distinction. Styron was intensely competitive—all good young novelists are—but over the years envy began to eat into his character. Months before James Jones's *Some Came Running* was published (and it had the greatest advance publicity of any novel I remember—for publicity seemed to begin two years before publication), Styron obtained a copy of the galleys. There were long nights in Connecticut on "Styron's Acres" when he would entertain a group of us by reading absurd passages from Jones's worst prose. I would laugh along with the rest, but I was a touch sick with myself. I had love for Jones, as well as an oversized fear for the breadth of his talent, and I had enough envy in me to enjoy how very bad were the worst parts of *Some Came Running*. But there were long powerful chapters as well; some of the best writing Jones has ever done is found in that book. So I would laugh in paroxysms along with the others, but I was also realizing that a part of me had wanted *Some Came Running* to be a major book. I was in the doldrums, I needed a charge of dynamite. If *Some Came Running* had turned out to be the best novel any of us had written since the war, I would have had to get to work. It would have meant the Bitch was in love with someone else, and I would have had to try to win her back. But the failure of *Some Came Running* left me holding onto a buttock of the lady—if she had many lovers, I was still one of them. And so everything in me which was slack and conservative could enjoy Styron's burlesque readings. Yet I also knew I had lost an opportunity.

A few months later, I ceased seeing Styron—it would take a chapter in a novel to tell you why. I liked the boy in Styron, disliked the man, and had vast admiration for his talent. I was hardly the one to read *Set This House on Fire* with a cool mind. Nine years had gone by since *Lie Down in Darkness* was published, and the anticipation of the second novel had taken on grandiloquent proportions among his friends and his closest enemies. One knew it would be close to unbearable if his book were extraordinary; yet a part of me felt again what I had known with *Some Came Running*—that it would be good for me and for my work if Styron's novel were better than anything any of us had done. So I read it with a hot sense of woe, delighted elation, and a fever of moral speculations. Because it was finally a bad novel. A bad maggoty novel. Four or five half-great short stories were buried like pullulating organs in a corpse of fecal matter: overblown unconceived philosophy, technicolor melodramatics, and a staggering ignorance about the passions of murder, suicide and rape. It was the magnum opus of a fat spoiled rich boy who could write like an angel about landscape and like an

adolescent about people. The minor characters were gar-
goyles, and badly drawn. Here and there quick portraits
emerged, there was one excellent still-life of an Italian
police official who was Fascist, the set pieces were laid out
nicely, but the vice of the talent insisted on dominating.
Whenever Styron didn't know what to do with his men
and women (which was often, for they repeated themselves as endlessly as a Southern belle), Styron went back
to his landscape; more of the portentous Italian scenery
blew up its midnight storm. But Styron was trying to write
a book about good and evil, and his good was as vacuous as
the spirit of an empty water bag:

> I can only tell you this, that as for being and nothingness,
> the one thing I did know was that to choose between them
> was simply to choose being, not for the sake of being, or
> even the love of being, much less the desire to be forever—
> but in the hope of being what I could be for a time.

Which is a great help to all of us.

His evil character took on the fatal sin of an evil
character: he was not dangerous but pathetic. A fink.
Styron was crawling with all ten thumbs toward that ogre
of mystery who guards the secrets of why we choose to kill
others and quiver in dread at the urge to kill ourselves. But
like a bad general who surrounds himself with a staff which
daren't say no, Styron spent his time digging trenches for
miles to the left and miles to the right, and never launched
an attack on the hill before him. It was the book of a
man whose soul had gotten fat.

And yet, much as I could be superior to myself for
having taken him thus seriously, for having written predictions in *Advertisements for Myself* that he would write a
very good book which the mass media would call great,
much as I would grin each day after reading a hundred
pages of hothouse beauty and butter bilge, much as I
would think, "You don't catch the Bitch that way, buster,
you got to bring more than a trombone to her boudoir,"
much so much as I was pleased at the moral justice which
forbids a novelist who envied too much the life of others to

capture much life in his own pages, I was still not altogether happy, because I knew his failure was making me complacent again, and so delaying once more the day when I would have to pay my respects to the lady.

And indeed I lost something by the failure of *Some Came Running* and *Set This House on Fire*. I never did get going far on my novel. I wrote a four-hour play and essays and articles, two hundred thousand words accumulated over the years since *Advertisements for Myself*, and I showed a talent for getting into stunts, and worse, much worse. Years went by. Now once again, in this season, ready to start my novel about the mysteries of murder and suicide, I found by taking stock of psychic credit and debit that I had lost some of my competitive iron. I knew a bit of sadness about work. I did not feel sure I could do what I had now settled for doing, and to my surprise I was curious what others were up to. If I couldn't bring off the work by myself, it might be just as well if someone else could give a sign of being ready to make the attempt. In this sad dull mellow mood, feeling a little like a middle-aged mountaineer, I read at one stretch over three weeks the novels I want to write about here.

There was a time, I suspect, when James Jones wanted to be the greatest writer who ever lived. Now, if *The Thin Red Line* is evidence of his future, he has apparently decided to settle for being a very good writer among other good writers. The faults and barbarities of his style are gone. He is no longer the worst writer of prose ever to give intimations of greatness. The language has been filed down and the phrases no longer collide like trailer trucks at a hot intersection. Yet I found myself nostalgic for the old bad prose. I never used to think it was as bad as others did, it was eloquent and communicated Jones's force to the reader. It is not that *The Thin Red Line* is dishonest or narrow; on the contrary it is so broad and true a portrait of combat that it could be used as a textbook at the Infantry School if the Army is any less chicken than it used to be. But, sign of the times, there is now something almost too workmanlike about Jones. He gets almost everything in, horror, fear, fatigue, the sport of combat, the hang-ups, details, tactics, he takes an infantry company through its early days in combat on Guadalcanal and quits it a few weeks later as a veteran outfit, blooded, tough, up on morale despite the loss of half the original men, gone, dead, wounded, sick or transferred. So he performs the virtuoso feat of letting us know a little about a hundred men. One can even (while reading) remember their names. Jones's aim, after all, is not to create character but the feel of combat, the psychology of men. He is close to a master at this. Jones has a strong sense of a man's psychology and it carries quietly through his pages.

The Thin Red Line was of course compared to *The Naked and the Dead,* but apart from the fact that I am the next-to-last man to judge the respective merits of the two books, I didn't see them as similar. *The Naked and the Dead* is concerned more with characters than military action. By comparison it's a leisurely performance. *The Thin Red Line* is as crammed as a movie treatment. No, I think the real comparison is to *The Red Badge of Courage,* and I suspect *The Red Badge of Courage* will outlive *The Thin Red Line.* Yet I don't quite know why. *The Thin Red Line* is a more detailed book; it tells much more of combat, studies the variations in courage and fear of not one man but twenty men and gets something good about each one of them. Its knowledge of life is superior to *The Red Badge of Courage*; *The Thin Red Line* is less sentimental, its humor is dry to the finest taste, and yet . . . it is too technical. One needs ten topographical maps to trace the action. With all its variety, scrupulosity, respect for craft, one doesn't remember *The Thin Red Line* with that same nostalgia, that same sense of a fire on the horizon which comes back always from *The Red Badge of Courage.*

No, Jones's book is better remembered as satisfying, as if one had studied geology for a semester and now knew more. I suppose what was felt lacking is the curious sensuousness of combat, the soft lift of awe and pleasure that one was moving out onto the rim of the dead. If one was not too tired, there were times when a blade of grass coming out of the ground before one's nose was as significant as the finger of Jehovah in the Sistine Chapel. And this was not because a blade of grass was necessarily in itself so beautiful, or because hitting the dirt was so sweet, but because the blade seemed to be a living part of the crack of small-arms fire and the palpable flotation of all the other souls in the platoon full of turd and glory. Now, it's not that Jones is altogether ignorant of this state. The description he uses is "sexy," and one of the nicest things about Jim as a writer is his ease in moving from mystical to practical reactions with his characters. Few novelists can do this, it's the hint of greatness, but I think he steered *The Thin Red Line* away from its chance of becoming an American classic of the first rank when he kept the mystical side of his talents on bread and water, and gave his usual thoroughgoing company-man's exhibition of how much he knows technically about his product. I think that is the mistake. War is as full of handbooks as engineering, but it is more of a mystery, and the mystery is what separates the great war novels from the good ones. It is an American activity to cover the ground quickly, but I guess this is one time Jones should have written two thousand pages, not four hundred ninety-five. But then the underlying passion in this book is not to go for broke, but to promise the vested idiots of the book reviews that he can write as good as anyone who writes a book review.

When you discuss eight or ten books, there is a dilemma. The choice is to write eight separate book reviews, or work to find a thesis which ties the books together. There is something lick-spittle about the second method: "Ten Authors in Search of a Viable Theme," or "The Sense of Alienation in Eight American Novelists." A bed of Procrustes is brought in from the wings to stretch and shorten the separate qualities of the books. I would rather pick up each book by itself and make my connections on the fly. The thesis of the Bitch is thesis enough for me. Its application to Jones would say that *The Thin Red Line* is a holding action, a long-distance call to the Goddess to declare that one still has one's hand in, expect red roses for sure, but for the time, you know, like there're contacts to make on the road, and a few Johns to impress.

Another Country, by James Baldwin, is as different from *The Thin Red Line* as two books by talented novelists published in the same year can turn out to be. It does not deal with a hundred characters, but eight, and they are very much related. In fact there is a chain of fornication which is all but complete. A Negro musician named Rufus Scott has an affair with a white Southern girl which ends in beatings, breakdown, and near-insanity. She goes to a mental hospital, he commits suicide. The connection is taken up by his sister who has an affair with a white writer, a friend of Rufus' named Vivaldo Moore, who in turn gets into bed with a friend named Eric who is homosexual but having an affair with a married woman named Cass Silenski, which affair wrecks her marriage with her husband Richard, another writer, and leaves Eric waiting at the boat for his French lover Yves. A summary of this sort can do a book no good, but I make it to trace the links. With the exception of Rufus Scott who does not go to bed with his sister, everybody else in the book is connected by their skin to another character who is connected to still another. So the principal in the book, the protagonist, is not an individual character, not society, not a milieu, not a social organism like an infantry company, but indeed is sex, sex very much in the act. And almost the only good writing in the book is about the act. And some of that is very good indeed. But *Another Country* is a shocker. For the most part it is an abominably written book. It is sluggish in its prose, lifeless for its first hundred pages, stilted to despair in its dialogue. There are roles in plays called actor-proof. They are so conceived that even the worst actor will do fairly well. So *Another Country* is writer-proof. Its peculiar virtue is that Baldwin commits every *gaffe* in the art of novel writing and yet has a powerful book. It gets better of course; after the first hundred pages it gets a lot better. Once Eric, the homosexual, enters, the work picks up considerably. But what saves the scene is that Baldwin has gotten his hands into the meat and won't let go. All the sex in the book is displaced, whites with blacks, men with men, women with homosexuals, the sex is funky to suffocation, rich but claustrophobic, sensual but airless. Baldwin understands the existential abyss of love. In a world of Negroes and whites, nuclear fallout, marijuana, bennies, inversion, insomnia, and tapering off with beer at four in the morning, one no longer just falls in love—one has to take a brave leap over the wall of one's impacted rage and cowardice. And nobody makes it, not quite. Each of the characters rides his sexual chariot, whip out, on a gallop over a solitary track, and each is smashed, more or less by his own hand. They cannot find the juice to break out of their hatred into the other country of love. Except for the homosexuals who can't break into heterosexual love. Of all the novels talked about here, *Another Country* is the one which is closest to the mood of New York in our time, a way of saying it is close to the air of the Western World, it is at least a novel about matters which are important, but one can't let up on Baldwin for the way he wrote it. Years ago I termed him "minor" as a writer, I thought he was too smooth and too small. Now on his essays alone, on the long continuing line of poetic fire in his essays, one knows he has become one of the few writers of our time. But as a Negro novelist he could take lessons from a good journeyman like John Killens. Because *Another Country* is almost a major novel and yet it is far and away the weakest and worst near-major novel one has finished. It goes like the first draft of a first novelist who has such obvious stuff that one is ready, if an editor, to spend years guiding him into how to write, even as one winces at the sloppy company which must be kept. Nobody has more elegance than Baldwin as an essayist, not one of us hasn't learned something about the art of the essay from him, and yet he can't even find a good prose for his novel. Maybe the form is not for him. He knows what he wants to say, and that is not the best condition for writing a novel. Novels go happiest when you discover something you did not know you knew. Baldwin's experience has shaped his tongue toward directness, for urgency —the honorable defense may be that he has not time nor patience to create characters, milieu, and mood for the revelation of important complexities he has already classified in his mind.

Baldwin's characters maim themselves trying to smash through the wall of their imprisonment. William Burroughs gives what may be the finest record in our century of the complete psychic convict. *Naked Lunch* is a book of pieces and fragments, notes and nightmarish anecdotes, which he wrote—according to his preface—in various states of delirium, going in and out of a heroin addiction. It is not a novel in any conventional sense, but then there's a question whether it's a novel by any set of standards other than the dictum that prose about imaginary people put between book covers is a novel. At any rate, the distinction is not important except for the fact that *Naked Lunch* is next to impossible to read in consecutive fashion. I saw excerpts of it years ago, and thought enough of them to go on record that Burroughs "may conceivably be possessed by genius." I still believe that, but it is one thing to be possessed by genius, it is another to be a genius, and *Naked Lunch* read from cover to cover is not as exciting as in its separate pieces. Quantity changes quality, as Karl Marx once put it, and fifty or sixty three-page bits about homosexual orgies, castration, surgeon-assassins, and junkie fuzz dissolving into a creeping green ooze leaves one feeling pretty tough. "Let's put some blue-purple blood in the next rape," says your jaded taste.

This is, however, quibbling. Some of the best prose in America is graffiti found on men's-room walls. It is prose written in bone, etched by acid, it is the prose of harsh truth, the virulence of the criminal who never found his stone walls and so settles down on the walls of the john, it is the language of hatred unencumbered by guilt, hesitation, scruple, or complexity. Burroughs must be the greatest writer of graffiti who ever lived. His style has the snap of a whip, and it never relents. Every paragraph is quotable. Here's a jewel among a thousand jewels:

> Dr. Benway . . . looks around and picks up one of those rubber vacuum cups at the end of a stick they use to unstop toilets . . . "Make an incision, Doctor Limpf. . . . I'm

going to massage the heart." . . . Dr. Benway washes the
suction cup by swishing it around in the toilet-bowl. . . .

Dr. Limpf: "The incision is ready, doctor."

Dr. Benway forces the cup into the incision and works it
up and down. Blood spurts all over the doctors, the nurse
and the wall. . . .

Nurse: "I think she's gone, doctor."

Dr. Benway: "Well, it's all in the day's work."

Punch-and-Judy. Mr. Interlocutor and Mr. Bones. One,
two, three, bam! two, four, eight, bam! The drug addict
lives with a charged wire so murderous he must hang
his nervous system on a void. Burroughs' achievement, his
great achievement, is that he has brought back snowflakes
from this murderous void.

Once, years ago in Chicago, I was coming down with a
bad cold. By accident, a friend took me to hear a jazz
musician named Sun Ra who played "space music." The
music was a little like the sound of Ornette Coleman, but
further out, outer space music, close to the EEEE of an
electric drill at the center of a harsh trumpet. My cold
cleared up in five minutes. I swear it. The anger of the
sound penetrated into some sprung-up rage which was
burning fuel for the cold. Burroughs' pages have the same
medicine. If a hundred patients on terminal cancer read
Naked Lunch, one or two might find remission. Bet
money on that. For Burroughs is the surgeon of the novel.

Yet he is something more. It is his last ability which en-
titles him to a purchase on genius. Through the fantasies
runs a vision of a future world, a half-demented welfare
state, an abattoir of science fiction with surgeons, bureau-
crats, perverts, diplomats, a world not describable short of
getting into the book. The ideas have pushed into the
frontier of an all-electronic universe. One holds onto a
computer in some man-eating machine of the future which
has learned to use language. The words come out in
squeaks, spiced with static, sex coiled up with technology
like a scream on the radar. Bombarded by his language,
the sensation is like being in a room in which three radios,
two television sets, stereo hi-fi, a pornographic movie, and

two automatic dishwashers are working at once while a mad scientist conducts the dials to squeeze out the maximum disturbance. If this is a true picture of the world to come, and it may be, then Burroughs is a great writer. Yet there is sadness in reading him, for one gets intimations of a mind which might have come within distance of Joyce, except that a catastrophe has been visited on it, a blow by a sledgehammer, a junkie's needle which left the crystalline brilliance crashed into bits.

Now beyond a doubt, of all the books discussed here, the one which most cheats evaluation is Joseph Heller's *Catch-22*. It was the book which took me longest to finish, and I almost gave it up. Yet I think that a year from now I may remember it more vividly than *The Thin Red Line*. Because it is an original. There's no book like it anyone has read. Yet it's maddening. It reminds one of a Jackson Pollock painting, eight feet high, twenty feet long. Like yard goods, one could cut it anywhere. One could take out a hundred pages anywhere from the middle of *Catch-22*, and not even the author could be certain they were gone. Yet the length and similarity of one page to another gives a curious meat-and-potatoes to the madness; building upon itself the book becomes substantial until the last fifty pages grow suddenly and surprisingly powerful, only to be marred by an ending over the last five pages which is hysterical, sentimental and well-eyed for Hollywood.

This is the skin of the reaction. If I were a major critic, it would be a virtuoso performance to write a definitive piece on *Catch-22*. It would take ten thousand words or more. Because Heller is carrying his reader on a more consistent voyage through Hell than any American writer before him (except Burroughs who has already made the trip and now sells choice seats in the auditorium), and so the analysis of Joseph H.'s Hell would require a discussion of other varieties of inferno and whether they do more than this author's tour.

Catch-22 is a nightmare about an American bomber squadron on a made-up island off Italy. Its hero is a bombardier named Yossarian who has flown fifty missions and wants out. On this premise are tattooed the events of the novel, fifty characters, two thousand frustrations (an average of four or five to the page) and one simple motif: more frustration. Yossarian's colonel wants to impress his general and so raises the number of missions to fifty-five. When the pilots have fifty-four, the figure is lifted to sixty. They are going for eighty by the time the book has been done. On the way every character goes through a routine *on every page* which is as formal as a little peasant figure in a folk dance. Back in school, we had a joke we used to repeat. It went:

"Whom are you talking about?"
"Herbert Hoover."
"Never heard of him."
"Herbert Hoover."
"Who's he?"
"He's the man you mentioned."
"Never heard of Herbert Hoover."

So it went. So goes *Catch*-22. It's the rock and roll of novels. One finds its ancestor in Basic Training. We were ordered to have clean sheets for Saturday inspection. But one week we were given no clean sheets from the Post laundry so we slept on our mattress covers, which got dirty. After inspection, the platoon was restricted to quarters. "You didn't have clean sheets," our sergeant said.

"How could we have clean sheets if the clean sheets didn't come?"

"How do I know?" said the sergeant. "The regulations say you gotta have clean sheets."

"But we can't have clean sheets if there are no clean sheets."

"That," said the sergeant, "is tough shit."

Which is what *Catch*-22 should have been called. The Army is a village of colliding bureaucracies whose colliding orders cook up impossibilities. Heller takes this one good joke and exploits it into two thousand variations of the same good joke, but in the act he somehow creates a rational vision of the modern world. Yet the crisis of reason is that it can no longer comprehend the modern world. Heller demonstrates that a rational man devoted to reason must arrive at the conclusion that either the world is mad and he is the only sane man in it, or (and this is the weakness of *Catch-22*—it never explores this possibility) the sane man is not really sane because his rational propositions are without existential reason.

On page 178, there is a discussion about God.

". . . how much reverence can you have for a Supreme Being who finds it necessary to include such phenomena as phlegm and tooth decay in His divine system of creation . . . Why in the world did He ever create pain?"

"Pain?" Lieutenant Scheisskopf's wife pounced upon the word victoriously. "Pain is a useful symptom. Pain is a warning to us of bodily dangers." . . .

"Why couldn't He have used a doorbell instead to notify us, or one of His celestial choirs?"

Right there is planted the farthest advance of the flag of reason in his cosmology. Heller does not look for any answer, but there is an answer which might go that God gave us pain for the same reason the discovery of tranquilizers was undertaken by the Devil: if we have an immortal soul some of us come close to it only through pain. A season of sickness can be preferable to a flight from disease for it discourages the onrush of a death which begins in the center of oneself.

Give talent its due. *Catch-22* is the debut of a writer with merry gifts. Heller may yet become Gogol. But what makes one hesitate to call his first novel great or even major is that he has only grasped the inferior aspect of Hell. What is most unendurable is not the military world of total frustration so much as the midnight frustration of the half world, Baldwin's other country, where a man may have time to hear his soul, and time to go deaf, even be forced to contemplate himself as he becomes deadened before his death. (Much as Hemingway may have been.) That is when one becomes aware of the anguish, the existential *Angst*, which wars enable one to forget. It is

that other death—without war—where one dies by a failure of nerve, which opens the bloodiest vents of Hell. And
that is a novel none of us has yet come back alive to write.

With the exception of *Another Country*, the novels
talked about up to now have been books written for men.
Catch-22 was liked, I believe, by almost every man who
read it. Women were puzzled. The world of a man is a
world of surface slick and rock knowledge. A man must
live by daily acts where he goes to work and works on the
world some incremental bit, using the tools, instruments,
and the techniques of the world. Thus a man cannot
afford to go too deeply into the underlying meaning of a
single subject. He prefers to become interested in quick
proportions and contradictions, in the practical surface of
things. A book like *Catch-22* is written on the face of
solemn events and their cockeyed contradictions. So it has
a vast appeal: it relieves the frustration men feel at the
idiocy of their work. *Naked Lunch* fries the surface in a
witch's skillet; the joy in reading is equal to the kick of
watching a television announcer go insane before your eyes
and start to croon obscenely about the President, First
Lady, Barry Goldwater, Cardinal Spellman, J. Edgar.
Somewhere in America somebody would take out his
pistol and shoot the set. Burroughs shatters the surface
and blasts its shards into the madness beneath. His rips the
reader free of suffocation. Jones wrote a book which a
dedicated corporation executive or an ambitious foreman
would read with professional avidity because they would
learn a bit about the men who work for them. *The Thin
Red Line* brings detail to the surprises on the toughest part
of the skin. So these three books are, as I say, books for
men. Whereas *Another Country*, obsessed with that
transcendental divide keeping sex from love, is a book
more for women, or for men and women. So too is *Set
This House on Fire*. And much the same can be said of
Rabbit, Run and *Letting Go*.

On record are the opinions of a partisan. So it is
necessary to admit that John Updike's novel was approached with animus. His reputation has traveled in

convoy up the Avenue of the Establishment, The New York Times *Book Review* blowing sirens like a motorcycle caravan, the professional muse of *The New Yorker* sitting in the Cadillac, membership cards to the right Fellowships in his pocket. The sort of critics who are rarely right about a book—Arthur Mizener and Granville Hicks, for example—ride on his flanks, literary bodyguards. *Life* magazine blew its kiss of death into the confetti. To my surprise, *Rabbit, Run* was therefore a better book than I thought it would be. The Literary Establishment was improving its taste. Updike was not simply a junior edition of James Gould Cozzens. But of course the Establishment cannot nominate a candidate coherently. Updike's merits and vices were turned inside out. The good girlish gentlemen of letters were shocked by the explicitness of the sex in *Rabbit, Run*, and slapped him gently for that with their fan, but his style they applauded. It is Updike's misfortune that he is invariably honored for his style (which is atrocious—and smells like stale garlic) and is insufficiently recognized for his gifts. He could become the best of our literary novelists if he could forget about style and go deeper into the literature of sex. *Rabbit, Run* moves in well-modulated spurts at precisely those places where the style subsides to a ladylike murmur and the characters take over. The trouble is that young John, like many a good young writer before him, does not know exactly what to do when action lapses, and so he cultivates his private vice, he *writes*. And there are long over-fingered descriptions in exacerbated syntax, airless crypts of four or five pages, huge inner exertion reminiscent of weight lifters, a stale sweet sweat clings to his phrases.

Example: Redbook, Cosmopolitan, McCall's.

Boys are playing basketball around a telephone pole with a backboard bolted to it. Legs, shouts. The scrape and snap of Keds on loose alley pebbles seems to catapult their voices high into the moist March air blue above the wires. Rabbit Angstrom, coming up the alley in a business suit, stops and watches, though he's twenty-six and six-three. So tall, he seems an unlikely rabbit, but the breadth of white face, the pallor of his blue irises, and a nervous flutter under his brief nose as he stabs a cigarette into his mouth partially explain the nickname.

Example: True Confessions.

Outside in the air his fears condense. Globes of ether, pure nervousness, slide down his legs. The sense of outside space scoops at his chest.

Example: Elements of Grammar.

His hands lift of their own and he feels the wind on his ears even before, his heels hitting heavily on the pavement at first but with an effortless gathering out of a kind of sweet panic growing lighter and quicker and quieter, he runs. Ah: runs. Runs.

It's the rare writer who cannot have sentences lifted from his work, but the first quotation is taken from the first five sentences of the book, the second is on the next-to-last page, and the third is nothing less than the last three sentences of the novel. The beginning and end of a novel are usually worked over. They are the index to taste in the writer. Besides, trust your local gangster. In the run of Updike's pages are one thousand other imprecise, flatulent, wrynecked, precious, overpreened, self-indulgent, tortured sentences. It is the sort of prose which would be admired in a writing course overseen by a fussy old nance. And in Updike's new book, *The Centaur*, which was only sampled, the style has gotten worse. Pietisms are congregating, affirmations à la Archibald MacLeish.

The pity is that Updike has instincts for finding the heart of the conventional novel, that still-open no-man's-land between the surface and the deep, the soft machinery of the world and the subterranean rigors of the dream. His hero, Rabbit Angstrom, is sawed in two by the clear anguish of watching his private vision go at a gallop away from the dread real weight of his responsibility. A routine story of a man divided between a dull wife he cannot bear to live with, and a blowsy tough tender whore he cannot make it with, the merit of the book is not in the simplicity of its problem, but in the dread Updike manages to convey, despite the literary commercials in the style, of a young man who is beginning to lose nothing less than his good American soul, and yet it is not quite his fault. The power of the novel comes from a sense, not absolutely unworthy of Thomas Hardy, that the universe hangs over our fates like a great sullen hopeless sky. There is real pain in the book, and a touch of awe. It is a novel which could have been important, it could have had a chance to stay alive despite its mud pies in prose, but at the very end of the book drowns in slime. Updike does not know how to finish. Faced with the critical choice of picking one woman or another (and by the end, both women are in fearful need), his character bolts over a literal hill and runs away. Maybe he'll be back tomorrow, maybe he'll never be back, but a decision was necessary. The book ends as minor, a pop-out. One is left with the expectation that Updike will never be great, there is something too fatally calculated about his inspiration. But very good he can be, a good writer of the first rank with occasional echoes from the profound. First he must make an enemy or two of the commissioners on the Literary Mafia. Of course a man spends his life trying to get up his guts for such a caper.

Letting Go, by Philip Roth, has precisely the opposite merits and faults. As a novel, its strategy is silly, tiresome, and weak. But its style, while not noteworthy, is decent and sometimes, in dialogue, halfway nice. It is good time spent to read any ten pages in the book. The details are observed, the mood is calm, the point is always made. It is like having an affair with a pleasant attentive woman, the hours go by neatly. It is only at the end of a year that one may realize the preoccupations of the mistress are hollow, and the seasons have been wasted.

Letting Go is a scrupulous account in upper Jewish New Yorker genre of a few years in the lives of two English Department college instructors, one married to that most coveted of creatures, a fragile dreary hangup of a heroine, the other a bachelor and lover of worried proportions.

Very little happens. The wife goes on being herself, the husband remains naturally frozen and stingy, and the instructor-lover has a small literary breakdown. One can say, well isn't this life? didn't Chekhov and de Maupassant write about such things? And the answer is yes they did, in five pages they did, and caught that mood which reminds us that there is sadness in attrition and grinding sorrows for decency. But Roth is not writing a book with a vision of life; on the contrary, one could bet a grand he is working out an obsession. His concentration is appropriated by something in his life which has been using him up in the past. Virtually every writer, come soon or late, has a cramped-up love affair which is all but hopeless. *Of Human Bondage* could be the case study of half the writers who ever lived. But the obsession is opposed to art in the same way a compulsive talker is opposed to good conversation. The choice is either to break the obsession or enter it. The compulsive talker must go through the herculean transformation of learning to quit or must become a great monologuist. Roth tried to get into the obsession—he gave six hundred pages to wandering around in a ten-page story—but he did it without courage. He was too careful not to get hurt on his trip and so he does not reveal himself: he does not *dig*. The novel skitters like a water fly from pollen spread to pollen spread, a series of good short stories accumulate en route, but no novel. The iron law of the conventional novel, the garden novel, is that the meaning of the action must grow on every page or else the book will wither. It is Updike's respectable achievement in *Rabbit, Run* that he writes just such a book, or tries to until the last three pages when he vanishes like a sneak thief. Roth never gets into the game. One senses a determined fight to maintain *Letting Go* as a collection of intricately intercollected short stories.

But the short story has a tendency to look for climates of permanence—an event occurs, a man is hurt by it in some small way forever. The novel moves as naturally toward flux. An event occurs, a man is injured, and a month later is working on something else. The short story likes to be classic. It is most acceptable when one fatal point is made. Whereas the novel is dialectical. It is most alive when one can trace the disasters which follow victory or the subtle turns that sometimes come from a defeat. A novel can be created out of short stories only if the point in each story is consecutively more interesting and incisive than the point before it, when the author in effect is drilling for oil. But Roth's short stories in *Letting Go* just dig little holes in many suburban lawns until finally the work of reading it becomes almost as depressing as must have been the work of writing it. Roth has to make a forced march in his next book, or at the least, like Updike, get around to putting his foot in the whorehouse door. If he doesn't, a special Hell awaits his ambition—he will be called the Rich Man's Paddy Chayefsky, and Paddy without his grasp of poverty is nothing much at all.

It is necessary to say that the four stories about the Glass family by J. D. Salinger, published in two books called *Franny and Zooey* and *Raise High the Roof Beam, Carpenters*, seem to have been written for high-school girls. The second piece in the second book, called "Seymour an Introduction," must be the most slovenly portion of prose ever put out by an important American writer. It is not even professional Salinger. Salinger at his customary worst, as here in the other three stories of the two books, is never bad—he is just disappointing. He stays too long on the light ice of his gift, writes exquisite dialogue and creates minor moods with sweetness and humor, and never gives the fish its hook. He disappoints because he is always practicing. But when he dips into Seymour, the Glass brother who committed suicide, when the cult comes to silence before the appearance of the star—the principal, to everyone's horror, has nausea on the stage. Salinger for the first time is engaged in run-off writing, free suffragette prose, his inhibitions (which once helped by their restraint to create his style) are now stripped. He is giving you himself as he is. No concealment. It feels like taking a bath in a grease trap.

Now, all of us have written as badly. There are nights

when one comes home after a cancerously dull party, full of liquor but not drunk, leaden with boredom, somewhere out in Fitzgerald's long dark night. Writing at such a time is like making love at such a time. It is hopeless, it desecrates one's future, but one does it anyway because at least it is an act. Such writing is almost always unsprung. It is reminiscent of the wallflower who says, "To hell with inhibitions, I'm going to dance." The premise is that what comes out is valid because it is the record of a mood. So one records the mood. What a mood. Full of vomit, self-pity, panic, paranoia, megalomania, *merde*, whimpers, excuses, turns of the neck, flips of the wrist, transports. It is the bends of Hell. If you purge it, if you get sleep and tear it up in the morning, it can do no more harm than any other bad debauch. But Salinger went ahead and reread his stew, then sent it to *The New Yorker*, and they accepted it. Now, several years later, he reprints it in book covers.

There is social process at work here. Salinger was the most gifted minor writer in America. *The New Yorker's* ability is to produce such writers. The paradox comes from the social fact that *The New Yorker* is a major influence on American life. Hundreds of thousands, perhaps millions of people in the most established parts of the middle class kill their quickest impulses before they dare to act in such a way as to look ridiculous to the private eye of their taste whose style has been keyed by the eye of *The New Yorker*. Salinger was the finest writer *The New Yorker* ever produced, but profoundly minor. The major writer like James Jones, indeed James Jones, leads the kind of inner life which enables him to study victories as well as defeats; Salinger was catapulted by a study of excruciating small defeats into a position of major importance. The phenomenon in the nation was the same those years. Men of minor abilities engaged America in major brinkmanships.

But it is always dangerous when the Literary Mafia (*The New Yorker, The Saturday Review,* The New York Times *Book Review, Time* magazine's book reviews, and the genteel elements in publishing) promote a minor writer into a major writer. A vested interest attaches itself to keeping the corpse of the violated standards buried. Readers who might be average keen in their sense of literary value find their taste mucked up. The greatest damage in this case, however, seems to have been to Salinger himself. Because a writer, with aristocratic delicacy of intent and nerves so subtle that only isolation makes life bearable for him, has been allowed to let his talent fester in that corrupt isolation. Salinger has been the most important writer in America for a generation of adolescents and college students. He was their leader in exile. The least he owed them for his silence was a major performance.

But it's a rare man who can live like a hermit and produce a major performance unless he has critics who are near to him and hard on him. No friend who worried about Salinger's future should have let him publish "Seymour an Introduction" in *The New Yorker* without daring to lose his friendship first by telling him how awful it was. Yet there was too much depending on Salinger's interregnum—he was so *inoffensive*, finally. So a suspension of the critical faculty must have gone on in the institutional wheels of *The New Yorker* which was close to psychotic in its evasions.

As for the other three stories in the two books, they are not as good as the stories in *Nine Stories*. Affectations which were part once of Salinger's charm are now faults. An excessive desire to please runs through his pages. There is too much sweetness. He is too pleased with himself, too nice, he lingers too much over the happy facility of his details in a way Fitzgerald never would. He is no longer a writer so much as he is an entertainer, a slim much-beloved version of Al Jolson or Sophie Tucker, the music hall is in the root of his impulse as much as the dungeons and mansions of literature. Does one desire the real irony? There is nothing in *Franny and Zooey* which would hinder it from becoming first-rate television. It is genre with all the limitations of genre: catalogs of items in the medicine chest, long intimate family conversations with life, snap with mother, crackle and pop. If I were a television producer I'd put on *Franny and Zooey* tomorrow. And indeed in ten years they will. America will have moved from One Man's Family to the Glass Family. Which is progress. I'd rather have the Glass Family on the air. But don't confuse the issue. The Glass stories are not literature but television. And Salinger's work since *The Catcher in the Rye* is part of his long retreat from what is substantial, agonizing, uproarious, or close to awe and terror. *The Catcher in the Rye* was able to change people's lives. The new books are not even likely to improve the conversation in college dormitories. It is time Salinger came back to the city and got his hands dirty with a rough corruption or two, because the very items which composed the honor of his reputation, his resolute avoidance of the mass media and society, have now begun to back up on him. There is a taste of something self-absorptive, narcissistic, even putrefactive in his long contemplation of a lintless navel.

The value of past predictions by this critic may be judged by the following about Saul Bellow. It is taken from page 467 in *Advertisements for Myself*.

> When and if I come to read *Henderson the Rain King*, let me hope I do not feel the critic's vested interest to keep a banished writer in limbo, for I sense uneasily that without reading it, I have already the beginnings of a negative evaluation for it since I doubt that I would believe in Henderson as a hero.

Well, one might as well eat the crow right here. Henderson is an exceptional character, almost worthy of Gulliver or Huckleberry Finn, and it is possible that of all books mentioned in this piece, *Henderson the Rain King* comes the closest to being a great novel. Taken even by its smallest dimension, and its final failure, it will still become a classic, a fine curiosity of a book quite out of the main stream of American letters but a classic in the way *The Innocents Abroad*, or *The Ox-Bow Incident, The Informer,* or *High Wind in Jamaica* is classic.

Bellow's main character, Henderson, is a legendary giant American, an eccentric millionaire, six-four in height, with a huge battered face, an enormous chest, a prodigious potbelly, a wild crank's gusto for life, and a childlike impulse to say what he thinks. He is a magical hybrid of Jim Thorpe and Dwight Macdonald. And he is tormented by an inner voice which gives him no rest and poisons his marriages and pushes him to go forth. So he chooses to go to Africa (after first contemplating a visit to the Eskimos) and finds a native guide to take him deep into the interior.

The style gallops like Henderson, full of excess, full of light, loaded with irritating effusions, but it is a style which moves along. *The Adventures of Augie March* was written in a way which could only be called *all writing*. That was one of the troubles with the book. Everything was mothered by the style. But Henderson talks in a free-swinging easy bang-away monologue which puts your eye in the center of the action. I don't know if Bellow ever visited Africa, I would guess he didn't, but his imaginative faculty—which has always been his loot—pulls off a few prodigies. I don't know if any other American writer has done Africa so well. As for instance:

> I was in tremendous shape those first long days, hot as they were. At night, after Romilayu had prayed, and we lay on the ground, the face of the air breathed back on us, breath for breath. And then there were the calm stars, turning around and singing, and the birds of the night with heavy bodies, fanning by. I couldn't have asked for anything better. When I laid my ear to the ground, I thought I could hear hoofs. It was like lying on the skin of a drum.

After a series of tragicomic adventures, Henderson reaches a royal almost Oriental tribe with a culture built upon magic and death. He is brought to the King, Dahfu, who lives in a wooden palace attended by a harem of beautiful Amazons. (One could be visiting the royalest pad in Harlem.) Dahfu is a philosopher-king, large in size, nobel, possessed of grace, complex, dignified, elegant, educated, living suspended between life and death. The King, delighted with his new friend, takes him into the secrets of his mind and his palace, and one begins to read the book with a vast absorption because Bellow is now inching more close to the Beast of mystery than any American novelist before him. Dahfu is an exceptional creation, a profoundly sophisticated man with a deep acceptance of magic, an intellectual who believes that civilization can be saved only by a voyage back into the primitive, an expedition which he is of course uniquely suited to lead.

As the action explores its way down into an underworld of plot and magical omens, one ceases to know any longer whether Dahfu is potentially an emperor who can save the world, or a noble man lost in a Faustian endeavor. The book is on the threshold of a stupendous climax—for the first time in years I had the feeling I was going to learn something large from a novel—and then like a slow leak, the air goes out of the book in the last fifty pages. Dahfu is killed in a meaningless action, Henderson goes home to his wife, and the mystery that Bellow has begun to penetrate closes over his book, still intact.

He is a curious writer. He has the warmest imagination, I think, of any writer in my generation, and this gift leads him to marvelous places—it is possible that Bellow succeeds in telling us more about the depths of the black man's psyche than either Baldwin or Ellison. He has a widely cultivated mind which nourishes his gift. He has a facility for happy surprises, and in Henderson, unlike Augie March, he has developed a nose for where the treasure is buried. Yet I still wonder if he is not too timid to become a great writer. A novelist like Jones could never have conceived Henderson, the Rain King (no more could I), but I know that Jones or myself would have been ready to urinate blood before we would have been ready to cash our profit and give up as Bellow did on the possibilities of a demonically vast ending. The clue to this capitulation may be detected in Bellow's one major weakness, which is that he creates individuals and not relations between them, at least not yet. Augie March travels alone, the hero of *Seize the Day* is alone, Henderson forms passionate friendships but they tend to get fixed and the most annoying aspect of the novel is the constant repetition of the same sentiments, as if Bellow is knocking on a door of meaning which will not open for him. It is possible that the faculty of imagination is opposed to the gift of grasping relationships—in the act of coming to know somebody else well, the point of the imagination may be dulled by the roughness of the other's concrete desires and the attrition of living not only in one's own boredom but someone else's. Bellow has a lonely gift, but it is a gift. I would guess he is more likely to write classics than major novels, which is a way of saying that he will give intense pleasure to particular readers over the years, but is not too likely to seize the temper of our time and turn it.

For those who like the results of a horse race, it should be clear that the novels I liked the most in this round of reading were *Henderson, Naked Lunch,* and *Catch-22. The Thin Red Line* if not inspired was still impressive. *Another Country* suffered from too little style but compensated by its force. *Rabbit, Run* was better than expected but cloyed by too much writing. *Set This House on Fire* was rich in separate parts, and obese for the whole. *Letting Go* gave a demonstration of brilliant tactics and no novelistic strategy at all. *Franny and Zooey* and *Raise High the Roof Beam, Carpenters* was a literary scandal which came in last.

It has been said more than once that Tolstoy and Dostoevsky divided the central terrain of the modern novel between them. Tolstoy's concern—even in the final pessimism of *The Kreutzer Sonata*—was with men-in-the-world, and indeed the panorama of his books carries to us an image of a huge landscape peopled with figures who changed that landscape, whereas the bulk of Dostoevsky's work could take place in ten closed rooms: it is not society but a series of individuals we remember, each illuminated by the terror of exploring the bad jungle of themselves. This distinction is not a final scheme for classifying the novel. If one can point to *Moby Dick* as a perfect example of a novel in the second category—a book whose action depends upon the voyage of Ahab into his obsession—and to *An American Tragedy* as a virile example of the first kind of novel, one must still come up short before the work of someone like Henry James, who straddles the categories, for he explores into society as if the world were a creature in a closed room and he could discover its heart. Yet the distinction is probably the most useful single guide we have to the novel and can even be given a modern application to Proust as a novelist of the developed, introspective, still-exploitive world, and Joyce as a royal, demented, most honorable traveler through the psyche. The serious novel begins from a fixed search for that reality in society, or else must embark on a trip up the upper Amazon of the inner eye.

It is this necessity to travel into one direction or the other up to the end which makes the writing of novels fatal for one's talent and finally for one's health, as the horns of a bull are final doom for the suit of tights. If one explores the world, one's talent must be blunted by punishment, one's artistic integrity by corruption: nobody can live in the world without shaking the hand of people he despises; so an ultimate purity must be surrendered. Yet it is as dangerous to travel unguided into the mysteries of the Self, for insanity prepares an ambush. No man explores into his own nature without submitting to a curse from the root of biology since existence would cease if it were natural to turn upon oneself.

This difficulty has always existed for the novelist, but today it may demand more antithesis and more agony than before. The writer who would explore the world must encounter a society which is now conscious of itself, and so resistant (most secretly) to an objective eye. Detours exist everywhere. There was a time when a writer had to see just a little bit of a few different faces in the world and could know that the world was still essentially so simple and so phrased that he might use his imagination to fill in unknown colors in the landscape. Balzac could do that, and so could Zola. But the arts of the world suffered a curious inversion as man was turned by the twentieth century into mass man rather than democratic man. The heart-land which was potential in everyone turned upon itself; people used their personal arts to conceal from themselves the nature of their work. They chose to become experts rather than artists. The working world was no longer a congeries of factories and banks so much as it was reminiscent of hospitals and plastic recreation centers. Society tended to collect in small stagnant pools. Now, any young man trying to explore that world is held up by pleasures which are not sufficiently intense to teach him and is dulled by injustices too elusive to fire his rage. The Tolstoyan novel begins to be impossible. Who can create a vast canvas when the imagination must submit itself to a plethora of detail in each joint of society? Who can travel to many places when the complexity of each pool sucks up one's attention like a carnivorous cess-fed flower? Of all the writers mentioned here, only Jones, Heller and Burroughs even try to give a picture of the world, and the last two have departed from conventional reality before financing the attempt. It may be that James Jones is indeed the single major American writer capable of returning with a realistic vision of the complex American reality. But by his method, because of the progressively increasing confusion and contradiction of each separate corner in American society, he will have to write twenty or thirty books before he will have sketched even a small design.

Yet a turn in the other direction, into the world of the Self, is not less difficult. An intellectual structure which is cancerous and debilitating to the instinct of the novelist inhabits the crossroads of the inner mind. Psychoanalysis. An artist must not explore into himself with language given by another. A vocabulary of experts is a vocabulary greased out and sweated in committee and so is inimical to a private eye. One loses what is new by confusing it with what may be common to others. The essential ideas of psychoanalysis are reductive and put a dead weight on the confidence of the venture. If guilt, for example, is neurotic, a clumsy part of the functioning in a graceful machine, then one does not feel like a hero studying his manacles, nor a tragic victim regarding his just sentence, but instead is a skilled mechanic trying to fix his tool. Brutally, simply, mass man cannot initiate an inner voyage unless it is conducted by an expert graduated by an institution.

Set This House on Fire, Another Country, Rabbit, Run, Letting Go, Henderson, and the Glass stories were all amateur expeditions into the privacy of the Self, but they are also a measure of the difficulty, because one could sense the exhaustion of talent in the fires on the way, as if a company of young untried men were charging a hill which was mined and laid across with fire lanes for automatic weapons.

Yet the difficulty goes beyond the country of psychoanalysis. There are hills beyond that hill. The highest faces an abyss. Man in the Middle Ages or the Renaissance, man even in the nineteenth century, explored deep into himself that he might come closer to a vision of a God or some dictate from eternity, but that exploration is suspect in itself today, and in the crucial climactic transcendental moments of one's life, there is revealed still another dilemma. God, is it God one finds, or madness?

The religious temper of these books is significant. Of them all, *The Thin Red Line, Naked Lunch, Another Country,* and *Letting Go* have no overt religious preoccupation. Yet altogether one could make a kind of case that *Naked Lunch* and *Another Country* are not divorced from religious obsessions. The suggestion of still another frontier for the American novel is here. A war has been fought by some of us over the last fifteen years to open the sexual badlands to our writing, and that war is in the act of being won. Can one now begin to think of an attack on the stockade—those dead forts where the spirit of twentieth-century irreligious man, frozen in flop and panic before the montage of his annihilation, has collected, like castrated cattle behind the fence? Can the feet of those infantrymen of the arts, the novelists, take us through the mansions and the churches into the palace of The Bitch where the real secrets are stored? We are the last of the entrepreneurs, and one of us homeless guns had better make it, or the future will smell like the dead air of the men who captured our time during that huge collective cowardice which was the aftermath of the Second War.

THE WAR WRITERS TEN YEARS LATER

John W. Aldridge

Just over a decade ago in *After the Lost Generation* I made certain cantankerous pronouncements on the work of the younger group of American novelists who began to appear immediately following the war. I felt at the time that these writers were becoming rather dangerously inflated values on the literary market, and I saw my job as essentially corrective and deflationary. What I had to say aroused considerable indignation in publishing and reviewing circles, partly because some of the writers I had hit hardest had been selected to replace Hemingway and Fitzgerald—or so their jacket blurbs said—and I seemed to be interfering with the democratic right of American literature to repeat itself. Yet the passage of time has hit most of them a good deal harder than I did, so much harder in fact that it now seems scarcely believable that they could ever have occupied the positions of prominence which they obviously did occupy in the literary life of the postwar period.

Norman Mailer, Irwin Shaw, Truman Capote, Frederick Buechner, Alfred Hayes, Robert Lowry, Merle Miller, Calder Willingham, Gore Vidal, Paul Bowles, Vance Bourjaily, along with James Jones, whose first novel appeared after my book was written—these were some of the apparently promising younger novelists of ten years ago. Today nearly all these writers give one the impression that their best work is behind them and that they can no longer be counted on to excite or command our attention with future work that is fresh, surprising, or very much more than a haggard recapitulation of the ideas and experiences with which they began their careers. As a group they have lost the critical standing their first books won for them, and most of them seem individually to have reached a creative impasse of one kind or another. Some have dropped out of sight completely. Others have abandoned the novel for less exacting and more lucrative forms of writing. One or two others have turned their baffled search for new materials into a topic of tabloid psychoanalysis and public confession. A few have continued, as if from habit, to bring out occasional books which, in spite of good intentions, one somehow never has the impulse to read. Every last one of them has suffered by comparison with a different and, in some cases, a younger set of contemporaries whose minds were not formed on the easy simplifications of wartime, and who seem to have a firmer grasp of the enormously subtle and complicated realities of the immediate present.

Perhaps because they aroused such high expectations to begin with, the authors of the classic war novels appear to have stood up least well under the pressures of the last ten years. Norman Mailer of course remains the strongest potential talent of the group and the best literary mind of the war generation. Yet his personal and polemical writings continue to seem more interesting than his novels, and his prejudices more interesting than his ideas. His failure to find his line after *The Naked and the Dead* has evidently caused him to seek in sheer raw experience the intensity he cannot create in art, and in the process to mistake the quick thrills of notoriety for the solid satisfactions of earned success.

Both James Jones and Irwin Shaw seem to have suffered in recent years quite simply from having lived too long abroad. The result for Jones appears to be that his experience of American life stopped with the period of the war and its immediate aftermath, and having so far been unable to put his European experience to creative use, he has been obliged since *From Here to Eternity* to keep returning obsessively to that period, first for the emotional background of *Some Came Running*, then in *The Pistol*, and most recently in *The Thin Red Line*. Shaw seems to have lost touch in Europe with the way present-day Americans talk and act, and a large part of his recent fiction has been seriously flawed by his tendency to make them talk and act in patterns which have been long out of date. Yet in Shaw's case one feels that the stoppage of experience occurred even earlier than the war, that in fact he has not really been creatively engaged with American life since the thirties—and then less with its actualities than with the fashionable representations of it to be found in certain modern novels.

As for some of the other young writers who were considered so promising right after the war, Truman Capote and Frederick Buechner continue to be the most potent arguments we have against the idea that the new fiction of the period was all done by men whose sense of language came out of an ouija board manipulated by the ghost of Theodore Dreiser. Both are highly sensitive and accomplished practitioners of the poetic "high" style, Buechner of the strain descending from Henry James, and Capote of the strain indemnified by Faulkner and then powdered and perfumed by the ladies' fashion magazines. But Buechner has done little of real interest since *A Long Day's Dying*, while Capote has become a classic example of precocity extended and professionalized into a career. In 1951, I said that as Capote grows older, he will undoubtedly have to stop writing solely about adult children and childlike adults. Apparently I was wrong, for he is still writing about them, and he has unquestionably grown older.

One can say almost exactly the same thing in slightly different terms about Vance Bourjaily. In the novels he has done since his first book *The End of My Life* one finds abundant evidence of advancing years, little evidence of creative development. He has continued to write from essentially the same assumptions about experience as those with which he began his career. The world has moved on, but he has not. Calder Willingham and Gore Vidal, on the other hand, *have* moved on, straight on out of the novel into the field of its more prosperous competitors. Willingham published several abrasively funny books after *End as a Man* and for a while seemed on the point of becoming established as a kind of crackerbarrel J. D. Salinger. But some years ago he turned to screen writing and has since done only one novel, about which nothing at all need be said. Vidal, who was once notable for the large number of books he had managed to produce before reaching the age of thirty, rather dramatically announced at about the same time that he had finally discovered the novel form to be unworthy of his talents. Then he too went off to Hollywood, later transferred to television, and has recently found success as a writer of light popular plays for the Broadway theatre.

There are of course any number of plausible explanations for the failure of these writers to develop artistically or to continue with their novelistic careers. The nervous strain of creative effort is very great; the will can grow tired and become paralysed; critics can be obtuse, unfriendly, or just indifferent once too often; the rent sooner or later must be paid. It is also entirely possible that I was right in thinking that at least some of these writers were not really so very talented to begin with, but rather were pushed into an undeserved prominence simply because they happened to be among the first younger novelists to appear after the war. Yet the group as a whole has done interesting enough work to make it clear that the problem for most of them has not been basically one of talent as such. What seems far more likely is that there was something about their initial orientation as writers, something limited or defective about their manner of first engaging life imaginatively, which seriously impaired their ability to function under the changed social and intellectual conditions of the last ten years.

The point may just be that except perhaps for Capote and Buechner these writers never really have engaged life imaginatively. From the beginning of their careers they have been singularly deficient in the power to work up their materials out of their own creative resources and, therefore, singularly dependent upon the social scene to provide them with those materials. So long as the issues of the war and the immediate aftermath seemed valid and fresh, this weakness was neither obvious nor particularly crippling. In fact, it could even masquerade as a kind of strength, for it gave to much of their work the cold realism of front page news and the documentary film. But the war was the last large-scale socially "given" subject to which these writers had access, and to an important extent it spoiled them for what came later. It was an experience in which not only they but their entire generation were meaningfully and dramatically involved, and it was so potently *there* as experience that it could be made into a novel by almost anyone with a good memory for details, a certain indignation, and only a fair competence in the language of fiction. The war in effect stood in the same relation to them as the great collective experiences of the first war and the Depression stood to the writers of the twenties and thirties, and like those occurrences it stirred into momentary life a number of talents that might under more normal conditions have remained dormant.

But the bleak period since the war has provided these writers with nothing comparable to the experience of the war years. It has been characterized by a curious failure to jell, by a lack of distinctive form and direction, and by an inevitable retreat of the old socially oriented literary mind on all fronts. In place of a tangible and readily usable subject the period has given us the indefinite suspensions and equivocations of the Cold War against an emotional background of alternating and even at moments co-existing anxiety and apathy. The central experience of the time has had the disconcerting effect of seeming to be shut off from relationship with the individual mind, of seeming to transpire on some plane of almost mythic abstraction far beyond the reach of human understanding.

The point about the Cold War is precisely that it *is* cold and not hot. It is by definition a state of action withheld,

of participation avoided, in the face of an endless recurrence of aborted crises followed by stalled negotiations
followed by more aborted crises—as if the broken record of
our years has become stuck forever in the groove of
incipient world catastrophe. In short, there can be no
question of *experiencing* the Cold War in any of the old
vigorous senses of the word. One simply endures it, waits it
out, and in the end gives over the mind to the protective
custody of its own resources, its own power to enforce
sanity and order within the closed precincts of the created
work of art. But for writers in whom that power is
unawakened or who have grown accustomed to having
their literary materials served up to them in the form of
hot wars, concrete social issues, and collective social
experience, such a condition of life can be baffling indeed.
It can even result in a fatal derangement of sensibility.

To deal effectively with the massive complications and
ambiguities of the Cold War period, to say nothing of the
present amorphous state of American society, a writer
would ideally need the artistic equipment of an Orwell, a
Kafka, Camus, Céline, or Dostoevsky. But since such
equipment is rather hard to come by these days, he ought
at the very least to have an artistic orientation sufficiently
similar to theirs to enable him to see that the task of the
novelist in a time like ours can no longer be confined to a
simple exploration of the social appearances and surfaces,
but must be expanded and deepened to take into account
the chaotic multiplicity of meanings which now confront
us both above and beneath the surfaces. He ought, in
other words, to be able to recognize that his task is
something far different from what it was and needed to be
in any previous time, and that he must bring to it far larger
resources of mind, imagination, and technical understanding than have ever been necessary before. If the experience
of the present age has failed to define itself in the form of
readily usable literary material, then he must be prepared
to define it imaginatively, and to make of the very
difficulty of definition one of the enriching values of his
art.

Yet it is just this more stringent view of the novelist's task which the majority of the war writers have shown themselves least capable of accepting and acting upon. From the beginning they have nearly all operated in accordance with the now outdated and vastly over-simplified view bequeathed them by their predecessors of the twenties and thirties. And they have remained arrested in this view even as the developments of recent history have doomed both it and them to a condition of almost quaint irrelevance to just about everything we now take to be real and true. In fact, one of the perplexing features of these writers as a group has been their apparent inability to see their experience except in terms of the literary stereo-types of the immediate past, their failure to discover new ways of seeing that would be more suited not only to their individual talents but to the changed realities of the present time.

The work of the war generation abounds in examples of this failure. There are all those novels—most of them by writers scarcely remembered today—in which Heming-way's war was fought all over again in a style so syn-thetically Hemingwayish that one was shocked to realize that at the time they were written, Hemingway had already ceased to sound like himself and was beginning to sound like them. Mailer, Jones, and Shaw were all indebted in their first novels to the panoramic-naturalist view of society which Dos Passos made fashionable in *USA* and *Manhattan Transfer*. This view functioned for them rather like a celluloid overlay on a military map: it got them to where somebody else had already been without requiring them to explore the uncharted and perhaps heavily mined territory of their own imaginations. As a systematic, if somewhat mechanical formulation of reality it served them well enough—so long as reality continued to fit the formulation. But in our day it evidently does not, and the writers who have failed to understand this are searching the map for an objective that no longer exists. Mailer of course does understand this, and one of the most encouraging things about him is that he has tried hard since *The Naked and the Dead* to break out of the naturalistic stereotype into fresh formulations of reality as he now sees it to be. Up to now none of his attempts has been quite successful, but one at least feels that wherever he is trying to get, nobody has been there before him. And one can be absolutely certain that in his case the route will be mined every step of the way.

Yet the solution for Mailer and the others does not consist simply in throwing off the influence of a specific writer or method of writing. It finally involves emancipation from the whole complex of stock responses to and literary arrangements of experience that belong to the past and have acted up to now as blinders on their vision of the present. Capote, for example, can certainly not be accused of imitating Faulkner in any sort of direct or literal way. Yet his early work represents an almost burlesque usage of the kinds of materials, and the modes of treating those materials, that have been previously patented and perfected by the official Faulknerian imagination of the South.

Mailer, Jones, Shaw, and Bourjaily have been trapped in another kind of burlesque by the official literary clichés of the twenties and thirties. Their fiction is always compulsively rehearsing the shopworn melodrama of their predecessors' discovery of the facts of life, always exulting in experiences which most of us have long since had and which fiction ought by now to have long since outgrown. In Bourjaily's novels in particular the standard characters all seem to be terribly young men who spend an inordinate amount of time thinking up elaborate practical jokes to play on one another or engaging in rather heavily witty fraternity-house repartee or drinking away their sense of the sickness of the age or naughtily smoking pot out behind the barn of conventional society or fighting down homosexual impulses for which their parents are somehow to blame or trying to get as many different girls into bed as they possibly can.

Cliché *Weltschmerz*, cliché psychology, cliché dipsomania, cliché satyriasis—these are among the counterfeit coins of the legacy left to the war writers by the twenties and thirties. At one time it was almost impossible to tell that they were counterfeit because there was so little else in circulation. But today there is a great deal else. In the last several years an altogether different group of younger writers have come to prominence, a group consisting of, among others, Saul Bellow, James Baldwin, Bernard Malamud, J. D. Salinger, Philip Roth, and James Purdy. And these writers are minting a new and genuine currency of the creative imagination, one that seems certain to remain the legal tender of the serious American novel for a long time to come.

EUDORA WELTY AND CARSON McCULLERS

Marvin Felheim

RICHNESS—of invention, of language, of method—is the chief characteristic of the writings of Eudora Welty and Carson McCullers. Yet their achievements are quite different: one feels that Miss Welty has succeeded in writing consistently at or near the top of her great talent, whereas a reading of the works of Mrs. McCullers leaves one with the impression that she has not yet altogether realized her undeniable abilities. Or, to put it another way, the stories of Eudora Welty, from the earliest examples in the thirties, are distinctively poetic and moving; the two dominant strains—a brilliant use of myth and symbolism and a magnificent humor—reach their logical pinnacles in *The Golden Apples* (1949) and *The Ponder Heart* (1953); the development is exact and the technique is sure. The literary career of Mrs. McCullers, on the other hand, is marked by no such consistent development. Her third novel, *The Member of the Wedding* (1946), is her best; *The Ballad of the Sad Café* (1951) and her most recent work, *Clock Without Hands* (1961), are exciting pieces that seem somehow to be the work of a young writer, whose potential is still to be wholly realized. Her major successes are in the novella form.

At the same time, both writers have had some notable failures. Miss Welty has not mastered the novel. *The Robber Bridegroom* (1942) is ephemeral and over-extended and *Delta Wedding* (1945) is inconclusive and vague; it leaves the memory of a dim atmosphere, imperfectly recollected. Mrs. McCullers' failure can, similarly, be identified with a form she has not dominated: *The Square Root of Wonderful* (1958), called by her publishers her "second" play because she had earlier made a stage adaptation of *The Member of the Wedding*, is simply a bad play to which both its stage history and a reading will testify.

A number of positive things can be said about both these writers. Both are southerners (Miss Welty is a Mississippian; Mrs. McCullers is from Georgia) and both write about the South. The richness which I mentioned earlier—the variety of characters, many of whom are brilliantly eccentric and/or grotesque, the use of symbolic language to suggest the mythological background of the events they picture, and, finally, the powerful senses of humor and of love which permeate their works—these are the characteristic trademarks of the best southern writing. These traits distinguish also the works of William Faulkner and Robert Penn Warren and they are a notable means by which we can label this truly significant aspect of American writing.

i

Miss Welty is a most self-conscious writer, deeply committed and astute. Her sensitivity appears in her attacks upon critics and their meticulous analyses (in an address, "The Reading and Writing of Short Stories," and in an essay, "How I Write"); here she posits the typical artistic rejection of the crudity of the non-artist, as when she states: "Beauty may be missed or forgotten sometimes by the analyzers because it is not a means, not a way of getting the story along, or furthering a thing in the world." But her statements also incorporate a positive faith: in beauty, in love, in poetry; "it's hard for me to think that a writer's stories are a unified whole," she proclaimed, "in any respect except perhaps their lyrical quality."

Here, then, a place of departure: lyricism. It is a pervasive "quality," obvious from the beginning, the significant year, 1936, when she first exhibited her unposed photographic studies of Mississippi Negroes in the Lugene Gallery in New York and when she published her first story, "Death of a Traveling Salesman," in *Manuscript*. The beginnings are sure. The eye, the heart, and the hand: these are the organs she depends upon. And the fact that they add up to an intelligent whole is the critic's observation.

A good example of her early work is her second published story, the provocative "A Piece of News." Quite simply, Miss Welty tells of an afternoon adventure of Ruby Fisher ("She must have been lonesome and slow all her life, the way things would take her by surprise"); when Clyde, her husband, "would make her blue, she would go out onto the road, some car would slow down, and if it had a Tennessee license, the lucky kind, the chances were that she would spend the afternoon in the shed of the empty gin." So much, so explicit and clear. Also, specific enough the rewards for Ruby: "a sack of coffee, marked 'Sample' in red letters" and a newspaper. There, she reads that a "Mrs. Ruby Fisher had the misfortune to be shot in the leg by her husband this week." This item leads to a series of fantasies during which Ruby imagines herself dead and buried. When Clyde returns, she fixes his supper, then delightedly shows him the paper. He reads. An awful moment of helplessness overcomes them both ("Rare and wavering, some possibility stood timidly like a stranger between them and made them hang their heads"). Then he burns the paper. They admit the obvious truth that "it was another Ruby Fisher—in Tennessee." And after his good-humored spank across her backside, Ruby sits at her supper. These are the actual events.

The Freudian symbolism—of the gun, of the shot, of Clyde's once black-haired handsomeness now turned to damp bald-headedness—is an obvious device of the story. But equally significant is Miss Welty's handling of two images: the fire and the rain storm; the blazing up of both of these natural symbols parallels and deepens the story's meaning and clarifies that "still moment" of awareness between human beings, which here, as elsewhere in her fiction, is the transcendent point of revelation. Further, the transgression of Ruby, her dalliance and Clyde's ultimate acceptance are the essential materials of all human mythology. Related with a powerful restraint and with a compassionate humor, the story is a model of method: first, her camera-like eye, which sees and records with precision the surface reality; then, by the inclusion of lights and shadows and by the arrangement of the details, the author manages to suggest the poetic depths which underlie and surround the human condition.

It is true that Miss Welty offers no facile answer to the enigmas she exposes. She does not suggest, for example, that either recognition or love will make Ruby and Clyde Fisher "better" or "different" or "happier." They are caught in their essential humanity; an unexpected moment of fantasy enables them to see each other in a new light; the moment is brief, ecstatic and beautiful; it offers no more than a flash of light or a song. It is simply there; it happens. The compassion and the humor which the author lends to that moment, however, raise it to the level of art. Miss Welty's technique reminds one of an impressionistic painting or a recording of an impromptu jazz session (her stories, "A Memory" and "Powerhouse," explore such phenomena). She makes the experience available. And although the sequential nature of language, as Keats observed, cannot reproduce ecstasy and the flash of beauty, the story is nevertheless all that we have (maybe, even, all that we need).

This sense is nowhere captured more profoundly and more beautifully by Miss Welty than in her poignant story, "A Still Moment." Briefly, three strangers—Lorenze Dow, evangelist, Murrell, outlaw, and Audubon, naturalist—meet by a "great live-oak tree" somewhere on the Natchez Trace. They all have a great need to communicate and are filled with a burning urgency to wrest knowledge and meaning from life. "But instead of speech there happened a moment of deepest silence." And "in that quiet moment, a solitary snowy heron flew down not far away and began to feed beside the marsh water." There stood the bird, "lighter and more serene than the evening

. . . the circuit of its beauty closed . . . ," offering to each of them its flight, its ecstasy, its essence of life. And "what each of them had wanted was simply *all*. To save all souls, to destroy all men, to see and record all life that filled this world—all, all—." Audubon kills the bird in order to paint its beauty. What he will reproduce will be "a dead thing and not a live thing, never the essence, only a sum of parts." His action exposes to him "for the first time . . . horror in its purity and clarity . . . in the bright blue eyes" of Lorenze. Murrell, unmoved, returns to his faith—"Travelers were forever innocent"—and his knowledge—"of ruin," Lorenze, horror-stricken, comes to realize that "God Himself, just now, thought of the Idea of Separateness" after having given Love first. Love, for Lorenze, should have come afterwards to "heal in its wonder." He can resolve his dilemma only with a shout: "Tempter!" And he rides furiously on.

Miss Welty closes the story with the calm assurance of the great poet: "Then the sun dropped below the trees, and the new moon, slender and white, hung shyly in the west." There is faith here, a trust in beauty as well as an artist's confidence in her own awareness and in her skill.

The same techniques, much more elaborately manipulated, characterize all the stories in *The Golden Apples*. Here the myths, classical and literary, are an obvious device to add dimension to the stories by placing them in a tradition. This is something about which Miss Welty has always been most careful: her settings. Physically, except for some of the stories in *The Bride of the Innisfallen* (1955) her settings are almost exclusively the Delta region of Mississippi. In *The Golden Apples*, Miss Welty uses this locale (with one exception: the story, "Music from Spain," takes place in San Francisco) to create her own world (the town of Morgana) and her own time (a forty-year span in the lives of the leading and some lesser citizens); the relevance of Morgana to Faulkner's Yoknapatawpha is obvious; but there is one difference: Faulkner's word is derived from the Indian background, whereas Morgana harkens back to Morgan le Fay and the world of magic. Both authors proceed freely to mingle pagan, Christian and folk myths in their respective realms. By means of such literary devices—the use of myths and the references to literature (Yeats's poem, "The Song of the Wandering Aengus," for example)—Miss Welty extends the implications of her plots. Further poetic techniques—the symbolic use of music and time, of birds and flowers—add another dimension. Finally, Morgana is all the world, both in time and space (consequently, the title of one story, "The Whole World Knows").

Throughout these masterful tales, Miss Welty weaves the threads of her constant themes: loneliness, awareness, love. So, "June Recital" ends as we are told of Cassie Morrison's newly awakened consciousness, a mixture of her memories of the Yeats poem and of her childhood experiences. What she has learned is that "Both Miss Eckhart and Virgie Rainey were human beings terribly at large, roaming on the face of the earth. And there were others of them—human beings, roaming, like lost beasts." The pessimism is as apparent as the beauty; both are swallowed up in Miss Welty's compassion.

The theme, as in music, is repeated with variation in "Moon Lake." Easter, the orphan girl, evidently one of King McLain's "scattered" children, is tickled, literally by a green willow switch, and falls from the diving-board into the lake. Rescued from the bottom, she is revived (with vulgar and comic overtones) by Loch Morrison. Her resurrection becomes the central episode of the story. But afterwards, Nina and Jinny Love watch Loch, his heroism past, slowly undress "in his tent of separation in the middle of the woods, in the night." Jinny Love suddenly becomes aware of the human condition, isolation. "You and I will always be old maids," she says to Nina. But "they went up and joined the singing."

Just before this final scene, however, Miss Welty has inserted a description of the reaction of the other girls:

Some of them looked back and saw the lake, rimmed around with its wall-within-walls of woods, into which the dark had already come. There were the water wings of Little Sister Spights, floating yet, white as a bird. "I know another Moon Lake," one girl had said yesterday. "Oh, my child, Moon Lakes are all over the world," Mrs. Gruenwald had interrupted. "I know of one in Austria . . ." And into each fell a girl, they dared, now, to think.

Expansion of the theme here, to universality, emphasizes both the pathos and the wonder. The final sentence becomes not merely an extension in time and space, it is a poetic observation of truth and judgment.

Finally, in the last story, "The Wanderers," the whole sad truth about existence bursts upon Virgie Rainey. She has just returned to Morgana on the "slow train from Memphis"; "she had come back to something." " 'You're back at the right time to milk for me,' her mother said when she got there." Virgie, running, by the back way,

> never saw it differently, never doubted that all the opposites on earth were close together, love close to hate, living to dying; but of them all, hope and despair were the closest blood—unrecognizable one from the other sometimes, making moments double upon themselves, and in the doubling double again, amending but never taking back. For that journey, it was ripe afternoon, and all about her was that light in which the earth seems to come into its own, as if there would be no more days, only this day—when fields glow like deep pools and the expanding trees at the edges seem almost to open, like lilies, golden or dark. She had always loved that time of day, but now, alone, untouched now, she felt like dancing; knowing herself not really, in her essence, yet hurt; and thus happy. The chorus of crickets was as unprogressing and out of time as the twinkling of a star.

A still moment, indeed. Miss Welty, like any true lyric artist, poet or painter, has put her finger upon the exact and singing truth, first the overwhelming, inevitable sadness of life and then the surge of redeeming ecstasy. This is her triumph and the glory of her art. "To be capable of passion, of love, of wisdom, perhaps of prophecy, toward his material": this, she wrote, was the sum of Faulkner's achievement. "Isn't that enough?" she asked Edmund

Wilson. Yes, we answer. Enough both for Faulkner and for Eudora Welty who wrote the words out of the depths of her heart and understanding.

ii

The central emphasis in Mrs. McCullers' stories and novels is upon loneliness, particularly the loneliness of love and its consequent pain and suffering. She makes this point not only in her first novel, *The Heart Is a Lonely Hunter* (1940), where every character is alone and unhappy and searching—and doomed, but also, explicitly she sets forth her thesis in an authorial statement in *The Ballad of the Sad Café.*

"First of all, love is a joint experience between two persons—but the fact that it is a joint experience does not mean that it is a similar experience to the two people involved. There are the lover and the beloved, but these two come from different countries. Often the beloved is only a stimulus for all the stored-up love which has lain quiet within the lover for a long time hitherto. And somehow every lover knows this. He feels in his soul that his love is a solitary thing. He comes to know a new, strange loneliness and it is his knowledge that makes him suffer. So there is only one thing for the lover to do. He must house his love within himself as best he can; he must create for himself a whole new inward world—a world intense and strange, complete in himself."

Intense and strange indeed is the world of the lover as portrayed in the fiction of Carson McCullers. And just as the "lover can be man, woman, child, or indeed any human creature on this earth," so "the beloved can also be of any description." No better examples of this idea could be found than the characters in her first work. Singer, the gentle deaf-mute, is the confessor and somewhat grotesque object of love of many others: the mad revolutionary Jake Blount, the socially conscious but frustrated and oppressed Negro doctor Benedict Copeland, the troubled tomboy Mick Kelly. "Each man described the mute as he wished him to be." But Singer, who wants to talk so passionately that he must double his hands up into fists in his pockets, in turn is an unfulfilled lover—of his fat, idiotic fellow mute, the Greek Antonapoulos.

In this very first work, Mrs. McCullers demonstrated two of her characteristic preoccupations: her fondness for grotesque characters and the necessity for violence. Her ability to write convincingly about such conditions makes *The Heart Is a Lonely Hunter* and *Reflections in a Golden Eye* (1941) interesting and readable on a realistic level where we see the accurate portrayal of eccentrics, but it is not sufficient to make them distinguished as works of art. In the second work, where everything is seen as though the "immense golden eye" of a "ghastly green" peacock, a point of view which renders everything "tiny" and "grotesque," the eccentricities become connected with behavior as well as with character: Captain Penderton who "had a sad penchant for becoming enamoured of his wife's lovers"; the frustrated Alison Langdon who cuts off the nipples of her breasts with the garden shears; the silent Private Ellgee Williams who rides bareback and nude through the green woods.

In every case, whether the lover is grotesque or whether the grotesquerie is in the nature of his love (we remember that Frankie Addams has, in the words of Berenice, fallen "in love with a wedding"), the result is not only suffering but violence. Singer kills himself. The Captain shoots Private Williams. And in the later works the violence persists. In *The Ballad of the Sad Café,* the climax is a horrifying wrestling-boxing match between Miss Amelia and Marvin Macy, after which Macy and the hunchback, Cousin Lymon, systematically destroy and violate everything. The concluding action of *Clock Without Hands* starts with the bombing of Sherman Pew's house and his death, events which are followed by the complete collapse of old Judge Clane as he tries to make a speech on the radio; after these bizarre details, the death from leukemia of J. T. Malone provides a quiet and pathetic ending. Indeed the novel is set within a framework of sickness and death which thus become the symbolic symptoms of the

society (a punishment for the failure to recognize the
existence of time and the necessity of change?).

Grotesque characters and lurid events are not all of Mrs.
McCullers' stock-in-trade. She has, as well, a sense of form.
In a curiously dead-pan style, she begins each of her longer
works with an exact statement of what is going on. "In the
town there were two mutes, and they were always together" is the opening sentence of *The Heart Is a Lonely
Hunter*. *Reflections in a Golden Eye* begins with this
astute observation: "An army post in peacetime is a dull
place." Before the end of the first short paragraph she has
told us that at a certain fort in the South a murder was
committed. And she concludes that paragraph: "The
participants of this tragedy were: two officers, a soldier, two
women, a Filipino, and a horse." *The Member of the
Wedding* starts out: "It happened that green and crazy
summer when Frankie was twelve years old." The summer's boredom and the heat are subsequently described.
"And then, on the last Friday of August, all this was
changed: it was so sudden that Frankie puzzled the whole
blank afternoon, and still she did not understand." The
opening description of *The Ballad of the Sad Café* is in
the same vein: "The town itself is dreary," she notes, and
then she gives the evidence, continuing with an account of
the boarded-up leaning building which was once the café
and the terrible face of grief that sometimes appeared in a
second-floor window. She concludes the opening section
with a short factual paragraph: once there was a café, with
tables and cloths and paper napkins. The owner was Miss
Amelia Evans. "But the person most responsible for the
success and gaiety of the place was a hunchback called
Cousin Lymon." The one other person who had a part in
the story was "the former husband of Miss Amelia, a
terrible character who returned to the town after a long
term in the penitentiary, caused ruin, and then went on his
way again." The assertion—"Death is always the same,
but each man dies in his own way"—starts *Clock Without
Hands*. J. T. Malone's condition is then described as of
March, 1953.

Each of these openings is exact, economical, dramatic. Information is presented with journalistic efficiency and objectivity. The events of the story unfold in orderly detail. The first three chapters of *The Heart Is a Lonely Hunter* neatly introduced the three chief groups of characters and the three chief settings of the novel. *Reflections in a Golden Eye* is meticulously arranged in four sections, and *The Member of the Wedding* is just as precisely divided into three parts. The three-part structure of this latter novel is, indeed, one of its glories: in section one we meet Frankie Addams, she of the crusty elbows, noisy and restless, aimlessly wandering but with a life centered in the kitchen where she communes with Berenice and John Henry; in the middle section, she is F. Jasmine, the exotic woman of the world, who flirts with a soldier as she wanders through the town to proclaim her relationship to Janis and Jarvis and the wedding; her horizons are extended to include other characters both from the white and Negro worlds; finally, in part three, she becomes simply Frances Addams; John Henry dies; Berenice prepares to go off and marry T. T.; Frances and her father will depart the old house to move out to the new suburb; and she has a friend, Mary Littlejohn, braided, brown-eyed, and intimate. The structure of each work thus emerges from a literal statement or set of facts. The movement is then from order into disorder. In only one of her novels are the tragic details resolved, or is order restored. The works are thus all of a piece, all part of Mrs. McCullers' vision, which is not so much tragic as pathetic and lyric. The wounded cry of the lonesome and/or hurt lover reminds us of his state: particularly are the young left desolate (Mick Kelly and Jester Clane): only in *The Member of the Wedding* is there any resolution as Frankie successfully undergoes the adolescent metamorphosis into Frances.

In working out her plots (themes) Mrs. McCullers utilizes typical poetic symbols. Her two chief images are music and time (also recurring symbols in the stories of Miss Welty). Mick Kelly learns to love Mozart, as contrasted with Baby Wilson, whose tap-dancing epitomizes the most vulgar aspirations of the society. Alison Langdon and her Filipino servant, Anacleto, both love ballet. Sherman Pew and Jester Clane play the piano. And all that remains of the gay and terrible events which took place in the sad café is the ballad mournfully but magnificently sung by the chain gang. In fact the characteristic impression created in and by all of Mrs. McCullers' works is that somewhere there is music, a kind of tuneful accompaniment which somehow makes the suffering a bit more bearable. This notion, again, is based upon a lyrical principle; also, these sad songs of mankind relate both to folk ballads and to the blues. In all respects the mood is nostalgic and lyric.

Time is another important symbol for Mrs. McCullers. The life of Singer and Antonapoules is curiously timeless, and hence lovely, until suddenly the Greek is put away into a state institution; then, Singer doesn't know what to do with his time any more than with his hands. Jake Blount and Benedict Copeland are "driven" by their awareness of the shortness of time in which to accomplish their goals: Jake is mad, Copeland is ultimately victimized not only by the stupidity of his fellow Negroes ("For forty years his mission was his life and his life was his mission. And yet all remained to be done and nothing was completed") but by the time of his disease, tuberculosis. All of the events of *The Member of the Wedding* transpire in one summer, the year when Frankie is twelve. The happenings of *Reflections in a Golden Eye* seem to float in time and space, but actually they take place within a month. The days of joy in the café, too, were numbered, ironically dependent upon Marvin Macy's term in the penitentiary; then came the time of preparation as Miss Amelia and Marvin trained for their inevitable confrontation. Finally in *Clock Without Hands*, the very subject of the novel is time. The framework concerns the time it takes for leukemia to kill its victim; this strange blood disease has its own symbolic relevance; the fifteen months it takes for J. T. Malone to die parallel and dramatize the exciting times during which Judge Clane tries to turn the

clock back and Sherman Pew seeks to advance the slow
tick-tock of integration. Both are doomed, the Judge to
madness, Sherman to a violent death. The two extremists,
Sammy Link who hates the Negroes and throws the bomb,
and Jester who loves and tries to understand, meanwhile
go for an airplane ride, into the timeless skies; they must
return, however, to reality: reality is the timely death of
Malone, who represents the ordinary man in the South.
But all of the characters are caught up in time's inexorable
march. This is the burden of Mrs. McCullers' most recent
song. It represents not only her sensitive awareness of the
world and her lyric cry of sympathy with the lonely and
the victimized, but it suggests as well a philosophic
resolution: just as a summertime of pain allows for
Frankie's growth, so, here, more tragically, out of a year of
cruelty and disease and death will emerge a more meaningful world.

THE DISSECTIONS OF
MARY McCARTHY

Paul Schlueter

ALMOST EVERY DESCRIPTION of Mary McCarthy's fiction
includes such terms as "honest," "intellectual," "savage,"
"witty," "satiric," or "dispassionate." Notwithstanding the
dangers inherent in attaching labels to a writer, it is
certainly accurate to point out that Miss McCarthy
reflects all of these qualities, and that her reputation as a
writer is based as much on her relentless pursuit of these
traits as it is on the purely external trappings of her novels
and stories—the competition (usually in bed) between
the sexes, for instance. In one sense, she is not even a
novelist; the autobiographical content and extraneous
padding found in some of her books would appear to place
her in a category all her own, that of a highly intelligent
woman reflecting upon her own past life, and able,
through some kind of near-total recall, to incorporate such
nostalgic glimpses into highly competent short stories,
some of which are expanded, printed, and sold as novels.
In this respect, she is not unlike some other writers
(Hemingway and John O'Hara come to mind) who were
also masters of the shorter form, but who were sometimes
able (not always satisfactorily) to develop a short narrative
into novelette or novel length. Further similarities between
Miss McCarthy and other contemporary writers, however,
are difficult to make; her attraction for both popular and
critical audiences is partly a result of her combination of
sex-and-intellect, and partly a result of the difficulty of
classifying her. In short, Miss McCarthy has something in

her fiction for almost everybody, but all of these audiences, I believe, would agree in describing her approach to writing as reflective of the Modern American Bitch. The best term to describe her particular approach to writing, however, is dissection: ruthlessly, she cuts beneath the layers of accumulated social pretense and hypocrisy, to the core of contemporary man and woman. Lying thus, naked to the marrow, that man and woman become experiments in which Miss McCarthy attempts to determine why certain patterns of behavior occur; but after the dissection, it is no wonder that the pieces rarely fit together well enough to make a recognizable human being again. Her interest, then, is not in human beings *qua* human beings, but as objects from which a better understanding of human psychology and physiology can be derived.

Miss McCarthy's first published book, *The Company She Keeps* (1942), is a loosely linked collection of semi-autobiographical short stories, of which at least two ("The Man in the Brooks Brothers Shirt" and "Portrait of the Intellectual as a Yale Man") are certainly among the best written in our time. It was immediately clear, after this collection appeared, that Miss McCarthy had unique talents for probing into and analyzing character, especially that of a woman like herself, who seems—no matter what her fictional name—to appear in almost all of her fiction. In *The Company She Keeps,* this recurring character is called Margaret Sargent; she is a New Yorker, a Trotskyite, born a Catholic but raised under both Protestant and Catholic influences, who, when we first meet her, is in the process of getting a divorce. Subsequently, she works in an art gallery run by an idiosyncratic confidence-man; she travels via Pullman to the west coast and back for her divorce, and, incidentally, makes love with a man she meets; attaches herself to a fashionably intellectual literary-political crowd; and, finally, goes through analysis, concluding that "she did not believe in God." This last section, in particular, seems especially moving, almost as if Miss McCarthy saw in Margaret Sargent more than a fictional alter ego; whatever it is that bothers Miss Sargent (certainly a mixture of religion-politics-sex-intellect) would seem to lead Miss McCarthy to identify with her more than is the case with her other "heroines." In a *Paris Review* interview, Miss McCarthy admitted that most of the stories in this collection (with the specific exception of the one about the Yale man) had a basis in her own experience; in particular, "The Man in the Brooks Brothers Shirt" described something that "actually happened," with, of course, names and locales changed.

The Company She Keeps also serves to introduce a theme which is, to a greater or lesser extent, suggested or developed in everything Miss McCarthy has written: the disillusionment in the lives of the professional liberals of the 1930's who find out belatedly that society is not ready for salvation from the left. Instead of a firm adherence to a doctrinaire, somewhat bohemian liberalism, Miss McCarthy's central characters, such as Margaret Sargent, revert to a skeptical, cynical, even pessimistic middle-class standard of living and behavior, perhaps best seen in the story about the Yale man, in which a conventionally liberal young writer moves from a struggling left-wing magazine to a weekly news-magazine, a move closely matching the metamorphosis in his own social views. Such a conversion, of course, somewhat approximates Miss McCarthy's own, and can also be seen in one character or another in all her fiction.

The Oasis (1949), the first of Miss McCarthy's novels (although really more of a long short story or novelette), is a cold and analytical glimpse into a utopian society of artists and intellectuals. As with most other societies of this sort, however, this Utopia seems foredoomed to failure, not so much for the inadequacy of the theory behind such a cooperative community, but rather because even intellectuals are incapable of overcoming the petty and bothersome trifles inherent in such a society. More purely satiric than her previous book, *The Oasis* makes it perfectly clear from the outset that she has little sympathy with such escapists; although all the residents in the community believe theoretically in the rightness of their brand of utopianism, when it comes to a practical test of that theory, the society crumbles. Suitably enough, the incident that brings matters to the breaking point is a dispute over some intruders attempting to pick some strawberries, as if a few berries more or less would in itself invalidate the philosophy behind the community. It seems obvious that Miss McCarthy believes that men among other men (especially intellectuals holding all the "right" views among other intellectuals) are far too complex and uncertain to live together harmoniously. Cliquish, incapable of action, stubborn, anachronistically left-wing, lethargically pacifistic (except for the one member whose gun, itself out of place in Utopia, serves to frighten away the interlopers), and unable to cope with the primitive conditions of their surroundings, the Utopians are doubtlessly intended to represent, in Miss McCarthy's mind, the *reductio ad absurdum* of the advanced ideas of the 1930's. Among the reasons why the society crumbles is certainly the attempt at removing one middle-aged manufacturer from the society, because, in some indefinable way, he "just doesn't fit." The theory, then, is not sufficient for them to make of Utopia the ideal society they had dreamed of. That, along with the strawberry incident and an abortive, fantastic, and short-lived plan to consolidate all the peace-loving peoples of the world, effectively diminishes the possibility of Utopia surviving beyond that season. Because the group had considered Utopia as a means of arriving at "collective security," while at the same time separating themselves from the real world, it was doomed to failure; and this is particularly so in this utopian society because of the "ugliness" each member sees in himself and the others. Such idealists, Miss McCarthy seems to say, must at last remain ineffective individualists; when such individualism is given up, even in part, for the sake of a utopia, something is bound to break, and, in *The Oasis*, it is the society itself.

Miss McCarthy switched locales in her next work of fiction, *The Groves of Academe* (1952), although the same preoccupation with the inadequacies of doctrinaire liberalism is evident. Set in a fictional progressive college in Pennsylvania, *The Groves of Academe* concerns Henry Mulcahy, a professor at once comical and villainous, who, because of obvious incompetence, is threatened with dismissal. The professor, however, lets word drop that he had been a Communist during the 1930's, and this is sufficient to get the professional liberals on the Jocelyn College faculty and administration to support him, since, of course, a "witchhunt" is anathema in such a setting, particularly during the McCarthy era when this novel appeared. Handled as a satire, as this is, the theme is highly successful; handled more heavily, as one might have expected, the book would have become a polemic about academic freedom. But the professor is so adept a scoundrel that, in the end, he is rehired and the academic-freedom-defending president of the college is forced to resign. In short, justice and freedom are both inverted; the issue becomes, not whether or not a one-time Communist should or should not teach, but rather whether or not the liberal world of academe is a world in which such qualities as integrity, freedom, and intellectualism really mean anything, or if they are merely part of the jargon of the classroom, and as such, deserve to be exposed for what they are. Unquestionably, the reflex-action in supporting the professor with the would-be past is part of the liberal-intellectual-idealistic mentality which Miss McCarthy seems to take such delight in assaulting, but, in this novel, it is done with what must be called a more humorous and less savage satire than in her other novels. What makes *The Groves of Academe* so delightful is the irony in the circumstances of a liberal making himself seem to be a victim of conservative persecution, thus forcing the liberal administration to out-liberal him by rehiring him.

Miss McCarthy's satire in *The Groves of Academe* not only is less caustic than in her other books, it is also considerably more knowledgeable about the jargon, the pet beliefs, the occurrences on a college campus, than, for instance, is the case with Utopia. Almost every stereotype of personality to be found on real "progressive" campuses is found on that of Jocelyn College: the president is the epitome of the well-meaning, rugged, thoughtful, liberal administrator; the poetry conference held on Jocelyn's campus has all types of poets represented (with Miss McCarthy's sympathies obviously lying with a "poet of the masses" who hitchhiked to the conference, and who puts the lie to Mulcahy's claims of earlier Communist affiliation); the faddish preference on the students' part for particular writers; the narrow specialist (Mulcahy himself, a Joycean, fits this category) who cannot understand why everyone doesn't appreciate his speciality; and so on, down the list of academic habitués. The target of the satire, however, is considerably larger than this listing would indicate. In the essential conflict between Mulcahy and the administration, such major issues are raised as the impossibility of the academic mind either being free or knowing what to do with freedom, the professional liberal whose liberalism is shaken by not being able to champion another liberal, and the liberal who is at heart an opportunist using liberalism for his own advantage. Essentially, the weakness Miss McCarthy sees in the shallow philosophy held by the characters in *The Groves of Academe* is an inability to see a "darker truth about human nature" than they think they should believe in. Thus, Mulcahy manipulates people and liberalism for his own benefit, and the others, liberals one and all, cannot adjust to and handle the results of that "darker truth."

A *Charmed Life* (1955) is also concerned with intellectuals and artists, but instead of the setting being a college campus or escapist colony, it is New Leeds, a New England summer artist-colony; and the characters, instead of being itinerant visitors to the town, as one would expect, are the permanent residents of the community. Martha Sinnott is the central character; she had been married to a sometime writer in the town, and comes back, with a new husband, to attempt to make a success of her second marriage on the site of the first. The story, what there is of it, concerns Martha's relationships with the various odd members of New Leeds, her seduction by her first husband, her discovery of her pregnancy, and a fatal drive to Boston for an abortion. Quite caustic and bitter, A *Charmed Life* reveals even in its title an obsession on Miss McCarthy's part with a sarcastic stripping-away of her characters' psyches and lives; although Martha is, at the end of the novel, the only character who has died, it can validly be said that none of the characters has any real life left, so clinically complete has been Miss McCarthy's dissection. Those bohemians are clearly types, even down to the great original, but undiscovered, artist, the virginal rich girl, and the universal genius, expert in all fields but recognized in none. The characters, however, do not seem at all believable. Even Martha, for instance, seems quite contradictory; in her college days, she had had many sexual flings, without the least concern over conscience or consequences, so, the reader wonders, why the mania for an abortion when the slim chance exists that her first husband is the father? If the intent in this novel is satire (and no other term seems to fit), then what, exactly, is being satirized? If it is Martha who is being satirized, there is certainly not as much on which to base the satire as, say, with Margaret Sargent; the satire seems more forced, more contrived, more uncertain. Norman Podhoretz once commented that Miss McCarthy's characters are either intelligent or stupid, and that the intelligent are those "who refuse to harbor illusions about themselves," and who persistently self-analyze themselves. But for Martha, as for some other heroines, an increase in self-awareness does not mean greater self-control, but the opposite; and Martha, instead of knowing what she is and has been, reacts in a totally unexpected manner, and then, conveniently, is killed.

Several lengthy digressions are included in A *Charmed Life*, giving the reader the distinct feeling that this should be a much shorter story. As with the prolonged poetry discussion in *The Groves of Academe*, the digressions are usually of a literary nature; Racine's *Bérénice* is the major topic in A *Charmed Life*, with other digressions along the way about Hamlet, Kant, and Shaw—in short, the kind of "arty" discussion typical of New Leeds and its inhabitants. And even Martha, despite her claims to "not fitting in," seems as typically a New Leedsian as anyone else, only, perhaps more blatantly amoral. The novel, then, seems more a mélange of pseudo-artistic and literary chit-chat, coated with sarcasm and invective, than an effective satire or novel. Really a collection of related scenes, the book, had it been considerably shorter, might have been another excellent story; instead, it seems an occasionally boring, always witty, usually acid, collection of ugly cadavers on which Miss McCarthy has unleashed her fury. The sense of characters being introduced, not because of stylistic necessity, but rather whimsically, cannot but strike the reader; perhaps this is nowhere more obvious than in the character of Eleanor Considine, who, introduced two pages from the end of the book, is described at length, only to serve as the awkwardly contrived means of "accidentally" killing Martha.

Although *The Group* (1963), Miss McCarthy's latest novel, has received considerable popular attention (more, one suspects, because of the sensationalism of Chapter II than because of interest in the author as a novelist), it too demonstrates some of the same faults to be found in *A Charmed Life*. Eight Vassar graduates (class of 1933, Miss McCarthy's own class) enter into the real world of the depression (which scarcely affects them personally), and, along the way, discover contraceptives, lesbianism, death, divorce, fashionable literary and artistic poseurs, and the rest of the trappings with which we are already familiar. The emphasis shifts from one girl to another, but with most attention given to Kay, who is introduced first—at her sudden marriage—and who serves at the end—at her death by defenestration—to bring "the group" together again. Little real action occurs; as with the earlier books, but to a far greater degree, the characters just talk. Their conversations, however, serve quite effectively to characterize them—so well, in fact, that one might say that in this respect Miss McCarthy is unexcelled. The treatment of the several characters is considerably more varied than in the earlier novels; not only is there actually a character whom Miss McCarthy seems content to describe approvingly (Polly), but there are also several lesser characters (Dottie, Helena, Priss) whose idiosyncracies, although vividly portrayed, nonetheless seem muted by contrast with Kay's.

The same sharp, ruthless satiric touch is seen in *The Group* as in earlier books. Bohemianism, the literary world, would-be dramatists, the brainlessness of certain rich families whose every action is determined by the butler, and marriage itself—all these are touched upon, all are shown in their gruesome extremity, and all become self-consciously real. But this kind of satire, to be effective to the maximum, cannot be *saeva* without being *indignatio*; and even in this book, where a greater spectrum of characterization is present than previously, ideas and character traits with which Miss McCarthy is not in favor get reduced to a pulpy puddle not unlike Kay at the end of the novel. Even the funeral scene, a conclusion fittingly contrasted to the wedding scene with which the book opens, seems less an occasion for the author to demonstrate the changes and maturation in the remaining members of "the group," than it is for her to pin-point once again the girls' shortcomings—their desire for security, their fashionable marriages, their concern not for the dead girl but for their own interests, their self-consciousness at the ostentation of having three psalms at the funeral instead of a more "proper" number.

It might legitimately be asked, then, whether or not Miss McCarthy is really a novelist. Her dependence on autobiographical or semi-autobiographical materials is not in itself a deficiency (although one wonders whether she could write a novel not based on events in her own life), but her technique is. Her enormous vocabulary and erudition show on every page; indeed, scarcely a page appears without some italicized French phrase or esoteric term. But this witty, highly intelligent fondness for words for their own sake sometimes makes of a relatively short narrative a book of several hundred pages. Her treatment of characters, with rare exceptions, serves as a pulpit or platform from which she can lecture on some evil in humanity or some *cause célèbre* with which she is no longer personally involved. Indeed, so cavalier is she with characters, even central ones, that she disposes of them in the best *deus ex machina* fashion; when all else fails, kill them off; it's neater that way, and its saves her the chore of figuring out some logical means of ending the novel. When Miss McCarthy is not attempting a novel, as in her excellent stories in *The Company She Keeps*, or her semi-autobiographical narratives in *Cast a Cold Eye* (1950, later incorporated in *Memories of a Catholic Girlhood* [1957], in many ways her best book), she has no noticeable trouble winding things up; there is none of the sometimes forced attempts at polemicizing; there is none of the artificial intrusion of the author in literary or political digressions. In short, whatever strengths are to be found in her novels—vigor, honesty, straightforwardness, intelligence, to name a few—are more than adequately represented in the shorter pieces as well, and not a few additional strengths are added.

The shorter pieces, moreover, do not seem to be especially propagandistic about a particularly amoral attitude toward sex, although this can certainly be found; sex in the longer works, aside from whatever explicitness with which it is presented, seems always to be something done more as a whim than because of passion. In *The Group*, Dottie's curiosity, not any feelings of love, leads to her seduction; and when it is over, she thinks of the dichotomy of sex and love. In *A Charmed Life*, Martha at first resists Miles's attempts at making love; then, stoically, she "takes a deep breath, like a doomed person," and says "all right." In "The Man in the Brooks Brothers Shirt," Margaret eventually gives in: "She had felt tired and kind, and thought, why not?" Then: "There was to be no more love-making, she saw, and from the moment she felt sure of this, she began to be a little bit in love." Sex, then, serves not as an expression of love, but as an amoral encounter between man and woman in their eternal struggle for superiority over one another. Even the act of love coincides with the clinical, dispassionate, acerbic dissection Miss McCarthy performs on her fellow human beings, a dissection evident not only in the perfunctory and illogical behavior patterns of these humans, but, more's the pity, in the deepest emotional recesses of humanity. This dissection, then, serves less as a means of examining in detail other human beings, and more as an immolation of and by Mary McCarthy herself.

Despite the intellectualism, the clarity of insight into character, the satire of others' foibles, the dispassionate wit of her books, they ultimately lack a foundation, perhaps a moral foundation, on which great art must be based. Without this foundation, Miss McCarthy's novels are as ultimately sterile and animalistic as, say, the world Lear saw (the parallel is obvious) when he shouted, "Let copulation thrive!" Or, in other words, dissection sometimes requires more than enthusiasm and a sharp knife.

BERNARD MALAMUD AND THE
NEW ROMANTICISM

Charles Alva Hoyt

"SUFFERING is like a piece of goods," says Frank Alpine, the dogged hero of *The Assistant*; "I bet the Jews could make a suit of clothes out of it." The suffering of the Jews is to Bernard Malamud the stuff and substance of his art; from it he has fashioned works of surpassing beauty and integrity, and a sure place among the best writers of his time.

"The other funny thing," Alpine continues, "is that there are more of them around than anybody knows about." This emphasis upon the universality of the Jew—even the identity of Jew and Gentile, for the two merge in some of Malamud's more interesting characters, including Frank Alpine—and thus, the insistence upon the community of human suffering, lifts Malamud's work from his own period and place and sets it in competition with the best writing of any time. This is as it should be. One hears Malamud referred to as a "Jewish writer." He is a Jewish writer in the same sense that Dickens is a social-protest writer, or Jane Austen a domestic novelist.

Suffering is Malamud's theme, and upon it he works a thousand variations: some comical, some menacing; some austere, some grotesque; some imaginative, others classic. The Jew as symbol for suffering mankind is hardly an original idea. In Malamud there is considerable individuality, however: in his style, for example, which is highly personal yet generous and attentive to the requirements of outsiders, the public; in his characterization, variegated, kaleidoscopic, but in essence shifting combinations of only two or three basic forms. Most of all Malamud reveals his personality in his attitude, which is strikingly and overwhelmingly Romantic.

Because criticism has to stalk its prey from a distance, its dicta sometimes fall to the ground well behind the retreating quarry, the live work of art. In the museum they arrange these things differently. Just at present there is particularly noticeable one of these gaps between the classifier and the classified. The New Critics, sunk into dotage, have bequeathed to their disciples an assortment of missiles which although effective in the nineteen-thirties, have proven totally inadequate when directed at the bounding Romanticism of the sixties. It is becoming increasingly evident that the inevitable has happened; that the athletic fatalism of Hemingway, the closed "realism" of the Naturalistic school, the chipped classicism of Eliot and T. E. Hulme, have engendered their opposites. Romanticism is by now abroad in all its traditional forms, and proliferating: Youth in Revolt (Kerouac and others of the Beat group; England's Angry Young Men), Glorification of Energy, and Passion Unconfined (the Picaresque romps of Saul Bellow and J. P. Donleavy), The Unleashed Imagination (Thomas Pynchon, Joseph Heller), Social Protest (James Baldwin and others above), and of course, the Cult of the Self, which so baffles the classicist critic (J. D. Salinger has certainly out-Wordsworthed Wordsworth here, drawing upon himself new Jeffreys, as has to a lesser degree Norman Mailer). To this exuberant ill-assorted group Malamud stands as philosopher, or deepest thinker, perhaps.

While it cannot be seriously suggested that the writers mentioned above are committed to any sort of concerted program, it is easily demonstrable that many or most of them hold certain principles in common. Instead of taking up these principles at their peripheral positions, I should prefer just at present to move to what I conceive to be their center, their common point of issuance: the fundamental Romantic Rejection of Objectivity. Classicism observes the arrangement of things—very likely records it—and wisely adapts itself to Order. Romanticism, refusing to accept a mere catalogue, reorders things to suit itself. Naturalism simply despairs.

Take the problem of suffering, for example. Naturalism can offer nothing better than this: "curse God and die." Classicism suggests graceful acquiescence, and an alternate problem, one better adapted to Man's limitations: "Know then thyself, presume not God to scan; / The proper study of Mankind is Man." Romanticism, finally, calls the problem itself into question: "How do you know but ev'ry Bird that cuts the airy way, / Is an immense world of delight clos'd by your senses five?" The tormented characters of Bernard Malamud's fiction, although fated often to despair, curse, submit, and turn aside, still cling to the Romantic's determination to reject old evidence, to present a new solution that will be bigger than the sum of its parts. It is this highly characteristic Romantic drive that supplies the impetus of Malamud's greatness; it can be found, in one form or another, in each of his works to date.

Foremost among these is *The Assistant*, Malamud's second novel, an acknowledged masterpiece. Most of his readers discovered him in the year of its publication, 1958, or in 1959, when his first collection of short stories, *The Magic Barrel*, won the National Book award. These thirteen stories and the novel which crowns them are the products in the main, it would seem, of one intense period of creativity, the nineteen fifties. Early in this period, we have that curious work *The Natural*, published in 1952, Malamud's first novel; after it we have another burst of publication in the early sixties: a third novel, *A New Life*, 1961, and another collection of stories, *Idiots First*, 1963. These later works represent no departure; obviously some of them are partially or wholly products of the fifties. They are closely related in every way to the works published in 1958 and 1959. At least two of the stories in *Idiots First* belong to the early fifties; one, "The Cost of Living," is the source of *The Assistant*, which may explain why it was not published in the earlier collection. Most of the stories in *Idiots First*, however, would seem to date from the early sixties, as does *A New Life*. All of these works represent a continuous flow of ideas in the same direction; and since none of the recent ones has surpassed *The Assistant*, it must be with that novel that we begin our study.

One of Malamud's strongest and best claims to enduring recognition is his instinct for myth. From his first novel, which is at times almost entirely removed from the plane of ordinary reality, to his latest short story, he provides for his characters and their situations a ritual shadow of significance which never seems contrived, and at times is simply astonishing in its effectiveness. It is this quality which has time and again fascinated critics of *The Assistant*. Here Malamud has realized an age-old prophecy: the lion lies down with the kid. Once side by side, they look very much alike.

Frank Alpine, a drifting down-and-outer who has wandered into petty crime, becomes involved in the robbery and beating of Morris Bober, a luck-deserted Jewish grocer. *The Assistant* is the story of Alpine's slow, bitter self-subjection to his former victim; their lives become increasingly entangled until Alpine *becomes* Bober: at the grocer's death he takes his place, an assistant no longer. Out of the dirt and the deprivation of the novel's slum setting there has come, not the Naturalistic cry of pain, but an inescapable sense of mystic union: the identity of the oppressor and the oppressed.

The oppressed is presented as the Jew in this novel; Alpine is Italian—"I am of Italian extraction." But from the start these distinctions are blurred; there is nothing particularly "Italian" about Alpine, except that he understands the preparation of minestrone and pizza; and Bober has his Jewishness called into question at his own funeral. The Rabbi defends him: " 'Yes, Morris Bober was to me a true Jew because he lived in the Jewish experience, which he remembered, and with the Jewish heart. Maybe not to our formal tradition—for this I don't excuse him—but he was true to the spirit of our life—to want for others that which he wants also for himself.' " Thus defined, the Jewish spirit does not differ appreciably from the Christian. As for Alpine, he passes from scorn to wonder at Bober's plight; to sympathy, and finally to identification. Early in the book he stands aloof: "That's what they live for, Frank thought, to suffer. And the one that has got the biggest pain in the gut and can hold onto it the longest without running to the toilet is the best Jew. No wonder they got on his nerves."

But a short time later he is himself called a Jew, with some justice if little delicacy, by his former partner in crime. In some incomprehensible fashion Frank Alpine has taken Bober's fate upon himself, and even a cheap hoodlum like Ward Minogue can see it. Less perceptive and more fearful is Bober's wife, who dreads an entanglement between Alpine and her daughter: " 'But a goy, Helen, an Italyener' "—" 'A man, a human being like us.' " Helen is not always as charitable. Her feeling for Frank suffers a terrible revulsion; at the novel's end they are still estranged, although not hopelessly so. Bober himself frequently discourages his assistant—we are not to understand that any union of Man, even one in misery, is cheaply attained. But Frank Alpine, like most of Malamud's heroes, slogs ahead doggedly, often even in spite of himself. It is at Bober's funeral that he observes that suffering is like a piece of goods from which clothing may be made; shortly afterwards, at the novel's end, he puts it upon himself symbolically as he has already done in actual fact: "One day in April Frank went to the hospital and had himself circumcised . . . The pain enraged and inspired him. After Passover he became a Jew."

The relationship between two men is the heart of the book. They are the grocer and assistant, father and son, aggressor and victim, missionary and convert, even sacrifice and priest—if the idea seems farfetched, it may seem less so upon reconsideration of *The Natural:* the mystic slaughter of the king has apparently occupied Malamud's mind from the start. Quintessentially, both Alpine and Bober are true to one basic type, that which is at once both object and impulse of all Malamud's art: the *schlemiel*. Struggling, striving, always en route, but destined never quite to arrive, the *schlemiel* is both the butt and terror of the Gods. At heart he is decent, but whatever he touches turns to ashes; because he *cares*, he exposes himself continually to rebuffs, absurdities, humiliation. He is well-known to art: as Chaplin's tramp he loves too well, but rarely wisely, so that his love is scarcely ever reciprocated. The *schlemiel's* relationships with women are tragicomic. He intends nothing but good to his fellow creatures; yet because of his naïveté, his awkwardness, his obstrusiveness, and worst of all, his consistent bad luck, he embroils them in nothing but heartbreak and confusion. They are not slow to learn to avoid him, but he will never know why.

In *The Assistant* both the aggressor and his victim are fundamentally *schlemiels*. Consider Frank Alpine:

> I've been close to some wonderful things—jobs, for instance, education, women, but close is as far as I go. Don't ask me why, but sooner or later everything I think is worth having gets away from me in some way or other. I work like a mule for what I want, and just when it looks like I am going to get it I make some kind of stupid move, and everything that is just about nailed down blows up in my face . . . I want the moon so all I get is cheese . . . what I mean to say is that when I need it most something is missing in me, in me or on account of me. I always have this dream where I want to tell somebody something on the telephone so bad it hurts, but then when I am in the booth, instead of a phone being there, a bunch of bananas is hanging on a hook.

Frank's actions throughout the novel are nothing more than exposition of this theme, his introduction of himself in the second chapter. As for Bober, his is a classic case. Here is his daughter's evaluation of him:

> The grocer, on the other hand, had never altered his fortune, unless degrees of poverty meant alteration, for luck and he were, if not natural enemies, not good friends. He labored long hours, was the soul of honesty—he could not escape his

honesty; it was bedrock; to cheat would cause an explosion
in him, yet he trusted cheaters—coveted nobody's nothing
and always got poorer. . . . He was Morris Bober and could
be nobody more fortunate. With that name you had no sure
sense of property, as if it were in your blood and history not
to possess, or if by some miracle to own something, to do so
on the verge of loss. At the end you were sixty and had less
than at thirty. It was, she thought, surely a talent.

Struck down by his assailant's gun, Bober falls, "without a
cry. The end fitted the day. It was his luck, others had
better."

The curious thing is that these characters, who dominate
Malamud's fiction, are actually dignified, elevated by their
plight, or to be exact by their reaction to it. Classicism,
when it considers the downtrodden at all, utilizes them for
the sake of irony; that is, it is really looking at someone
else, someone important. Gay's footpads and whores, and
Swift's Clever Tom Clinch, losers all, are not presented on
the basis of their own merits. Naturalism, although it deals
almost exclusively with such figures, is no more genuinely
concerned with them; they are rather pawns, counters in a
contest of reproaches with the Deity. Only the Romantic
will wish to present them in such a way that they
epitomize Man's condition—struggling, stumbling ahead,
not winning, but not losing either. The reason the
schlemiel receives new rebuffs is that he always makes new
efforts; and once in a while these efforts are granted success.
If none of his triumphs is permanent, neither are his
failures.

The *schlemiel* is the proper figure to translate Malamud's theme into action. Anyone with any sense would
react differently; anyone with any luck would not have
been put in the position of reacting at all. But the
Romantic approach to suffering is bold; if logic is no help,
then logic must upon occasion be discarded. The brilliant
group of short stories surrounding *The Assistant* supports
and extends Malamud's findings. One of the most notable
among this new collection of *schlemiels* is Arthur Fidelman of "The Last Mohican." Fidelman is a "self-confessed

failure as a painter" and a Jew, although again mostly in name (his American background has gone a long way toward Gentilizing him). There is in him something of both Alpine and Bober, but he is in his vulnerable good-will and poverty closer perhaps to Bober. A certain bathetic streak in him reminds us however of Alpine, who slid into the grave during Bober's funeral. Fidelman is pursued relentlessly by Shimon Susskind, a dirty, sponging, obnoxious immigrant who manages to establish a claim upon his victim that both recognize. In despair Fidelman cries, "Am I responsible for you then, Susskind?" "Who else?" comes the answer.

I do not wish to suggest that all these *schlemiels* are identical. Fidelman is definitely Fidelman; in stressing his essential community with Malamud's other heroes—the critical element in Malamud's theme—I have to neglect such personal characteristics as his humor, which is much more pronounced than that of either Bober or Alpine. Fidelman is so delightful, in fact, that he is brought forward again in *Idiots First*, to general applause. But the *schlemiel*, football of the Gods (and symbol of undignified Man), is constantly in motion; one day up, the next into the mud. Wherever we may find Malamud's characters, we generally leave them on the upswing, usually a modest one, to be sure, but an upward movement nonetheless. Bober dies, but he has lived to see his fat and lucky neighbor offer hard cash for his run-down grocery. Alpine is low at the novel's end, but his new strength of purpose is clear. He has become a Jew and will eventually get the girl. Only rarely do we see a Malamud character on the downward swing. Fidelman is humiliated, robbed, blackmailed and insulted, yet at the story's end, chasing his tormentor (who will of course escape him), he has "a triumphant insight." " 'Susskind, come back,' he shouted, half sobbing. 'The suit is yours. All is forgiven.' " With such an attitude, the *schlemiel* is of necessity irrepressible. Fidelman is treated even worse in *Idiots First*, utterly squashed by a beautiful, hateful, ignorant bitch of a woman; yet at the end of the story he is in bed with her.

Most of Malamud's characters must content themselves with successes of a less climactic nature.

The story which gives the collection its title, "The Magic Barrel," obviously a favorite of its author, and of the critics, is not so hilarious. Its hero is a gentle rabbinical student, Leo Finkle, who engages in a series of adventures both ludicrous and touching with a down-at-the-heels marriage broker, one Pinye Salzman. Again the imperative contact between two men—one, like Bober, gentle, lovable; the other a hard-luck hustler, bowed but not quite broken. Again an ending of powerful affirmation: the student, rejecting all of Salzman's goods, fastens upon the broker's own daughter, a girl who is clearly marked as bad luck—her father weeps at the thought of her. (Many such bad-luck women occur in Malamud's fiction.) Yet the student embraces his fate; the close of the story finds him going to meet her where she waits, her eyes filled with "desperate innocence."

"The Magic Barrel" is one of the most beautiful recreations of Malamud's vision, but it is outdone in some respects at least by the remarkable "Angel Levine." Here the problem of suffering is formally stated, in almost Biblical, or to be more exact, Cabalistic terms. The struggles of its humble hero Manischevitz are those of Job: his business is wiped out, his wealth taken, even the insurance; his health is ruined, but he must work on for his wife, who is on her deathbed:

> "My dear God, sweetheart, did I deserve that this should happen to me?" Then recognizing the worthlessness of it, he put aside the complaint and prayed humbly for assistance: "Give Fanny back her health, and to me for myself that I shouldn't feel pain in every step. Help now or tomorrow is too late. This I don't have to tell you." And Manischevitz wept.

But help does come to him, in this enormously moving story, from a characteristically ludicrous source: a seemingly demented Negro who claims to be an angel sent from Heaven. At first Manischevitz rejects Levine, as the

Negro is called, out of hand, but finally he overcomes his logic and his pride and seeks for his own salvation: he goes up to Harlem and publicly confesses his faith in a saloon full of loafers and scorners. Like Job, he finds it is not enough simply to refrain from cursing. At the last his faith has restored his wife and his health to him; looking up, he is granted a vision of dark wings. " 'A wonderful thing, Fanny,' Manischevitz said. 'Believe me, there are Jews everywhere.' " The story ranks with the finest products of the Romantic imagination.

The Magic Barrel has other triumphs, other sufferings, other *schlemiels*. "The First Seven Years" gives us a glimpse of that rare figure, the Malamud villain, in this case a hard-working young man who hopes to be a certified public accountant. He is first cousin both to Helen's suitor in *The Assistant*, the well-groomed Nat Pearl, and to the sell-out educator Gerald Gilley of *A New Life*. Malamud wastes little time with these All-American Boys; in the story at hand the tension derives, as usual, from a contest between two more familiar types, a shoemaker and his refugee assistant, over the shoemaker's daughter. The bemired graduate student hero of "Behold the Key" is much reminiscent of Fidelman: he too is a sufferer (but he has a wife and children to suffer with him); he too is stranded in beautiful, hostile Italy. This fellow Carl Schneider is one of the few *schlemiels* that we find on a definite downward course: at the story's end, having searched in agony for a key, and found it when it is no longer of any use, he is struck in the face with it. Even worse off is Henry Levin of "The Lady of the Lake." Because he tries to sell his Jewish birthright for a glamorous dream, both his past and his future are taken from him. He sees on a tapestry a figure tormented in Hell: " 'What did he do to deserve his fate?' " – " 'He falsely said he could fly.' "

The *schlemiel* is permitted to fly, but with his own wings, no borrowed plumage. Levin, a pathetic figure hoping for a new life, called himself "Henry R. Freeman." It was not his object that was wrong, the new life, but the lies he told looking for it. It is appropriate that we leave this most unhappy of all Malamud protagonists for a look at a close relation, the S. Levin who is the hero of the third novel, *A New Life*. Although he has come from afar, there is little of the escapist about this Levin: he is trailing visible clouds of glory from a past of the most unmitigated suffering. This is how the book begins: "S. Levin, formerly a drunkard, after a long and tiring transcontinental journey, got off the train at Marathon, Cascadia, toward evening of the last Sunday in August, 1950." He is a Jew, a wanderer—a *schlemiel* too? Well, he gets his pants wet twice in the first thirteen pages, and from that point— indeed from the first sentence—the book's import is predictable. *A New Life* has been called a departure for Malamud, a venture forth from his familiar ground. No judgment could be less true. Levin is the archetypal Malamud hero, emerged from his standard background to fight his eternal good fight for his place in the sun.

Structural differences are apparent, however. In *A New Life* Malamud abandons the two-man relationship which forms the basis of most of his best work and returns to the problem of the hero solo, much as he set it up in *The Natural*. In *A New Life*, however, and for the only time in his work, he puts some real effort into a heroine, Pauline Gilley, the married woman with whom Levin falls in love. She is a worthy replacement for the missing male *schlemiel*; she has suffered, she endures, she makes mistakes, she gives somewhat too liberally of her love. Yet she is not developed nearly as fully as is the second man of *The Assistant*, nor even, perhaps, as those of the short stories. To a *schlemiel*, a woman is usually simply bad luck. A female *schlemiel* seems a contradiction in terms. Nevertheless, Malamud explores the new avenues opened by the relationship between Levin and Pauline with insight and affection. The book, however, is fundamentally Levin's; his the principal suffering and his the principal triumph.

I don't know whether it has been much commented upon, but *A New Life* bears a curious resemblance in a number of ways to *Lady Chatterley's Lover*. In both we have a vibrant woman tied to a half-dead man, the intrusion of a virile newcomer (bearded in Levin's case) of a lower order, a powerful but beautiful sex-experience between the wife and the new man in the woods, the establishment of a meaningful relationship between them, and their eventual triumph over the forces of suspicion, guilt, mistrust and calumny. Both books are organized symbolically with the seasons, so that the lovers' awakening into their passion shall coincide with the spring. Both books work effectively in symbols throughout; both have stuffy villains, slightly unbelievable, or at least negligible, because both—and this is the most important of all—both books neglect other considerations to focus upon the necessity of the individual's protest against the forces in the modern world which operate so as to separate man from man and man from woman. Both books celebrate courage—in Lawrence's phrase, "the courage of tenderness," the courage to let down one's defenses. Both thus give utterance to the great Romantic cry against the Machine Age, which was first heard at the appearance of the satanic mills of the late eighteenth century, and has not diminished since.

S. Levin—he achieves the nickname Sam at the end of the book, after sacrificing his protective beard—is one of Malamud's most fortunate characters. Yet we realize, at the end of the book, that he has reached his apogee. Just as we know Frank Alpine must come up, so we know Levin must come down; but he will never again hit bottom. He has done that, and survived. He has his new life at hand, even if it may not be one of wine and song. His defeated adversary taunts him: Levin has now no money and no job, and no prospect of one; a wife of notorious weakness, poor health and inconsistency, and two expensive children not his own. " 'Why take that load on yourself?' " " 'Because I can, you son of a bitch.' " With that remark alone, Levin proves his right to the girl and to whatever suffering and joy may be waiting. We can leave him to fight his future battles without our scrutiny.

The recent short stories continue to investigate the problem of suffering. As usual, it is the problem and not the answer that absorbs Malamud—the answer is as tenuous as each man's sense of responsibility to his fellows, as fleeting as the moments of union among men. Certain of the old strains are sounded boldly in *Idiots First*. There is the return of Fidelman, more foolish than ever, and more indomitable. There are more *schlemiels*, professor Orlando Krantz of "The Maid's Shoes," like Fidelman victimized by the Italians; and most unhappy of the new group, Nat Lime, who wants to marry a Negro. "Black Is My Favorite Color" is an interesting new variation on Malamud's theme, a poignant account of the overwhelming difficulties in the way of honest relationships between different races. Yet at the end of the story Nat Lime, beaten, scorned and rejected by white and black alike for his pains, is trying again. There is "A Choice of Profession," either pilot study for, or overflow from, *A New Life*; and "The Cost of Living," related to *The Assistant*. Perhaps the high point of the collection is the fable called "The Jewbird." A progressive and ambitious Jewish family (the "progress" and ambition derive largely from the father, a seller of frozen foods whose aim is to send his son to the Ivy League) is visited by a ragged, rumpled old bird named Schwartz, who speaks in dialect and smells of herring. The father is embarrassed and wrathful. After much fencing he gets his hands on the bird—but not before it has yanked his nose half off—and wrings its neck. When the little boy asks who is responsible for the murder, the mother tells him "anti-semeets."

It is a strange fact that Malamud's first novel has absolutely nothing to do with the Jew. Strange in particular to those who fancy him as a Jewish writer, for is not the first novel supposed to lay down the bricks and flagstones and cinderblocks for all the edifice that is to come? In fact, that is exactly what *The Natural* does, which is why I have reserved it for last: it provides a valuable test for any theory of Malamud's art, both because it comes first, and because it seems so foreign to him. It is a baseball story, and yet baseball is not the heart of the book; I have it on good authority that Malamud knew little about the game as a young man, and cared less. (There are technical errors in the book, but they do not seem glaring to me.) No, at the center of the novel is nothing less than the myth of sacrifice, the killing of the sacred king. For some reason which will seem important to a biographer, Malamud chose to present his first allegory on suffering in the context of another great symbolic system: baseball, the all-American game. Only after he had stated the problem in these terms did he take up his more congenial image, the wandering, suffering Jew.

The young natural—the almost supernaturally gifted athlete—Roy Hobbs, begins his career by striking out the Whammer, greatest man in the game. This is not only pure American folklore, it is also right out of Frazer: the young God kills the old and takes his place. Roy thus earns the right to be cut down by a crazed woman assassin who wants to kill all the brightest and best men in sports, the heroes of the nation. He is not killed, however; only crippled; his luck turns and he drags on as a *schlemiel*, haunted by bad memories and evil women. After years, he pulls himself to the top again, only to be himself struck out by a new bright-faced boy. He is then plunged into a final scandal and humiliation, because of his own foolish lusts. But as he goes down he crushes the evil that has preyed on him; and there are the usual signs that he will rise again; a good woman waits for him.

Now all of this is open, evident, outspoken. Like many other artists, Malamud begins with the naked statement and spends later years clothing it. Suffering here is as blindingly apparent as the winter sun on a snowy field. The answer, too, falls as swiftly and completely over the scene as a storm front:

> "What beats me," he said with a trembling voice, "is why did it always have to happen to me? What did I do to deserve it?"
> "Being stopped before you started?"
> He nodded.

"Perhaps it was because you were a good person?"
"How's that?"
"Experience makes good people better."
She was staring at the lake.
"How does it do that?"
"Through their suffering."

The later works, though vastly more sophisticated, more complicated, more careful, as the author comes to realize the enormousness of the problem, are essentially reworkings of *The Natural*. Frank Alpine as the tarnished man of good will, Fidelman the silly saint, Sam Levin the *schlemiel* who gets up after his tenth beating: all these are more intelligible, more comprehensible reincarnations of Roy Hobbs, who is even at the end of his book a little larger than real life. But he is of necessity a titan, even if a fallen one, for he establishes the lowly *schlemiel's* divine origin, which is not seen again in Malamud, although constantly alluded to. Within this lowest of characters—Man—there is the God-given fire of decency and determination that enables him to overcome everything arrayed against him.

This is the oldest and finest Romanticism of all, that of Plato and his predecessors, who refused to estimate Man's worth by an objective reckoning of *things*. It is in that tradition, and for that ideal, that Malamud stands. As for the particular background of his sufferers—Jewish grocer, Anglo-Saxon athlete, Italian hobo, German immigrant—that does not matter at all.

THE FOOL OF EXPERIENCE:
SAUL BELLOW'S FICTION

Frederick J. Hoffman

IN Isaac Bashevis Singer's story, "Gimpel the Fool," which Saul Bellow translated for the *Partisan Review* and for *A Treasury of Yiddish Stories* (1953), the hero Gimpel is forced to accept many monstrous impositions upon his patience and good humor and belief. But he yields to the necessity; what's the good of *not* believing, he argues. "Today it's your wife you don't believe; tomorrow it's God Himself you won't take stock in." [1] Of course, this statement is mock-heroic, or—even worse—deliberately anti-heroic. Marcus Klein speaks of the European ghetto tradition of *dos kleine menschele,* or the *stetl,* "who is forced by the presence of perils everywhere to ingenious ways of personal survival." [2]

Whatever the influence of this creature, this "fool of reality," there is no question that Saul Bellow's great "affirmation" is in the struggle against chaos and "clutter," of a "too muchness" of everything, toward life and the freedom to live. This freedom includes the will to act eccentrically, to remain "dangling" before society's "normalcy"; but it is not the kind of attitude Dostoevsky eventually leaves to his underground man. Bellow's hero moves *into* society, with a desperate hope that the human dilemma will be solved in community recognition and action.

There is always an air of the ludicrous and the absurd in the world to which the Bellow creature seems committed. It is not the "absurd" of Camus's reading of Kafka, however;[3] the absurdity of Bellow's world is more likely to consist of a profusion of things, a clutter and surplusage of experience, the city world of Chicago and New York, where "things" and gestures and manners and knowledges are heaped upon one another because there isn't enough space to contain them or time to consider them separately. Bellow's heroes are therefore something less than ideally heroic; they are agonizingly at grips with their own personal and moral identity and security; with surviving the flux and contrarieties of experience; finally, with the overwhelming noumenal question of their relation to an unknown. We cannot expect from them either the large qualities of conventional heroism or the agonizing moral toothaches of the "alienated hero." For, as Marcus Klein says, alienation is "morally reprehensible."[4] To be separated from the rest of society is a condition wholly deplorable.

Bellow's novels therefore scan the human world for its types of separation, conformity, rebellion, and adaptation. Ultimately, he seeks for affirmation; it is a modest ambition, however, and he will not conclude it at the expense of novelistic virtues. In his own statement, in *The Living Novel*, he speaks of the necessity to affirm as equivalent to the need to survive. Modern writers, he says,

> are prone, as Nietzsche said in *Human, All Too Human*, to exaggerate the value of human personality. . . . Why should wretched man need power or wish to inflate himself with imaginary glory. If this is what power signifies it can only be vanity to suffer from impotence. On the nobler assumption he should have at least sufficient power to overcome ignominy and to complete his life.[5]

To overcome ignominy and to complete his life: surely these are modest ambitions? But of course in the world of World War II and after, perhaps they are not so modest after all?

ii

The phenomena of affirmation are variously called: "radical innocence," "dogmatic innocence," "beatitude," gestures of "the American existentialist," the hipster, etc. They require some form of general explanation. Of course it would be easy to say simply that writers of the present generation had come through an "ordeal" and were therefore pledged to affirm. But frequently affirmation seems too desperate, too viciously improvisatory, too bitterly anti-everything to be recognizable by any customary sight or definition. Further, recent literature is *not* all affirmative, by any means. The work of the new dramatists, the plays and the fiction of Samuel Beckett, the fantasies and the angry realism of much contemporary literature testify against any patent notion of spontaneous yea-saying in the teeth of an almighty Nay.

The fact is that recent experience is horrifying, frightening enough to dispel many notions of easy acceptance. Yet the *kind* of will that Bellow defines in his hero is not unusual; in Bellow's case it is the Yiddish comic or fool, the *schlemiel* or *schlimazl* of Yiddish humor.[6] One needs to remember that Bellow speaks, not of the grand affirmation or of the "beat-itude" of some contemporaries, but of "sufficient power to overcome ignominy and to complete [one's] life." Bellow, with Roth, Malamud and a growing number of other Jewish writers, is drawing upon the resources of humor, comedy, wisdom, and "secular prayer" that make up the modern Jewish personality in America. He is almost invariably an urban personality, though in at least one example (Bruce Friedman's *Stern*, 1962), he ventures into the suburbs. He is seldom any longer engaged in the struggle against anti-Semitism, because American Jews have enjoyed in recent years great freedom from persecution—perhaps because the experience of World War II and the discovery of Auschwitz and Dachau and its kind have proved traumatically useful; perhaps because the exercises of guilt of the current American have concentrated on problems of Negro integration.

All of these facts leave the way free to a phenomenal rise in the value of Jewish humor and wisdom: a middle-middle class form of manners, which penetrates every aspect of American life. In Bellow's case at least, it is the strategies of survival of *dos kleine menschele,* or the devices, at several levels of sophistication, of the *schlimazl,* that govern the "affirmation of life" and keep it from getting out of hand. The essential task is to fight against loss of identity, to make a "show" of virtue and a satisfactory life in this world, since the next world has been only nebulously indicated and surely does not inspire confidence. Bellow's great contribution lies in his ability to "socialize" the effort to survive in the modern world. Like Philip Roth and Bernard Malamud, he draws heavily upon Jewish manners for the scene and quality and style of his fictions. As in many of Malamud's short stories, the ultimate concerns of Bellow's novels are eschatological. The stratagems used to make a completed life seem an adequate surrogate of immortality. Also, they are not stuffily "fake profound," but produce the impression of ideas carefully sifted through nuances of human behavior.

iii

Bellow's novels began by examining life within a relatively narrow range of possibilities. The first two works seemed linked by various devices to several points in the "tradition of the new." *Dangling Man* (1944) seems at first glance to describe a diminished attitude toward a diminished world. The hero-narrator, Joseph, is waiting out his days before he will be called up to join the army; meanwhile, he fills his days rather aimlessly, observing the eccentricities of his fellow boarders in the manner of a Gogol observer. He does not stay locked up in his place of waiting, but moves out from time to time, though always with some reluctance. There is a form of obsessive narrowness in his observation of the life around him; he will have none of it, or he resists totally any "friendly" advice offered by brother Amos, or financial assistance from him.

Joseph, in short, wishes to save himself from the taint of the "outside." He exists in a marginal state. The very fact that he is dangling—waiting, and no longer of the ordinary world—gives him a special character. He examines others and himself, narrowly. The consequences are not that he loses his sense of himself, but rather that he is able to separate false from real identities. This is a world quite different from those Bellow was to describe in his later novels. It is narrowly conceived, and the narrator's sense of pain is personal, meditative, and withdrawn. He "suffers from a feeling of strangeness, of not quite belonging to the world, of lying under a cloud and looking up at it." [7] His brother's attempts to advise him concerning his future merely lead to a scoffing answer: " 'There are many people, hundreds of thousands, who have had to give up all thought of future. There is no personal future any more. That's why I can ony laugh at you when you tell me to look out for my future in the Army, in that tragedy.' "

Inevitably, Joseph appears to be moving toward the act of cutting himself off from life. That he rejects his brother's help is not unusual; almost all of Bellow's novels contain this family circumstance of the two brothers divergently interested and ambitious, alternately clashing with each other and trying to reach across their differences to each other. But the pall of the war hangs over him: we have accustomed ourselves to slaughter, he says in one journal entry: "We are all, after some fashion, the beneficiaries of that slaughter and yet we have small pity for the victims. This has not come with the war, we were ready before the war ever started; it only seems more apparent now." And he takes a narrowly righteous view of the affair: he would rather die in the war than profit from it, would rather be a victim than a beneficiary of it. Ultimately, he goes to the draft board, to hurry the day of his actual induction.

This strangely limited book is like a door slightly ajar; through the opening, the reader, with the narrator, is squinting at the world. But we should, I think, be on guard against dismissing *Dangling Man* for its gaudier and more lively successors. It is a bit like Dostoevsky's *Notes from Underground* and somewhat like the Kafkan story of the self-debasing person who, frightened, stares out at the world. In a few details as well it resembles Jean-Paul

Sartre's *Nausea*: both Bellow's and Sartre's heroes seek to cut themselves off from the past and to find an area in which self-choice may become effective. That Joseph should have hastened into the Army is not evidence of the failure of his wish to remain free, but rather a desire to move into the society of his fellows. This despite the final bravos recorded in his journal: "Hurray for regular hours! And for the supervision of the spirit! Long live regimentation!"

As among the several readings of this book available,[8] I prefer J. C. Levenson's; while his generalization concerning the "dangling man" in American literature is scarcely entirely accurate, it is nevertheless true that Bellow intends a form of "marginal free spirit" in Joseph's situation and his reaction to it. "The sick soul is the same anywhere," Levenson says, "but what the Bellow hero seeks is recovery, not rebirth." [9] Joseph's general attitude is dour and unforgiving and critical; and this tendency forces a monotony upon the book's scene. He is not helped by the malicious wryness of humor that helps us to accept the narrator of *Notes from Underground*. Nor is his preoccupation with the lively self graced by such philosophical rhapsodies as attend Sartre's *Roquentin*, as he discovers selfhood. Yet the self-exile within a rooming house has its own genuine *raison d'être*. Bellow's purpose throughout his career is to show that, however absurd his acts may be, a man must take his chances in society. Joseph's imprisonment is ended in his welcoming life in a form of society, the Army, which—though scarcely ideal—is a welcome relief from the agonies of waiting and the experience of glowering hatefully at the people who are not caught in the Army's net.

The Victim (1947), despite an almost equally narrow conception and setting, is multifold in its suggestiveness and rich in moral meaning. It is also the only one of Bellow's novels to have a tight, "neat" structure. It comes before the "moral picaresque" which is to characterize the next two works. *The Victim* is a superbly thorough examination of the complexities of moral guilt. That Asa

Leventhal's accuser (*and* victim) happens to invoke anti-Semitism is a part of the complex, but only a part; in other words, the novel is not "about" anti-Semitism, but rather examines Jewish insecurity and the Jewish attitude toward complicity in anti-Semitic behavior. The book does not bounce with vitality or gleam with variety; it is an "indrawn book," but it is so skillfully managed that it often convinces me that Bellow might have done worse than follow its model.

To begin with, Leventhal is living alone in a hot New York summer (his wife is South to visit relatives). Loneliness invites self-analysis, as it did in *Dangling Man*. Further, Leventhal's generous spirit (it can be generous, as he shows in his treatment of his sister-in-law on Staten Island) is hedged by feelings of insecurity, and these feelings very soon expand to include the awful sense of guilt concerning a New England gentile, Kirby Allbee, who begins by accusing him of responsibility for losing his job. Guilt and insecurity are, in fact, composite emotions, and they become inseparable as Leventhal and Allbee gradually become confused as one person: victimizer and victim in one.

Allbee is obviously on the way down, all the way, "like one of those men you saw sleeping off their whisky on 3rd Avenue." [10] But he is not without resources of guile, and has been "spying out" on Leventhal, to see how he might take his advantage. Asa had had him fired by telling tales on him, or so Allbee insists. In any case, the charge hits home, and Leventhal is never thereafter free of Allbee's accusation, and rarely of his presence. Allbee moves in on him, and makes himself at home with a freedom of privilege that distresses Leventhal. The implication is that no one is free of guilt; and there is the added suspicion that victim and assailant are hard to distinguish. In Leventhal's case, the sense of "being a Jew" is heightened by Allbee's New England gentile nature; so that they are easily and naturally enemies, each capable of saying or doing the incriminating thing.

The complexities of this relationship are masterfully

exploited by Bellow. The New York heat provides a suitably debilitating atmosphere, so that normal suscepti- bilities are aggravated and normal powers weakened in it. Leventhal at first rebels against the thought of complicity: "Admittedly there was a wrong, a general wrong. Allbee, on the other hand, came along and said '*you!*' and that was what was so meaningless." But the absurdity of the charges does not make him immune from them. The world was after all vicious, and men did unexplainable harm to one another: "Therefore hideous things were done, cannibalistic things. Good things as well, of course."

The struggle continues, between two moral views: that of assuming a man "got what he deserved," and that of assuming a moral web, in which both Leventhal and Allbee are caught. As the battle continues, it alternates serious with comic moments: Allbee's ludicrous excesses are matched by the mixture of blame and doubt that affects Leventhal's view. Allbee's assault upon his privacy becomes a matter of taking over his apartment, living in it, satisfying his vices in it, and leaving it in chaos after his debauches. "Leventhal felt Allbee's presence, all that concerned him, like a great tiring weight, and looked at him with dead fatigue, his fingers motionless on his thighs. Something would have to happen, something that he could not foresee."

The most disconcerting evidence of the collapse of sense is the disorder and filth Allbee seems always to bring with him. Yet his intrusions cannot be easily dismissed. For one thing, Asa permits them, and thereby seems in some way willing to admit their reasons. In other words, he seems to be conspiring with Allbee to admit guilt. The relationship of enemy to enemy and of accusation to guilt, is confused; and in the confusion Allbee acts to upset all of Leventhal's hopes and promise.

The most fully and masterfully contained person in the novel is Schlossberg, a journalist who writes "whatever comes to hand" for the Jewish papers. He believes in "fullness," in realizing selfness: " 'It's easy to understand. Here I'm sitting here, and my mind can go around the world. Is there any limit to what I can think? But in another minute I can be dead, on this spot. There's a limit to me. But I have to be myself in full.' " There is something large, ample, inclusive, in Schlossberg that makes Leventhal seem pale and weak in his presence.[11] Nevertheless, Asa Leventhal must fight his own battle, must lay the ghosts of his own insecurity and his imagined complicity in evil. That battle culminates in his discovering Allbee in the act of attempting suicide.

> The air was foul and hard to breathe. Gas was pouring from the oven. "I have to kill him now," he thought as they grappled. He caught the cloth of his coat in his teeth while he swiftly changed his grip, clutching at Allbee's face. He tore away convulsively, but Leventhal crushed him with his weight in the corner. Allbee's fist came down heavily on his neck, beside the shoulder. "You want to murder me? Murder?" Leventhal gasped. The sibilance of the pouring gas was almost deafening.

Here, in the two persons, accuser and victim come so close to being the same person that the twin acts of suicide and murder become almost indistinguishable. And Asa Leventhal ends by recognizing the horror of himself as Allbee has dragged him along, to the point where the two almost willingly connive in being the same morally confused person. This is the great mastery of *The Victim*, that it should have worked at so close a range with its subject that its fanciful conclusion comes near to being the real one. While the question of anti-Semitism does come up at the beginning and is repeated later (Allbee, for example, is outraged that a Jewish scholar should write a book on Thoreau and Emerson), it is no more important than that of "anti-anti-Semitism"; and the ultimate issue is one of general morality specifically grounded.

iv

In 1953, Bellow turned to an entirely different kind of work, the "moral picaresque." The form has its advantages over that of *The Victim*, in which every detail is precisely balanced against every other. *The Adventures of Augie March* presents the Jewish hero in an entirely different pattern. March is not a great hero, but rather a man who fails repeatedly to realize the possibilities in any given situation. As Goldberg says of him, "Unlike most picaresque heroes, Augie is basically a passive figure. He is a drifter who falls into situations, and when they become untenable he either votes himself out or circumstances conspire to force his withdrawal." [12]

One is tempted to say "Amen" to this and to go on, to assert that only the form has changed, not the hero. It is true that, while in *Dangling Man* and *The Victim* the author squints at his hero and his situation, here he sets things in motion from the beginning and doesn't permit them to slow down to the end. But the form and the hero are here interrelated. Augie March is a disciple of "life" in the sense of choosing to experience so much of it. The fact that he also is "passive" is significant, but only in the sense that he will not come to great or heroic or even definite decisions about himself. The ultimate decision about him has already been made: that he will be closely tied to the range, nature, and scope of his experiences, and that they will define him.

Almost, the charm of *The Adventures of Augie March* comes from the minor personages rather than from the titular hero. There are men and women who grapple furiously and ingeniously with circumstance, and who gain power from the effort expended. March is himself a bastard; he knows his mother but not his father, a fact which already throws the Jewish family off center. The *pater familias* is lacking, the man who holds the family together by command and by love. So, Augie must look for other men, for examples of the father image. William Einhorn is the first, "the first superior man I knew." [13] He is a "pioneer" builder and planner, a form of the grotesque, who collects vast quantities of mail, pamphlets, copies of the *Congressional Record:* everything that is free. In his sexual relationships, "he was single-mindedly and grimly fixed on the one thing, ultimately *the* thing, for which men and women come together."

While there is something about Einhorn that might strike a young man with awe, there is also something grotesquely "over-complete" about him. Augie March avoids implication with the grotesque, though he permits it and even admires it. To say that he is "passive" may simply mean that he frequently chooses against the grotesque, and indeed against extremes of any kind. They are measured against his sense of limit. He is an ingratiating hero, though not necessarily an impressive one. Above all, March thinks of the *possibility* of human renewal; hence the novel takes the form of a spiral, in which recurrence and change somehow combine subtly and steadily to alter the model. ". . . for each separate person too, everyone beginning with Eden and passing through trammels, pains, distortions, and death into the darkness out of which, it is hinted, we may hope to enter permanently into the beginning again."

It is important that the setting of this novel be known as the 1930s, the decade of soup lines and organizers and clashes with scabs. The entire vision of the picaresque is modified and limited by economic and political circumstances. Augie March is forced to work, to steal, to adjust his way through school and college; he doesn't complete the latter, though he tries several times. In the end there is something wrong with the picture: there is too much to know, and the knowing and the living have too little to do with each other.

Part of the picaresque comes from Augie's move from job to job: from a "luxury dog service on North Clark" to a private entrepreneurship as a "gifted crook," a lifter of expensive textbooks from the University of Chicago bookstore. He is not successful at the latter "work" because he finds it difficult to give up a book to a customer. His brother Simon suggests the "surest employment" of all, to marry the plain daughter of a wealthy merchant; he succeeds in bringing it off, but Augie characteristically fails—in effect, chooses to fail. Augie, in fact, fails rather consistently in his affairs, fails to pursue them or to gain his objective in them. Until the last, that is, when he is on his way to the wars and stops over to see Stella, a woman he has already known in Mexico: "My body, which is maybe all I am, this effortful creature, felt subject to currents and helpless."

This is obviously *it*, as opposed to many others, which were not complete or were held back from completion for one reason or another. In effect, Bellow's novel moves in a pattern of incompletions, but toward the ultimate completion, which is to have "sufficient power to overcome ignominy and to complete [one's] own life." [14] Meanwhile, Augie's brother Simon proceeds toward the master design of the Bellow antagonist: a man of skill and cunning, he succeeds in marrying the merchant's daughter and builds a fortune for himself, quickly. He becomes prosperous and generally well-liked, and fat. But the source of dissolution lies there also—"from circus games to private dissoluteness." In the vast world of American upper middleclass, Simon exemplifies the mysterious desire for luxury, "for no matter what, just so its scope is vast . . . and always ulterior."

As in earlier works, there is a clash of brothers, the one successful and trying to urge success upon the others. But Augie March is the dedicated *schlimazl*. His failures are not only accidental; they are in a sense *designed* as commentary upon the successful. For this and other reasons, he attracts eccentrics to him, and the range of possible experience grows simply because, in a sense, he does not *choose* to succeed. His decision always leaves him a margin of belief:

> Me, I couldn't think all was so poured in concrete and that there weren't occasions for happiness that weren't illusions of people still permitted to be forgetful of permanent disappointment, more or less permanent pain, death of children, lovers, friends, ends of causes, old age, loathsome breath, fallen faces, white hair, retreated breasts, dropped teeth; and maybe most intolerable the hardening of detestable character, like bone, similar to a second skeleton and creaking loudest before the end.

This elaborate sentence is a sign of the disorder of the book as a whole. Augie's experiences quickly succeed one another, as do his thoughts. What remains constant in the whole is his conviction of the "privilege of illusion," despite the fact that most experience consists of smashing illusions. In a real sense, March survives in the manner of the "fool" who believes because not to believe is a move toward a desperate and calamitous end.

v

There is something very ingratiating about this "saving grace," this act of *credo quia absurdum est*. Bellow's heroes are always engaged on the frontiers of phenomena, where noumena "hover and threaten." Eugene Henderson (*Henderson the Rain King*, 1959) goes into darkest Africa to find out about what he calls the "noumenal department." [15] He had first retired to the country, because the city confused him; but he found that the country became similarly crowded and cluttered. A move to Africa—*not* Joseph Conrad's, but a much simpler world—seemed the next logical step. "There was a disturbance in my heart, a voice that spoke there and said, *I want, I want, I want!* It happened every afternoon, and when I tried to suppress it it got even stronger."

Specifically, Henderson goes to Africa to see if he can encounter life without the clutter and chaos with which it is surrounded in America. In Africa, he feels that he "was entering the real past, no history or junk life that. The prehuman past." He is received with wonder and graciousness in "a beautiful, strange, special place." And he is determined that he will carry his life "to a certain depth." In short, Henderson will test Man in his (Henderson's) own image. He must find the "pure image" of life; and it appears in the figure of the lion, which the King Dahfu displays before him: " 'When the fear yields, a beauty is disclosed in its place. This is also said of perfect love if I recollect, and it means that ego-emphasis is removed.' " The novel concludes on a vigorous moral note. Henderson, who is throughout the strong, uncertain, "violent" creature trying to find a precise meaning for himself, concludes that for America, " 'All the major tasks and the big conquests were done before my time. That left the biggest problem of all, which was to encounter death.' "

There is a kind of frenetic honesty in all of these gestures.[16] Henderson is perhaps the most vigorous of all of Bellow's "selves," even though the novel is more than halfway a fantasy. His preoccupation with the "Real," and with what underlies and overlies fact, is genuine enough. Bellow has now come about to the statement that a curiosity about life (measured in terms of degree), a seriousness about it, is an earnest of life itself. Beyond this, he asserts that speculations about the Real and the experiencing of it are indispensably related.

vi

The question is if Bellow hasn't exceeded his terms. *Henderson* is an entertaining novel, but it fails to convince just when it would be most serious. *Is* the act of *expanding* the universe of human experience necessarily guaranteed to produce more profound observations about it? *The Victim* and the title story of *Seize the Day* (1956) suggest to one at least that limiting the scope of action might yield the more satisfactory results. *Seize the Day* is one of the great short novels of our time. It is, furthermore, an almost perfect vehicle for the use of Jewish wisdom and humor. Scarcely a moment of it is wasted. The *schlemiel* of the piece, Tommy Wilhelm, suffers from such a multitude of adversities and such great uncertainty about himself that he is forced into an ecstasy of self-recrimination. Fortyish, an unemployed father, he is growing unpleasantly, shapelessly fat. "He looked down over the front of his big, indecently big, spoiled body. He was beginning to lose his shape, his gut was fat, and he looked like a hippopotamus." [17] He feels how ridiculous, how contemptible he is, through the contempt his father shows him, but also on his own initiative. Wilhelm's agony is both retrospective and moral; that is, when he is willing to leave off accusing circumstances, he is left only with himself. Both self-rationalization and self-contempt are morally useful acts, since they lend equally to self-knowledge—in this case at least, because Tommy eventually goes the full way, to weep not for his bad luck but for himself as a pitiful figure. He wanders into a funeral parlor and there weeps bitterly, the only genuine mourner, who mourns the loss of himself.

> He could not stop. The source of all tears had suddenly sprung open within him, black, deep, and hot, and they were pouring out and convulsed his body, bending his stubborn head, bowing his shoulders, twisting his face, crippling the very hands with which he held the handkerchief. . . . [the music] poured into him where he had hidden himself in the center of a crowd by the great and happy oblivion of tears. He heard it and sank deeper than sorrow, through torn sobs and cries toward the consummation of his heart's ultimate need.

In this beautifully stated gem of human pathos, the full weight of Bellow's talent has effect. There is nothing staged or rhetorically "swollen" here; Tommy Wilhelm, a scapegrace and failure, bows in recognition of himself, weeps for the fact of his deterioration, and absolves himself of the failure he is because he becomes morally useful to himself in atonement.

Bellow has proved himself the master of the short tale as he is the artist of the large, uninhibited picaresque and the "moral fantasy." [18] The emphasis that critics have put upon his affirmation has sometimes been excessive. It is not so much the "avowal of life" that is important, but the analysis of lives. This analysis is feasible equally in the narrow-range and in the broad-scaled novels. *The Victim* succeeds often where *The Adventures of Augie March* doesn't quite. Tommy Wilhelm is a very different human being from Eugene Henderson, but both of them are equally valid human types. Above all, Bellow has made the move toward affirmation a process of some subtlety and a journey variously paced and affected by many useful digressive incidents. He has demonstrated that one cannot, or should not, affirm superficially. But he *has* maintained that it is possible and necessary to affirm.

THE SALINGER SITUATION

Richard Rees

DOUBTLESS there is a touch of the Puritan in everybody, even among the higher ranks of literary critics. So when the critics see an author's books swallowed in repeated gulps of half a million or more, with no difficulty and with an apparently uncritical relish, by innumerable young people in America, Europe, and even Russia, they naturally begin to suspect something unwholesome. "If they like it so much, it can't be good for them." That is a rough description of the Salinger situation, which is a very peculiar one for a serious writer to whom even the most puritanical critics allow considerable merit. To comment on this situation is a daunting assignment. A rather short novel, a few short stories, and a few fragments from what looks like a family saga in process of composition—that is all there is to go on. But at least two highly reputed critics, one English and one American, seem to have found it quite enough. From their reviews of Salinger's latest book I have gathered this posy of nettles: "false and senti-mental"—"lying"—"fake"—"mountebank Salvationist"—"beyond a joke"—"orgy of hatred for all those outside the cult"—"the club, for all its pep talks, is a closed corporation." J. D. Salinger is such an unusual phenome-non and for some people evidently such an awkward prob-lem that it is best, if one is confined to a short essay on him, to stick to generalities and not try to make more than one simple point. I propose to examine one of the most plausible complaints of his critics, to see whether it is justified. This complaint is implied in the foregoing quotations by the words "cult," "club," and "closed corporation."

In examining this complaint I must refer to two authors very unlike Salinger, and equally unlike one another: Ionesco and Orwell. In 1984 George Orwell foresees a horrifying future in which no one will dare to maintain or even to believe that two and two make four, unless authorized by the State; and he describes the torture and collapse of the last man who tries to resist. In his play, *Rhinoceros*, Ionesco more subtly and more frivolously shows a similar man, a little man like everybody, who is the last human being to survive in a town where everyone else turns into a rhinoceros. But that is the end of the resemblance between the play and the novel. Unlike 1984, *Rhinoceros* is brilliantly contrived to flatter the spectator's ego. It can hardly fail to please, because everyone enjoys indulging the mood in which one sees oneself as the only sensitive creature among a herd of pachyderms; and Ionesco makes it beautifully easy to identify oneself with the hero, and the rhinoceros with whatever type of human being happens to be one's own particular bête noire.

The criticism of Salinger that I want to refute is the one that accuses him of buttonholing the reader and enticing him into a cosy club of tender and sympathetic souls who see themselves as the only "real" people in a world full of pathetic phoneys, or as human beings among a herd of pachyderms. Now there is no doubt that Salinger does possess an almost hypnotic gift for creating a sense of exclusive intimacy between himself and his reader, and if he wanted to promote a cult of himself he could easily do so. If you agree at all with his outlook you cannot avoid the feeling that you have a specially intimate understanding of his mind and that if he knew your mind he would understand it in the same way. But this is not a unique phenomenon. A great many good writers have much the same effect on their readers, and Holden Caulfield was probably speaking for the majority when he said that the kind of book he liked was one that "when you're all done reading it, you wish the author that wrote it was a terrific friend of yours and you could call him up on the phone whenever you felt like it." But if an author makes his readers feel like this there is not the slightest reason to conclude that he wishes them to make a cult of him, and those who think there is are probably his competitors who would lack the power to inspire a cult if they wanted to.

It is obvious however that the hypnotic gift of intimacy will be resented, even if it is reluctantly admired on literary grounds, by those who do not sympathize with Salinger's general outlook. "Hold off! unhand me, graybeard loon!" These are almost the words of one of the critics I have quoted, when he admonishes Salinger that "writers should *keep their distance*" (his italics) —rather as if he had been indecently accosted by someone in the men's room. But what matters about a writer's outlook, taking his skill of presentation for granted, is not the degree of intimacy it evokes but its truth and relevance and the sincerity with which it is held. And as for the sense of exclusiveness, it is sometimes inevitable. Those who believe in the ersatz religion of Art for Art's Sake will admire rather than criticize the exclusiveness of the Joycean artist behind his barricades of "silence, exile, and cunning." And every didactic artist from Plato to D. H. Lawrence has urged his readers to dissociate themselves from the blind majority at least until it has become enlightened. I conclude therefore that all the talk about cults and clubs and corporations is quite beside the point and is no more than a cover for dislike and hostility toward Salinger's thought or outlook or subject matter.

When people dislike the thought or outlook or subject matter of a fiction-writer whose talent they cannot help recognizing, there are two obvious ploys available. They can praise the cooking and ignore the food, or they can praise the trimmings and ignore the main dish. How often one has heard D. H. Lawrence praised for his descriptive passages and his "lyrical" feeling for nature, to the total neglect of his subject matter and his ideas! In the same way, we are invited to admire Salinger's gift for dialogue and ear for contemporary speech, while ignoring or deploring his themes. In an age of comparative stability, when there is a general consensus of belief and feeling about life and death, artists of genius are not degraded by trimming and garnishing a ready-made theme. Virgil and Horace were court poets, and it is unlikely that they felt hampered in the exercise of their gifts through having to withhold some religious or social or philosophical challenge with which their souls were pregnant. And in the same way great artists have been able to express themselves without constraint as religious illustrators and decorators. But ours today is not an age of stability. Landmarks are continually shifting or being swept away, so it is seldom nowadays that literary genius can be neatly classified and directed into channels ready-made to control its flow.

To come to the point, which will turn out to be a surprise for hardly anybody: Salinger mixes religion and mysticism with his fiction. "People are already shaking their heads over me, and any immediate further professional use on my part of the word 'God,' except as a familiar, healthy American expletive, will be taken—or, rather, confirmed—as the very worst kind of name-dropping and a sure sign that I'm going straight to the dogs." Thus Salinger's fictional narrator, Buddy Glass, but all the same he keeps right on with the name-dropping.

To write anything about an author is always to risk misrepresenting him, and particularly when the author has obviously got so much more to say than he has yet said. But I doubt if Salinger will say anything in the future to prevent me from continuing to think of the Glass brothers and sisters, and their creator, as radical and irreconcilable critics of the ethos and ideals of their age. Whether the criticism has yet found or will ever find its own most appropriate form of expression is a different question, but whether it does or not, I believe it is potentially of the same order of importance as D. H. Lawrence's and is liable to meet with the same neglect, hostility or misrepresentation. In *The Catcher in the Rye* and in the earlier stories, most of which were not concerned with the Glass family, the criticism was mainly implicit. It only began to appear explicitly in "Franny" and since then it has seemed to relate itself to a comprehensive but rather rootless type of theosophy. But with an author who has written at least one exquisite short story and an epoch-making novel one ought surely to be prepared to await developments. And the more so when the waiting is made so pleasant by the jam with which the pills of anecdotal mysticism are administered.

Unlike Holden Caulfield, the Glass family can be quite irritating, but they are never dull, and if they tend to behave like a mutual admiration society, I can see no reason for supposing that the author means them to appear, so far, in any other light. It is no worse a scheme for a novel than the familiar one which depends upon a character strangely resembling the author himself who plays unconsciously the role of a mutual admiration society with a single member, or the equally familiar one in which the author plays that role in the background without actually appearing on the page at all. The common-or-garden Narcissus looks in only one glass; perhaps the Glasses are none the worse for being a collective Narcissus.

According to Nietzsche, if ever a great truth triumphs in the market-place you may be sure that some great lie has been fighting on its behalf. It is easy to talk about great truths, but it is very difficult to illustrate them; yet in *The Catcher in the Rye* Salinger really did succeed in illustrating truthfully the virtues of humility and generosity. And the book triumphed in the market-place. This is not the place to investigate all the great lies that may have fought on its behalf, but most of them would probably be found to have their roots in the narcissistic fantasy of its readers. What is more relevant to this discussion is the fact that the stories about the Glass family continue to triumph in the market-place although the proportion of truth-talked-about to truth-illustrated is much higher in them. However, a continued best-selling triumph for books which have anything to do with truth at all is a most extraordinary phenomenon. It is also remarkable how much popularity they continue to enjoy, despite the sort of dissenting opinions I have quoted, with the sophisticated public of "professional readers": critics, lecturers, commentators, writers about writers, and writers about writers about writers. Salinger himself, of course, as a man of letters, is a member of that public, but the other members might well regard him as a traitor of the same type as D. H. Lawrence: a rogue intellectual, a blackleg, a fouler of his own nest.

The best example of these characteristics is "Franny," a comparatively early story about the Glass family. In this story Franny and her boy-friend, Lane Coutell, argue at lunch about modern higher education among other things, and notwithstanding that Franny is a Glass—she is in fact the youngest member of the Chosen Family—Salinger does nothing at all to make things easy for her. He makes her unreasonable and hysterical, and afflicted with a bee in her bonnet about automatic prayer. Lane on the other hand argues patiently and reasonably, and all his opinions are the tolerant, broad-minded, intelligent ones which are accepted, "in the light of what we know today" as he puts it, in contemporary enlightened circles. It is true that he is a bit ludicrously self-satisfied about his paper on Flaubert, which was so well received by his tutor, "a big Flaubert man." But if there is any age at which one is entitled to be a bit ludicrous, surely it is during the first flush of excitement on discovering the world's treasures of art and literature. By contrast, Franny's behavior is impossible and yet Lane succeeds in keeping his temper. (Franny is, of course, on the verge of a nervous breakdown, but he cannot know that.) She objects to everything he says and in so far as she can be said to have any alternative point of view she seems to be against everything and everybody:

"I'm sick of just liking people. I wish to God I could meet somebody I could respect."

"I'm just sick of ego, ego, ego. My own and everybody else's. I'm sick of everybody that wants to *get* somewhere,

do something distinguished and all, be somebody interesting . . ."

She has given up her theatrical work at college, although
she is a brilliantly promising actress, and when Lane
shrewdly asks whether, perhaps, she is simply afraid of
competing, she retorts:

> I'm not afraid to compete. It's just the opposite. Don't you
> see that? I'm afraid I *will* compete—that's what scares me.
> That's why I quit the Theatre Department. Just because
> I'm so horribly conditioned to accept everybody else's val-
> ues, and just because I like applause and people to rave
> about me, doesn't make it right. I'm ashamed of it. I'm sick
> of it. I'm sick of not having the courage to be an absolute
> nobody . . .

What makes this passage so dramatic is that Franny is be-
having in such a way that neither Lane nor anybody else
would take her seriously, and yet what she is trying to say
is what everybody knows and always has known to be
the truth, and what everybody wants and always has
wanted to keep dark. *I'm sick of not having the courage to
be an absolute nobody.* The words are almost a summary
of the religious history of mankind. (Or if this seems farfetched in view of the fact that nine-tenths of humanity
have always perforce been absolute nobodies, it can be put
the other way round: how many have ever refused the
chance of becoming somebody at the expense of all the
nobodies? Who can resist the lure of status and prestige?
And is it not the essence of these privileges that the
more I have of them the less you have and vice versa?)
Small wonder that on her way to the ladies' room a few
minutes later Franny passes out in a dead faint.

Subjectively, no doubt she feels like the hero of 1984 or
Rhinoceros—a minority of one (or five, if she would
include her sister and brothers) against the world. The
whole world is out of step with Franny Glass, so of course
it is easy to make fun of her. Indeed, it is necessary to do
so in order to forget the uncompromising truth behind her
wild and extravagant words. What these words mean is
what Simone Weil meant when she said that there is a

natural alliance between truth and affliction, because both of them are mute suppliants, eternally condemned to stand speechless in our presence:

> Just as a vagrant accused of stealing a carrot from a field stands before a comfortably seated judge who keeps up an elegant flow of queries, comments and witticisms while the accused is unable to stammer a word, so truth stands before an intelligence which is concerned with the elegant manipulation of opinions.

This simile of Simone Weil's exactly fits the scene between Franny and Lane Coutell. The abyss between them is the same as that between the stammering vagrant and the elegantly literate judge.

It is remarkable how many of the outstanding writers of our time have been sceptical about our progressive educational ideals and about the kind of intelligence we set up as a standard. D. H. Lawrence, for example, would certainly have agreed with this passage in Simone Weil:

> A lot of people think that a little peasant boy of the present day who goes to primary school knows more than Pythagoras did, simply because he can repeat, parrot-wise, that the earth moves round the sun. In actual fact he no longer looks up at the heavens. The sun about which they talk to him in class hasn't, for him, the slightest connection with the one he can see. He is severed from the universe surrounding him . . .

and with this from one of her letters:

> The most beautiful poetry is the poetry which can best express, in its truth, the life of people who can't write poetry. Outside of that there is only clever poetry; and mankind can do very well without clever poetry. Cleverness makes the aristocracy of intelligence; the soul of genius is *caritas* . . .

And George Orwell used very nearly the same words:

> There is no lack nowadays of clever writers: the trouble is that such writers are so cut off from the life of their time as to be unable to write about ordinary people.

Ordinary people means the same as Franny's "absolute nobodies." But our whole conception of progress is based on the idea of turning everyone into an important somebody, and it is almost impossible for members of the "aristocracy of intelligence" not to assume that they themselves are the model to be copied for this purpose. On almost every page of Orwell, as of D. H. Lawrence, you can find this assumption questioned. And although Salinger resembles Orwell and Lawrence as little as they resemble one another, he seems to me to share their scepticism on this point.

I have dealt with "Franny" at some length because it seems to me that more than anything else that he has written—more than the subsequent Glass stories and more than *The Catcher in the Rye*—it sums up Salinger's problem as a writer. It is also, apart from "For Esmé—with Love and Squalor" and *The Catcher in the Rye*, probably his most successful piece of writing—though it is hard to foresee what the cumulative effect of the later Glass stories will be. I have had to omit much that ought to be mentioned. I would like to have shown that "For Esmé—with Love and Squalor" is an illustration of innocence, just as *The Catcher in the Rye* is an illustration of humility and generosity; and to have examined the extraordinary technical *tour de force* of the latter book. As Middleton Murry put it: "The effect of revelation is heightened by the apparently unexpressive medium: we are made to feel that the most fastidious utterance would be no more adequate to the spiritual simplicity of this generous soul than the barbarous lingo to which he is confined. To produce such an impression, of course, is a triumph of art." I would also like to have illustrated Salinger's delicate use of pathos without overbalancing into sentimentality (the story "Teddy" is an example), and to have shown that when he does wobble he does it in rather the same way as that other exquisite short story writer, Katherine Mansfield: "Eloise shook Mary Jane's arm. 'I was a nice girl,' she pleaded, 'wasn't I?'" (An alcoholic young matron remembering the past in "Uncle

Wiggily in Connecticut," a story whose title, too, recalls Katherine Mansfield not at her best.) And then one could say a lot in favour of, and a lot against, "A Perfect Day for Bananafish." In this story the effect seems stagily contrived when Seymour indulges in badinage with a small child on a Florida beach, kisses her little wet foot, and then immediately returns to the hotel and shoots himself. Nevertheless, Salinger's sympathetic understanding of children is one of his most original gifts, and his tact in presenting them, whether as leading characters or as extras, is usually infallible. (For example, when Zooey looks down into the street and is refreshed in his struggle with Franny's obsession by the sight of a little girl hiding behind a tree while her dachshund puppy runs around trying to pick up her scent.)

But I have been obliged to concentrate upon Salinger's more questionable or controversial aspects, because it is necessary to come to terms with them before one can decide if my view of him is correct. The obvious difficulty about my view is that it seems incompatible with his instantaneous and astonishingly widespread popularity. Even the smallest pill of bitter truth, however richly coated with sugar, could not be expected to go over so big and so easily. One might expect for *The Catcher in the Rye* a considerable success with a fairly large public of discerning readers, including "professional" ones, but when the book becomes a best seller in several continents and keeps it up year after year. . . . Is it just a freak of chance? Or must we go along with Nietzsche and suspect that some very big lie has been fighting on the book's behalf? And has Salinger lost his nerve, and is he now playing safe by doling out crumbs of the pre-digested Wisdom of the Ages, garnished with superior modern whimsy—an Ivy League beatnik, as somebody has called him? I do not believe it. But if I am right about the situation, it is one in which any writer might well be excused for losing his nerve. For if Salinger, like Franny, is protesting that the whole twentieth-century cavalcade of band-wagons is off its course, if he is down in the road arguing with the drivers, he will get lavishly bespattered with mud from the wheels.

When Franny insists that talent is of no avail for playing in Synge, because it calls for genius, she incurs the foreseeable snub: "You think *you're* a genius?" and the band-wagon rolls on, leaving Franny with a smear of mud on her face.

In the same way, the author of the Glass stories exposes himself to the sneer: "You think *you're* a prophet, a seer, a saint?"—and the only way for him to avoid the mud is to stop arguing and step aside. Perhaps that is what he will do. But then again, thank God, perhaps it isn't.

JAMES JONES—NORMAN MAILER

Edmond L. Volpe

IN 1943, during my second week of infantry training at Fort Wheeler, Georgia, my name appeared on the KP duty roster. Being a college graduate, I was put to scraping and scrubbing the giant pots and pans. Cursing my fate, the cooks, the army, the war, and the egg-encrusted pans, I listened with envy to the sounds of my fellow-recruits falling out for drill. A while later, I saw through the kitchen window a sight that left me shaken. On the prairie of the drill field were platoon after platoon of marching uniforms. Under identical helmets, not one man was distinguishable from another. Each uniformed figure was a stamped-out cog in a gigantic marching machine. At twenty, I had never doubted my significance and my future importance to the universe. But I knew suddenly I had metamorphosed into number 31337580. That day I enjoyed KP. At least for a few hours, I had escaped that inexorable maw that chewed up unsuspecting individualists and turned them into identical links in a never-ending human sausage for the delectation of the war gods.

Perhaps for my generation this vision of anonymity was the great trauma. We had grown up on Hemingway and Dos Passos and Cummings, and we had no illusions about heroism and glory, but we were not prepared to be swallowed up and lost in the massive organization of the army. It is this vision that has preoccupied two of the most talented fiction writers of the World War II generation—

James Jones and Norman Mailer. Their reactions to this threat to individuality have been different, mainly because Jones is essentially a realist, and Mailer is essentially a romantic. Jones's first novel describes the heroic struggle of an individualist to retain his integrity, but his later work contains no hero: the individual has been absorbed into the organization. Norman Mailer, on the other hand, continues to resist the sausage machine of modern society, and he continues his search for a twentieth century hero.

i

Despite the fact that Jones seems able to fulfill his talent only when he draws upon his army experiences, he has not remained static during the past fifteen years. Technically, his latest book is far superior to anything he has done before, and his vision has altered and matured. *The Thin Red Line* is set in Guadalcanal during World War II, but its attitudes and theme belong to the 1960's. This novel reveals that Jones has recognized and accepted his limitations and learned to work brilliantly with them. He has avoided the artistic errors of *Some Came Running* and the areas of human experience which that novel proved he was unable to handle. The absence of women in *The Thin Red Line* has much to do with its success. Jones cannot create complex female characters, and he cannot deal with the relations of men and women. Karen and Alma of *From Here to Eternity* are variations on the stereotypes of the embittered wife and the refined whore. The love affair in *Some Came Running* between the writer Dave and the teacher Gwen borders on the ludicrous. A college professor of English, Gwen has developed a naïve thesis about the relation of frustration in love and artistic creativity. When Dave, one of the writers about whom she has been theorizing, returns to his small midwestern hometown, Gwen immediately falls in love with him. Dave, who hates the town, has returned for a visit only to embarrass his brother. But after one meeting with Gwen, who has an undeserved reputation as a woman of the world, Dave decides to settle in the town until he succeeds in seducing her. After a visit or two, he is passionately in love with Gwen. The couple never do get together because the thirty-eight-year-old Ph.D. in literature would prefer to lose the man she loves rather than admit to him that she is still a virgin! The forty-year-old Dave, who has had plenty of experience with women, decides that Gwen will not sleep with him because she is a nymphomaniac!! The interminable philosophical digressions on life and love that inflate the novel are equally sophomoric. Jones is fictionally as far out of his orbit in a male-female society as a nun would be in a front-line platoon.

James Jones's fictional terrain is limited to that peculiar all-male world governed by strictly masculine interests, attitudes, and values. Into this world, no female can step without immediately altering its character. The female must remain on the periphery of male life—a powerful force in male consciousness, but solely as a provocative target for that intense sexual need that has nothing to do with procreation or marriage. In civilian life, the closest approximation to this all-male world is the camp of the weekend fisherman or hunter who becomes totally absorbed in technical details about sports and sporting equipment, who enjoys the comraderie of shared masculine interests, who competes for the distinction of being the toughest guy, the best shot, the bravest, boldest hunter, the greatest seducer. In this atmosphere, men strip themselves of the refinements of sensibility and language that they adopt in their life with women. Not intellect, nor manners, nor moral and aesthetic sensitivity, but technical skill and knowledge, physical strength and endurance, boldness and courage are the coveted virtues of this exclusively male world.

Individualism is identified, in *From Here to Eternity*, with this masculine life, as if the army were the final frontier of rugged individualism. There are two major threats to the masculine freedom of the enlisted man's existence—the bureaucracy represented by the officer class, and women. Robert E. Lee Prewitt, co-protagonist of the novel, loves not so much the army but the masculinity of barracks life. He wants to be a thirty-year-man because the raw violence, the drunken sprees, the sex without responsibility, the demands on physical endurance and technical skill express and challenge his maleness. Prewitt's war with the army is touched off by a breach of the freedom he expects in return for his loyalty and service as a soldier. The army can have no claim upon his skill at bugling and his ability in the boxing ring. These are voluntary activities, and when an inferior bugler is promoted above him, Prew chooses to transfer to an infantry outfit. A willing boxer until he inflicted a permanent injury on a sparring partner, Prew decides to keep a promise to a woman—his dying mother—not to hurt others unnecessarily, and he refuses to go out for the regimental team. At stake is Prewitt's self-defined integrity, his freedom to choose to do what he wants beyond his obligations as a soldier.

His assertion of individual rights sets into motion the juggernaut of the organization. As Jones makes clear throughout his story, Prew's quixotic struggle can only end in his destruction. Prewitt's history is an eloquent paean to a concept of individualism rapidly becoming anachronistic in an increasingly bureaucratic society. Milt Warden, the co-protagonist of the novel, embodies in his personality the masculine world of the enlisted man. He equates his integrity with the existence of the enlisted man, and when he falls in love with the company commander's wife, Karen, and finally refuses the commission which would make her permanently available to him, he preserves his integrity and his individualism. He does not sell out to the bureaucracy or to women. At the end of the novel, Prew is dead, but Warden drinks and brawls on the way to Mrs. Kipfer's brothel as the *Lurline* sails from Hawaii with Karen aboard.

Jones's second novel contains a facsimile of barracks life in the ménage of Dave and 'Bama. Like the soldiers in Schofield Barracks, the group of ex-GI's drink and gamble and brawl and whore, creating a masculine fortress in the very midst of a feminized, stifling bourgeois society. But this symbolic individualism has no chance of resisting for long the attacks of society and of women. *Some Came Running* presents the histories of a large number of characters, but though a few receive more attention than others, none emerges as a true protagonist. Jones's attitude toward his characters is also far more objective than it was in *From Here to Eternity*. It is almost impossible to feel sympathetic with any character in the entire 1,266 pages of the book. There are no loveable Maggios, nor are there any characters like the sadistic Judson whom one can hate. Jones has already discovered that "There's only a thin red line between the sane and the mad," the good and the bad.

The Thin Red Line has no protagonist. The story concerns an infantry company fighting in the jungles and hills of Guadalcanal. If a single character comes into focus momentarily, he quickly recedes into the background as Jones shifts attention to another soldier. The company encompasses the individuals that make it up. It is an abstract unit with a table of organization designating a variety of positions which human beings fill. In battle, the company, made up of platoons which are made up of squads, is deployed by the battalion commander according to a pre-established plan of attack. The battalions in the regiment are deployed by the regimental commander. The regiments are deployed by the division commander; the divisions deployed by the army commander, and the armies deployed all over the globe by a staff in Washington, D. C. Within this hierarchy, which gets larger and larger as it moves up the chain and farther and farther from the battle lines, the fighting soldier is a grain of sand on a beach encircling the globe.

Jones utilizes a number of effective techniques to dramatize the insignificance of the individual soldier in this massive organization. Concentrating most of his attention upon the activities of C-for-Charlie Company, he permits the reader to become a partisan rooter for the fighting unit. Then, he widens the angle of vision to make the reader aware of companies on each flank of C

Company also encountering severe hardships and fierce battles with the enemy. When C-for-Charlie reaches Boola Boola village, its final objective in the campaign, the effect of this dramatic climax is deliberately deadened: another company has already occupied the village and the fighting is about over. The over-enthusiastic C Company commander is relieved from his command because he had acted independently rather than as a unit in the organization.

Jones uses a similar technique in presenting the individual soldiers. By shifting from character to character, he gradually creates the impression that the individual is not only of little importance within the organization but he is of little importance to anyone but himself. When the men see wounded and dead for the first time they are shocked and horrified. During their first battle, they react intensely to the suffering and death of their comrades. But as the fighting continues, the dead bodies of their fellow-soldiers no longer really bother them, and they lose all compunction about killing enemy soldiers. The starving Japanese prisoners are treated inhumanly, but only because the combat situation has revealed to their captors the insignificance of the individual human life except to the being who possesses it. Dead, the grotesque uniformed figure is a piece of carrion to be buried before its stench becomes nauseating.

Jones's existential novel strips away all inherited concepts and all illusions, metaphysical or social, about man's inherent dignity and being. Atheistic or religious, brave or cowardly, these men are equally vulnerable to the indiscriminate governance of chance. Even those incalculable forces within man which make him a coward or a hero under fire are beyond the individual's control. The same men who zig zag bravely through enemy fire on an heroic mission will know soul-shaking terror a week later when, safe in a noncombat area, they hear bombs dropping miles away. Occasionally courage is psychologically explicable; most often it is not. Circumstances create values, and a man's sense of himself comes from his actions in these circumstances. Each man contains within his being the potential for every human virtue or vice, heroism and cowardice, compassion and sadism. The same men who under other conditions would show compassion for any living thing, in the feverish aura of combat are capable of murdering and torturing prisoners without the slightest qualm of conscience. No cause and effect relationship exists between virtue and destiny. The spattering mortar fragments slash the brave and the cowardly.

The ultimate insignificance of individual man is conveyed at the end of the novel. The campaign for Guadalcanal has ended and C-for-Charlie Company begins training for the coming attack on New Georgia. The great battle is reduced to one of a series of battles. Most of the men who made up the company are dead or dispersed. The dead and the evacuated wounded are replaced to fill out the table of organization. The individual men may live or die, come or go, but the abstraction C-for-Charlie Company remains.

Jones's vision of human existence is brutal and unsentimental, and he conveys it with superb artistry. His story of battle is fast-paced, tightly structured, painfully realistic. James Jones's fictional terrain is limited, but within that limited area he has presented a frightening twentieth-century view of individual man's insignificance in society and in the universe.

ii

Norman Mailer, in contrast to Jones, has continued to rage against the vision of anonymity. In his first novel, *The Naked and the Dead,* Mailer confronted a fundamental conflict in the modern American conception of individualism. This conflict has defined the social and political development of twentieth-century American society, and it has, to a great extent, defined the literary development of Norman Mailer.

The conflict, greatly simplified, concerns the meaning of individualism. Does it mean that each man in a society is free to live his own life, work toward his own ambitions, express his sense of self without assistance or interference? Or does it mean that each man must be guaranteed the economic security that will free him to express his sense of self? Few Americans have not embraced both definitions depending upon the circumstances and issues involved, but generally speaking, the political conservatives champion the first and the political liberals favor the second. Mailer began his career as a militant liberal, but like most of his fellow citizens, he has vacillated between the two persuasions. Psychologically he is drawn to the conservative interpretation, intellectually and emotionally, he is liberal. This dualism is probably the result of his fascination with power as an expression of self. *The Deer Park,* his third novel, contains a statement about the artist which Mailer's public career and his journalism would indicate is an accurate self-analysis: "The artist was always divided between his desire for power in the world and his desire for power over his work." It would probably be difficult to find validity for such an observation in the careers of most artists, particularly in America, but it does seem to apply to Mailer, who told one interviewer, "I suppose I write because I want to reach people and by reaching them influence the history of my time a little bit." To another interviewer he said, "I feel that the final purpose of art is to intensify, even, if necessary, to exacerbate, the moral consciousness of people." Norman Mailer obviously wants to inscribe the legend "Mailer was here" in the annals of history—and not just literary history. He wants to leave his mark, even if it has to be a scar, upon his time. This ambition has probably had much influence on the direction his career has taken. His bitterness and frustration at the failure of his second and third novels to impress the society from which he sought acclaim and power, he stridently expressed in the snarling columns he wrote for *The Village Voice.* Too often, he has sounded like a little boy who would rather be spanked for being naughty than ignored. His crusade for the right to be vulgar in print has had a liberating influence, but one wonders if it were not partially motivated by the desire to shock. The deflection of his creative energy from fiction to the essay is probably due, to some extent, to his unquenchable ambition to be a power in American society. One may question his maturity but hardly the sincerity of his aspirations in considering his claim to having won John Kennedy the presidency with an essay. The titles of his last two books, *Advertisements for Myself* and *The Presidential Papers* are only partly ironical.

Mailer's personal desire for power in the world would naturally make attractive to him the kind of man who can seize and wield power over others. And that is precisely what is evident in *The Naked and the Dead*. This fine novel, deservedly remembered and still widely read as one of the great World War II novels, is actually less about war than about the conflicting interpretations of individualism. Despite the detailed, realistic descriptions of army life and jungle combat, the excellent analyses of the combat soldier's responses and feelings, *The Naked and the Dead* is fundamentally, as Norman Podhoretz has observed, a political novel.

The division in society between the economically privileged and the economically deprived is reflected in the military caste-system. Mailer's enlisted men are, in fact, from the lower economic strata of society. The two officers upon whom he focuses attention are from well-to-do families. General Cummings, representing the conservative position at its most extreme, sees life as a chess game, a continual maneuvering for positions of power with success going to the cleverest and strongest. The general is coldly rational, considering the compassion of the liberal morally debilitating and sentimental. Cummings wields the power his rank gives him with an unassailable conviction in his right and duty to do so. His opponent in the dialectic is his aide, Lieutenant Hearn, the scion of a wealthy man. As a civilian, Hearn forsook the power his father offered him because he subscribed to the liberal interpretation of individualism. Responsive to the integrity and the feelings of all men, and sensitive to all the nuances that a liberal mentality can uncover in any social or intellectual issue,

Hearn is vacillating and weak. His exasperated, childish assertion of self against the general by grinding his cigarette butt on the immaculate tent floor is a romantic gesture that ends with his transfer to a combat platoon and his eventual death.

The counterparts of the officers among the enlisted men, Sergeant Croft and Red Valsen, validate by their experiences and personalities the intellectual positions of Cummings and Hearn. General Cummings derives his power from his rank, but Platoon Sergeant Croft does not command, he leads. His physical stamina, his courage, his will power, and his implacable need to dominate make him the most powerful man in the platoon and its natural leader. Hearn was educated to liberalism, but Red's grudging compassion for his fellow man was wrought out of his experiences in civilian life.

Clearly, Mailer's sympathy is with Hearn and Valsen, but his admiration goes to the men of power, Cummings and Croft. This fascination with power is also apparent in the repeated descriptions in this and other works of the reactions men experience when they kill. The exercise of man's ultimate power over others brings with it for Mailer's killers a heady exhilaration. Most of the men shrink from the truth of this experience, but Sergeant Croft does not. As much as Mailer is repelled by the cruelty and sadism of Cummings and Croft, he is also awed by the mystique of power. In this early novel, he attempts to relate the actions and reactions of his characters to their psychological past, but it is apparent that he has already detected the arcanum of being that many years later he will seek to explore.

Croft's determination to lead his squad over the mountain is an expression of power. He does not hesitate to send Hearn to certain death when the officer becomes a threat to the enterprise. The mountain challenges Croft's endurance and his leadership and, in attempting to scale it, he is pitting his will against the reluctance of the men, their physical limitations, and against the forces of nature. Mailer's admiration for Croft and Cummings led him into a fictional situation that his liberalism would not allow him to follow to its logical conclusion. The defeat of the general and the sergeant is contrived. Cummings' absence during the finale of the campaign deprived him of a victory he earned, and it is too obviously a plot manipulation. Croft's defeat by the hornets introduces a naturalistic theme—man's ultimate weakness against the forces of nature—that does not develop from the rest of the novel and that, judging from the rest of Mailer's work, was probably not intended.

Mailer came close to finding in Croft a twentieth-century hero, but he was not yet ready for him. He had to do a great deal of conscience appeasement before he could rediscover Croft in the existential hero who refuses to succumb to the dictates of an inherited moral and social code, who savors the freedom to exist in the present and to explore the extreme limits of personal power, who responds to the irrational forces in his being, and who creates his own meaning and identity through action.

Barbary Shore, though intellectually sincere, is a sop to a sorely beleaguered liberal conscience. At the end of this political allegory, Lovett heroically assumes the burden of the socialist ideal, but he is too shadowy a figure to emerge as a hero. Probably Mailer had already begun to sense that the socialist ideal would stifle the very individualism it was intended to provide. Whatever the causes, he failed to transmute his ideas into art. The first part of the novel, with its Kafkaesque atmosphere, is interesting, but the rest is smothered by the dialectic.

The Deer Park is a novel of personal discovery. Though much better than its critical reception indicated, it is considerably marred by intellectual confusion. As he wrote, Mailer seems to have made a series of discoveries that undermined his artistic control. His decision, when the book was in galleys, to strengthen the role of his narrator makes Sergius a transitional hero—part liberal, part existential hero—and hence an ill-conceived character. Sergius begins as an admirer of the liberal Eitel, develops a friendship with Marion Faye and, at the end of the novel, he cuts himself off from his society. The book seems to have begun with the plan of making Eitel, the movie director who defies the Congressional Investigating Committee by refusing to reveal names, a hero. But once again Mailer's sensibility, which runs far ahead of his intellect, interfered. He had begun to sense that the liberal was as much a part of the American society as the members of the investigating committee. The roots of the anti-welfare-state essays in *The Presidential Papers* are in this novel.

Mailer also discovered sex as an expression of power. As the title and epigraph indicate, he set out to reveal the corruption of a capitalistic society and the wide chasm between American sexual mores and practices—which he effectively accomplished—but in the process he began to view sex as a key to the mystery of being. Sergius, for instance, made impotent by his war experiences, regains his sexual power and psychological stability in his affair with the movie sex goddess, Lulu. The Sergius O'Shaugnessy of *The Deer Park* is not quite the same character as the Sergius of "The Time of Her Time," but the hero of that excerpt from the novel in progress explores the secrets of will and power in the sexual act, an exploration begun in *The Deer Park*.

Marion Faye seems also to have led Mailer into areas which are structurally and thematically tangential to his novel but which bring him closer to his future interests. Marion deliberately tests his own will power by violating the codes of his society and by exposing himself to his worst terrors. Deathly afraid of being attacked while he sleeps, he forces himself to leave his door unlocked. And though he has no need of the money, he chooses to be a pimp, an occupation held in utmost contempt by his society. Faye is no Croft, but he is an individualist seeking to discover himself through the exercise of will.

Both Marion and Sergius have roles in Mailer's projected novel. It is difficult to ascertain what that novel will be like from the two excerpts included in *Advertisements for Myself,* but it is apparent that Mailer has given up the idea of a social hero. Individualism cannot exist within the confines of twentieth-century society, and Mailer has found in the asocial, apolitical hipster—the existential hero—the sole remaining hope for individualism. The repetitious essays included in *The Presidential Papers* reveal that Mailer now sees the welfare state as a faceless totalitarian force impoverishing the psychic life of the nation, making the American a weak, bland automaton, a psychic neuter. The society, according to Mailer, is dying of cancer—that disease in which malignant cells surround and destroy the functioning organ. By standardizing the American's manner of living, his thinking, his emotional responses, his very needs, the society is strangling individualism. Mailer's criticism of American society and culture brings him very close to the position of the political conservative, but he recognizes that the pallid version of nineteenth-century rugged individualism advocated by the conservative is anachronistic. Unfortunately, Mailer insists upon writing political essays without a practical program for the restitution and growth of individualism. His hipster is an underground man and cannot exist in the sphere of practical politics. What Mailer calls existential politics is simply a very effective device for criticism, for dramatizing the loss of individualism in society and for proclaiming the sanctity and mystery of the human being. Mailer is an artist not a politician. As weapons to exacerbate the consciousness of the American people, his essays are forceful and effective. But Mailer confuses art with politics. His championing of violence, for example, to dramatize the refusal of society to recognize the force of the irrational in the human being is artistically justifiable but politically irresponsible. What these essays make clear is that Mailer thinks not as a politician but as an artist, and that in continuing to cater to his desire for power in the world he is wasting a precious talent.

His passion for individualism has led him to view man as an infinitely mysterious and infinitely fascinating being.

And he has taken as his fictional province the mystery of the human psyche. Norman Mailer has great talent, and he may yet provide a work of fiction to offset the terrifying view of human insignificance that James Jones has translated into art.

THE SINGULAR WORLDS OF
JACK KEROUAC

Howard W. Webb, Jr.

"EVERYTHING that he had ever done in his life, everything
there was—was haunted now by a deep sense of loss,
confusion, and strange neargrief. He had known a boy's
life in Galloway, he had grown up there and played
football and lived in the big house with his family, he had
known all the gravities and the glees and the wonders of
life. Now all that was lost, vanished, haunted and
ghostly—because it was no more." Thus young Peter
Martin, hero of *The Town and the City* (Harcourt, Brace,
1950), the first book by Jack Kerouac, reflects as he stands
observing the motley crowd on Times Square. The year is
1944: the remnants of the Martin family have recently
moved into a cramped basement apartment in Brooklyn,
and Peter, who serves in the Merchant Marine, has just
returned from a sad pilgrimage to the Massachusetts town
of his boyhood. As he stands musing and watching, his
melancholy disappears, for he sees three of his New York
friends coming up the street. "They were a strange trio:
one was a hoodlum, one was a dope addict, and the third
was a poet."

This scene, a crucial one in the work of Jack Kerouac,
brings together the two areas of experience which consti-
tute his subject matter and in large part explain the
meaning of what he writes. One of these areas is Lowell,
Massachusetts, where Kerouac spent his boyhood and
adolescence in the 1920's and 1930's as a member of a
large, happy, middle-class family of French-Canadian

origin and as one of a slightly smaller circle of boisterous, good-natured male companions. The other is the sub-terranean life—in New York, Denver, New Orleans, Mexico City, and San Francisco—of petty criminals and dope addicts, prostitutes and "chicks," writers and Truth bums, what has come to be called the "beat generation."

Never again in Kerouac's work do the two stand face to face, but each impinges on and gives color and significance to the other. The works that present the beat world carry references to Doctor Sax, Gerard, and other figures and sights of Lowell; those which present the Lowell world are cast in the "spontaneous prose" of the beat generation and carry mysterious allusions to Fellaheens and Sutras.[1] But Kerouac's loyalties are not divided. He celebrated Lowell because it remains for him a place of unsullied beauty; he celebrates the beat generation because he finds in it what he, like Peter Martin, had once thought was forever lost. Both his worlds contain the qualities he finds most important in life: joy, tenderness, and spirituality.

Since the beat generation is a constant in Kerouac's writing but a different and shifting concept everywhere else, let us start with some historical clarifications and distinctions. In the beginning, in New York in the mid-1940's was a group which apparently included Kerouac, Allen Ginsberg, William S. Burroughs, Clellon Holmes, Carl Solomon, and Neal Cassady, the Dean Moriarty of *On the Road*. They were haunted by their inability to believe in anything, convinced that this faith-lessness was unbearable, and driven by the tension arising from their conflicting views to a craving for excess. In 1948, Kerouac said to Holmes of this group and their situation: "You know, this is really a *beat* generation."[2] In *The Town and the City* he devotes almost a hundred pages to them, emphasizing their faithlessness and their excesses, but he does not give them a name. Clellon Holmes's first novel, *Go*, is an examination of the same group, but far more then Kerouac's book it stresses their tortured need for something to believe in. And Holmes's protagonist gives the group a name; he is both attracted and repelled by what he calls "this beat generation, this underground life." Shortly after the appearance of his novel, Holmes published an article (N. Y. *Times Magazine*, Nov. 16, 1952) in which he sought to define the term as he and, he presumed, Kerouac had used it: "More than mere weariness, it implies the feeling of having been used, of being raw. It involves a sort of nakedness of mind, and, ultimately, of soul; a feeling of being reduced to the bedrock of consciousness. In short, it means being undramatically pushed up against the wall of oneself." Holmes also extended the term to cover all young people "who went through the war, or at least could get a drink easily once it was over." The whole age group, he argued, was afflicted with "beatness." But they had had enough of "homelessness, valuelessness, faithlessness"; more and more they were occupied with the need for some kind of faith.[3]

Since neither Holmes's book nor his article provoked much interest, and since publishers would not accept Kerouac's second book, for the next five years little was heard of the beat generation. In 1955, *New World Writing* published "Jazz of the Beat Generation," actually a section of *On the Road*, under the pseudonym of "Jean-Louis"; and that same year Malcolm Cowley devoted a paragraph to a group of writers who "refused to conform and waged a dogged sort of rebellion," identifying them as "the beat generation" and asserting that Kerouac's "unpublished long narrative, *On the Road*, is the best record of their lives." Lawrence Lipton and Kenneth Rexroth wrote several articles describing the attitudes and works of a group of San Francisco writers, some of whom were members of the original New York group. Richard Eberhart, in 1956, reported that "San Francisco teems with young poets" and proclaimed that "the most remarkable poem of the young group . . . is 'Howl,' by Allen Ginsberg." [4] The next month *Howl and Other Poems* with its dedication to Jack Kerouac, William Seward Burroughs, and Neal Cassady, was published.

Then 1957, *annus mirabilis*: Kenneth Rexroth's article

on the art of the beat generation; Lawrence Ferlinghetti's trial for selling an obscene book, *Howl*; and in September the publication of *On the Road*.[5] At this point, the beat generation erupted into our midst with the suddenness and impact of a new volcanic isle, and for the next two years the isle seemed to be expanding to the size of a continent. Everywhere—on campuses and city streets, on television and in the movies, in *Time* and *Partisan Review*, the *Atlantic Monthly* and *Playboy*, the *New York Times* and the *Village Voice*—it loomed. Anthologies appeared, social psychologists and old Bohemians made studies, colleges opened their forums.[6] The "beatnik" threatened to replace the "organization man" as the American type. Then, by 1960, the new isle began to settle, and now it has apparently disappeared from view.

But in the work of Jack Kerouac the beat generation remains, not an island nor a continent, not an image of despair, a threat to society, nor an object of ridicule, but a created world. It began to take shape in 1947, when Kerouac decided that he must choose "between the drawing rooms full of Noel Cowards and the rattling trucks on the American highways."[7] His first two books converge on this point. *The Town and the City* ends with Peter Martin starting out on a new life "in his black leather jacket, carrying the old canvas bag in which all his poor needments for a long journey were packed." *On the Road* begins with Sal Paradise shaking off his feeling that everything is dead and heading west to join Dean Moriarty, who has contributed significantly to his recovery. The Kerouac protagonist, Jack, thus enters the beat world in the company of the Kerouac hero, Dean.[8] By this act, he sheds his haunting sense of "homelessness, valuelessness, faithlessness," but without a clear recognition, at the start, of why this happens. His adventures during the next few years supply the answer.

Part of his discovery lies in his expanding knowledge of Dean Moriarty, whose intelligence is "every bit as formal and shining and complete" as that of Jack's intellectual New York friends and whose criminality "was not something that sulked and sneered; it was a wild yea-saying overburst of American joy." Dean always races, "eager for bread and love," and responds to any experience—eating, making love, driving a car, listening to jazz, smoking marijuana—with vibrancy and zest. "We gotta go and never stop going till we get there," he tells Jack, who has already had a vision of him "running through all of life just like that—his bony face outthrust to life, his arms pumping, his brow sweating, his legs twinkling like Groucho Marx, yelling, 'Yes! Yes, man, you sure can go!'" Gradually Jack realizes that Dean is as he is because he has left behind all "bitterness, recriminations, advice, morality" and has always ahead of him "the ragged and ecstatic joy of pure being." In his experiences with this "new kind of American saint," considerably extended in *Visions of Cody*, which is "a vertical, metaphysical study of [Dean's] character and its relationship to the general 'America,'"[9] Jack recaptures joyfulness. He discovers the value of an open, unreserved response to events and people on the American highways and city streets.

Perhaps equally important, he finds on the concrete and asphalt what he had been unable to locate in the drawing rooms: people for whom he can feel compassion, affection, and love. They are warm, honest persons, quick to share their pleasures and pads, like Mississippi Gene and Montana Slim, Jack's companions on his first trip west, and on a trip east the Ghost of the Susquehanna, "a shriveled little old man with a paper satchel who claimed he was headed for Canady"; Remi Boncoeur and his girl Lee Ann, with whom Jack lives for a time near San Francisco; and Terry, the Mexican girl with whom he spends several intimate weeks. In *The Dharma Bums* Japhy Ryder, the "Oriental scholar" and mountain climber from Oregon; Beaudry, the truck driver who goes into Mexico with Jack and then, against company rules, carries him all the way to Ohio; Sean Monahan and his wife, owners of a shack in the Sierras where Japhy and Jack spend happy days, all have the same geniality and directness.

Possessing some of the characteristics of these people

but in a category by herself is Mardou Fox in *The Subterraneans*. As much, perhaps more than Jack, she is open and unreserved, prepared for tenderness and love. Even more thoroughly than in the case of Dean, we learn why she is a sharer in the underground life as we listen to her story of being naked and afraid in the San Francisco night. Jack, who has never heard such a tale "except from the great men I'd known in my youth, great heroes of America I'd been buddies with, with whom I'd adventured and gone to jail and known in raggedy dawns," believes that she has been "an angel wandering in hell and the hell the selfsame streets I'd roamed in watching, watching for someone just like her." His relationship with Mardou is deeper and more personal than are his ties with any other person in the beat world. But their affair crumbles. Jack's selfishness, his guilts and jealousies and doubts, his concern over the fact that she is a Negro, destroy her love for him.

At no other point in the entire saga does the Kerouac protagonist come so close to merging fully with the beat world. He fails and his failure reveals that while he may move about in this world he is never a part of it. Jack is not a reporter or a participant in the beat generation Kerouac creates; he is a responding spectator. His stance is evident even in one of the elements of style, the frequent use of such words as "wild," "great," "tragic," or "sad" preceding sights, sounds, activities, and the names of people; for this device, of course, describes the observer, not the thing observed. The boy from the large, happy, middle-class family of Lowell, Massachusetts, has simply not been shaped to fit the molds that contain a Dean or a Terry or a Beaudry or a Mardou Fox.

Jack's essential apartness is nowhere more obvious than in *The Dharma Bums*, the work in which he seeks and finds a new spirituality. In the earlier books he leaves the beat world occasionally to stay with his mother or sister, but these breaches are made to seem quite unimportant. In *The Dharma Bums* he spends a long stretch of time at home communing with nature and his soul, and on the

West Coast his search for Truth takes him further and further from human contact, at the end to a summer of complete isolation on a mountain top. In another sense, too, this book is a strange one. Jack's honesty in seeing himself as a "religious wanderer" and in believing that he has "become a Buddha" need not be challenged, but the success with which he communicates this new spirituality may certainly be questioned. As Warren Tallman observes: "Representation of the final trip to the Northwest, where the protagonist attempts to live in the Zen way on Desolation Peak, is so sketchy as to amount to a default." [10] What is convincing in *The Dharma Bums* is not Jack's effort to live in the Zen way but his response to the experience of mountain-climbing. As he nears the end of his first expedition, he writes:

> I had never had a happier moment in my life than those lonely moments coming down that little deer trace and when we hiked off with our packs I turned to take a final look up that way . . . It had been like when you're a little boy and have spent a whole day rambling alone in the woods and fields and on the dusk homeward walk you did it all with your eyes to the ground, scuffling, thinking, whistling, like little Indian boys must feel when they follow their striding fathers from Russian River to Shasta two hundred years ago, like little Arab boys following their fathers, their fathers' trails; that singsong little joyful solitude, nose sniffling, like a little girl pulling her little brother home on the sled and they're both singing little ditties of their imagination and making faces at the ground and just being themselves before they have to go in the kitchen and put on a straight face again for the world of seriousness.

Jack's response transports us from the Sierras and the Buddhistic realms of pure egolessness to the childhood world of Lowell; [11] for the function of the beat world for Kerouac's protagonist, and doubtless for Kerouac himself, has been to renew and sustain the virtues of the Massachusetts town in which he grew up. He will not go back to the drawing rooms; but then, in spite of that melancholy moment in Times Square, he has never really left Lowell.

The point is made again and again in Kerouac's writing. Looking back to the last year of his older brother's life (*Visions of Gerard*), Jack realizes that the truth to which he has come as an adult was first foretold in Gerard's sad eyes: "I see there in the eyes of Gerard the very diamond of kindness and patient humility of the Brotherhood Ideal propounded from afar down the eternal corridors of Buddhahood and Compassionate Sanctity, in Nirmana (appearance) Kaya (form)." Even Kerouac's understanding of what he had originally meant by the word "beat" came to him in Lowell:

> I went one afternoon [in 1954] to the church of my childhood (one of them), Ste. Jeanne d'Arc in Lowell, Mass., and suddenly with tears in my eyes had a vision of what I must have really meant with "Beat" anyhow when I heard in the holy silence in the church (I was the only one in there, it was five P.M., dogs were barking outside, children were yelling, the fall leaves, the candles were flickering along just for me), the vision of the word Beat as being to mean beatific.[12]

Just as the Lowell world is the source of the spirituality which Jack finds revivified in the beat generation, so it is the place where tenderness begins. The Martins of *The Town and the City* are a well-knit family; each member is "wrapped in his own vision of life," but they all have "the family stamp somehow imprinted upon each of their lives." Before the family begins to break up under the pressures of poverty, maturity, and war, Kerouac presents image after image of the love and compassion which are the keys to the Martins' unity: their shared pleasure when Peter is the hero of the Thanksgiving football game; Mickey's glorious day when he, the baby of the family, goes to the races and dinner in Boston with his father; fourteen-year-old Charley's exhilaration when his older brother and sister, Joe and Liz, discover him secretly collecting junk to pay for a broken window and spend the afternoon helping him; Peter's deep but unstated affection for Liz as he assists in her plans to elope. The tenderness that Kerouac associates with Lowell is perhaps best summed up in Peter's rush of love and grief and disbelief as he finds his father dead; for bluff, hearty George Martin is Kerouac's fullest portrait of the father who taught him tenderness, who "never lifted a hand to punish me, or to punish the little pets in our house, and this teaching was delivered to me by the men in my house and I have never had anything to do with violence, hatred, cruelty, and all that horrible nonsense." [13]

Tenderness and spirituality aside, Lowell is pre-eminently the place of joy, of "the glees and the wonders of life." In Lowell, joy is the result of Jack's open and unreserved response to a wide spectrum of influences, chief among them sports, movies, comic strips, pulp magazines, friends, and girls. These are the influences Kerouac refers to when he tells us that the beat generation

> goes back to the wild and raving childhood of playing the Shadow under windswept trees of New England's gleeful autumn, and the howl of the Moon Man on the sandbank until we caught him in a tree (he was an "older" guy of 15), the maniacal laugh of certain neighborhood madboys, the furious humor of whole gangs playing basketball till long after dark in the park, it goes back to those crazy days before World War II when teenagers drank beer on Friday nights at Lake ballrooms and worked off their hangovers playing baseball on Saturday afternoon followed by a dive in the brook—and our fathers wore straw hats like W. C. Fields. It goes back to the completely senseless babble of the Three Stooges, the ravings of the Marx Brothers (the tenderness of Angel Harpo at harp, too). [14]

In the beat world such memories become for Jack an almost private symbolism by means of which he comprehends his response to people and events. He understands, for example, that the first days of Dean's mysticism "lead to the strange ragged W. C. Fields saintliness of his later days"; he has "further Three Stooges adventures" with Henry Morley in *The Dharma Bums*. In the world of Lowell, however, these matters are not imported; they are an integral part of life. The phantasy of *Doctor Sax*, for example, appears to be a mixture of the comedians, Bela

Lugosi as Count Dracula, and "Lamont Cranston so cool and sure suddenly becoming the frantic Shadow going mwee hee hee ha ha in the alleys of New York." [15] By the time Jack is seventeen, in *Maggie Cassidy*, the line between phantasy and reality is clear, but materials from the movies and comic strips still provide him and the rest of his gang with games and poses for mocking the "world of seriousness." [16]

The joyfulness of Lowell is brought most sharply into focus in *Maggie Cassidy*. In this book Jack tastes the sweet success of sweeping the field at an indoor track meet; he knows the tormenting pleasure of being sought by two girls; he goes through the exquisite agony of loving Maggie in a tender and erotic affair that is never consummated; and he revels in the warm companionship of the friends he is soon to leave, G. J. Rigopoulos, Scotty Boldieu, Albert Lauzon, and Vinny Bergerac. Indeed, *Maggie Cassidy* is almost a reprise of *On the Road* and *The Subterraneans*, but its repetitions are not so important as its variations. Its "spontaneous prose" has an evocative force less often found in the beat world books, and the gang and Maggie are less frenetic, warmer and more innocent, than Dean Moriarty and Mardou Fox. Most different of all is the situation of Jack. In Lowell he is not merely a responding spectator, and he is certainly not a casual reporter; he is, instead, a fully involved participant.

His position as participant is underlined by Kerouac's use of narrative point of view. As the book opens, the gang, watched by an omniscient observer, are laughing and roughhousing through the snow on their way to a New Year's Eve dance; and Jack is simply one of them, no more special or separate than G. J., Scotty, or any of the others. We see him, in fact, as immersed in the world of Lowell. His total involvement continues even after he meets Maggie and takes over the narration himself. In Chapters IX through XVI, for instance, he tells us about a typical day in the eighteenth year of his life. He speaks of times with his family, in school, with the gang, and with Maggie; but in no case are these associations simply events to be reported or observed. They are, rather, experiences in which he participates. This experiential quality is further emphasized by frequent and extended use of present tense verbs which break the line between narrator-Jack and actor-Jack. Still, narrator-Jack is telling of a world he feels he has lost, and the mood of the book is essentially nostalgic. Toward the end, he leaves Lowell to attend prep school in New York; and when Maggie comes to a dance there, they have a bitterly "unsuccessful night." The next day she pleads with him: "Jacky. Lowell Jacky Duluoz. Come on home leave here." But he cannot, and the story proper concludes with the fragments of Jack's frantically social spring, and at the very end his sudden lament: "Maggie lost." In the last two chapters the time is three years later and the point of view is again that of an omniscient observer. We watch a cynical and joyless Jack try, cold-bloodedly but futilely, to seduce Maggie Cassidy.

Although the symbolism is perhaps a bit too obvious, his failure in this instance is as instructive as his failure with Mardou Fox. Just as he cannot fully merge with the beat generation, so he cannot violate Maggie, the symbol of Lowell. Here, as elsewhere in Kerouac's work, that Massachusetts town remains inviolate. Lost though it seemed, it was not irretrievably destroyed; and in that crucial moment in Times Square, Jack, in the person of Peter Martin, begins to find his way back. Thus the disparate but singular worlds that Jack Kerouac has created sustain one another, and his observation of one has enabled him to restore the other and to affirm them both.

At this point in his career, then, what evaluation can be placed on the ethical and artistic qualities of the works of Jack Kerouac? One critic, Norman Podhoretz, has argued that the beat ideology "is hostile to civilization; it worships primitivism, instinct, energy, 'blood'" and leads to the "notion that sordid acts of violence are justifiable so long as they are committed in the name of 'instinct.'" [17] For the Luce publications the beat generation has provided fine material for satire. Because of its "non-political radicalism," [18] it does not actively and directly threaten the established order; because of its apparent commitment only to drink, drugs, and sex, it can be ridiculed so as to give implicit affirmation to the comfortable conformity of a prosperous America. Actually, neither of these views has dealt with the beat world created by Kerouac. Podhoretz is really writing about the hipster figure described by Norman Mailer,[19] and the Luce publications have been concerned with the "beatnik" image manufactured by the mass media. Kerouac's own ethic is nonviolent; the values that he praises are peaceful and gentle ones. And his challenge is radical in the root sense of the word. He is not hostile to civilization, as his presentation of the Lowell world makes clear; but he is opposed to the destruction of joy, tenderness, and spirituality in American life and to the deification of "rows of well-to-do houses with lawns and television sets in each living-room with everybody looking at the same thing and thinking the same thing at the same time" [*Dharma Bums*]. He turns away from such a way of life because he finds in it no means for defining his individuality and his humanity, a view he can be said to share with a number of contemporary writers.

If comment on the ethical quality of Kerouac's work has been misdirected, discussion of its literary merit has been almost nonexistent. Warren Tallman's article, "Kerouac's Sound," studies seriously and in detail certain aspects of style; otherwise, critics have been content with remarks testifying to his "large talent" or scorning his books because they do not fit the novelistic pattern, "nothing that happens has any dramatic reason for happening." [20] Kerouac has doubtless contributed to this neglect with statements about his lack of any method other than the spontaneous. The preceding examination, however, directs attention to effects that are not the result of mere spontaneity. The beat generation and Lowell are vivid and convincing worlds, made so not only by an uncontrolled, run-away enthusiasm but also by a skillful use of controlling images and narrative point of view. And these worlds are inhabited by believable characters. Mardou Fox and Maggie Cassidy, particularly, are projected with remarkable roundness, no small accomplishment since we see them through the eyes of an emotionally-involved narrator; and Dean Moriarty, whether one approves of him or not, is fully created for us by his speech and his actions. A comparison of his language and rhythms with those of the Lowell gang or of the total character with Clellon Holmes's presentation of the same figure as Hart Kennedy in Go will reveal how effective Kerouac has been.

On both ethical and artistic grounds, then, he ought not to be too lightly dismissed. His challenge to society has substance and his literary accomplishment has merit. Any judgment of the work of Jack Kerouac must, however, be a qualified one for the present. One problem is that the relation between author and protagonist has not seemed consistent. Sometimes the two appear to be indistinguishable; at other times Jack is obviously a persona over which the author maintains a clear and sure control. Kerouac may have recognized this difficulty, for his recent practice of listing twelve of his works under the general title The Duluoz Legend indicates a desire to establish a firm, if thin, line between Jack and his creator. A more serious matter is the pace of productivity. Since 1957, Kerouac has published, including On the Road, fifteen books; but of this number no more than six were written after 1956, and only one of these, Big Sur, is in any way a major work.[21] The implication is that Kerouac is confronted with an intellectual and artistic crisis. Has he exaggerated the possibilities of self-realization in the beat world; has he sentimentalized the hoodlum, the dope addict, and the poet? After all, if Jack himself remains always separate from the beat generation, what chance is there for anyone else? And if the adulation accorded the strange trio is not truly warranted, what is the beat generation but a construct of Jack's disillusioned and haunted soul? Big Sur indicates that Kerouac has not come to terms with these questions. In that book the beat world no longer has its old meaning and function for Jack; Dean and some of the others are present, but joy, tenderness, and spirituality are not. The controlling images involve death; and at the end Jack is preparing to return to the East Coast, where "My mother'll be waiting for me glad—The corner of the yard where Tyke [a dead cat which Jack associates with Gerard] is buried will be a new and fragrant shrine making my home more homelike somehow." And where, we may well ask, do we go from here?

Jack Kerouac has thus far been an interesting, controversial, and in many ways effective writer. But the drawing rooms are now surely forever closed, life on the American highways and city streets seems to have lost its charm, and he would appear to be back on Times Square with no one coming toward him. He must either re-evaluate his worlds and his relation to them as man and artist, or he must find fresh experiential and literary means for reaffirming the virtues of Lowell.

JOSEPH HELLER'S *CATCH-22*:
ONLY FOOLS WALK IN DARKNESS

Frederick R. Karl

WHAT WE YEARN for in the post-war generation is fiction that seems "true"—or suggests whatever passes for truth—in its specifics as well as its generalities. While we all agree that the older great writers still move us profoundly, their vision in its particulars cannot appeal to us: Dostoyevsky was a reactionary, religious fanatic; Conrad, an anti-liberal; Lawrence, for blood, not social action; Mann, a disillusioned nationalist; Hesse, a mystic who recommended asceticism. We are still obviously affected by their psychological vision of man and the world, but repelled by what they offer in return, disturbed by the fact that they do not seem one of us. Perhaps because we have so assimilated their vision, we no longer turn to them for advice. They offer only a diagnosis, not a course of action true in its details. We read them with admiration, respect, even involvement. What they say is intensely true. But when we turn away from their printed pages, we face a different world. They are too idealistic for us. They want too much change, and at best they offer only spiritual rewards.

On the other hand, a novel like *Catch-22*, trailing recollections of Joyce, Nathanael West, and early, "funny" Céline, speaks solidly to those who are disaffected, discontented, and disaffiliated, and yet who want to react to life positively. With its occasional affirmations couched in terms of pain and cynical laughter, it makes nihilism seem natural, ordinary, even appealing. The very zaniness of its vision constitutes its attraction even to those who have compromised with most of the absurdities it exposes.

Catch-22 obviously appeals to the student, who beneath his complacency and hipster frigidity is very confused and afraid. It appeals to the sophisticated professional—the educator, lawyer, professor—who must work at something he cannot fully trust. It appeals to the businessman, who does not really believe that his empire primarily serves the public good. It certainly appeals to all the new professionals—the advertisers, publicity men, television writers—whose world is little different from the absurd one Heller presents.

Wartime life on Pianosa—whatever the veracity of its details—is a replica of life within any organization. Whether one is a lawyer, teacher, doctor, judge, union member, white collar worker, or writer attached to a magazine, advertising agency, newspaper, or television station, he finds himself in a similar kind of world. It is not simply a neurotic reaction to his surroundings that gives one this sense of absurdity: the absurdity is an actual fact, the consequence of many conflicting interests interacting and creating a world unfit for the individual.

This point is of course true of all good service fiction, but it is particularly true of *Catch-22*, beginning with its catchy title, its sense that the individual must always relinquish part of himself to the organization which chews him up and then eliminates him. Most people try to prevent becoming waste matter. The novel appeals to all those who want the good life and nevertheless reject its particularities, or even fear defining them. Beneath the surface, all its avid readers are afraid that "life"—whatever it is—is dribbling away from them in ways they can never dam. Calling themselves social animals, and arguing that every individual must be part of society, they hate society and distrust any individual who is a social animal.

For those who find given life nauseating, frustrating, and demeaning—that is, our sane citizens—*Catch-22* provides, at least temporarily, a moral, affirmative way out. So far do people diverge from their public image that their frustrated longings often consume their entire existence. They may wish to do right, but are compromised by the wrongness of their situation. They see themselves as defeated victims, but are forced to carry themselves as victors. They want to love, but find that hate is more sophisticated, and viable. They want to pursue self, but are admonished and shamed into embracing the public good. They desire to aid society, but are warned that only a fool puts self last. They wish for authenticity, good faith, decency, but find that inauthenticity brings immediate and often sensational results. Trying to believe, they more frequently are mocked by the very forces they desire to accept. Wishing to embrace the great world, they find themselves successes in the little.

What American novel of the last decade has spoken better to this type of individual—perhaps to all of us?—than *Catch-22*? Its surface extravagance masks a serious purpose: that in an impossible situation, one finally has to honor his own self; that in an absurd universe, the individual has the right to seek survival; that one's own substance is infinitely more precious than any cause, however right; that one must not be asked to give his life unless *everybody* is willing to give *his*.

It is the latter point—a kind of Kantian categorical imperative applied to survival—that has generally been neglected. When Yossarian decides that his life does count, he is making a moral decision about the sanctity of human existence. Life must not be taken lightly, either by others (military men, business manipulators, world leaders) or by oneself. Yossarian is a hero by virtue of his sacred appraisal of his future. To himself he is as valuable as a general or a president. Since he is so valuable, he has a right, an inviolable right, to save himself once he has done his share of the world's dirty business. The individual must consider himself supreme. What could be more democratic, American, even Christian!

Heller's point is always moral. The fact that many outraged readers saw Yossarian as immoral, cowardly, or anti-American simply indicates what falsely patriotic hearts beat sturdily beneath seemingly sophisticated exteriors. Yossarian is a great American—if we must have this point—an American of whom we should all be proud, even if Heller makes him an Assyrian (at times he seems like a Young Turk hiding behind an Armenian name).

The morality, in fact, both implied and stated, is somewhat pat. Despite the presence of so many seemingly "evil" characters, Heller believes implicitly in the goodness of man. Even the former (Cathcart, Dreedle, Milo, *et al.*), however, are not really evil in any sinister way: rather, they simply react to the given chance, the proffered opportunity. They could be professors, or even ministers. They are men on the make, and such is the quality of modern life *all* men are waiting for their chance. There are millions of Eichmanns, Hannah Arendt tells us. Yossarian is a Jesus among the money-lenders, without the mean sense of righteousness of a potential Messiah.

Yossarian is the man who acts in good faith, to use Sartre's often-repeated phrase. In Yossarian's situation— one in which war has turned all men into madmen— people float uneasily in a foreign world where human existence is feeble, contradictory, and contingent upon an infinity of other forces. Nothing, here, is certain except the individual's recurring assurance of his own response. All he can hope to know is that he is superior to any universal force (man-made or otherwise), and all he can hope to recognize is that the universal or collective force can never comprehend the individual. The only sure thing in a swamp of absurdity is one's own identity. "I think, therefore I am" has never seemed truer, distorted though Descartes' phrase may have become in the twentieth century.

Accordingly, the true hero of our era is the man who can accept absolute responsibility. He must act alone, and his faith—not in God, but in himself—must be good, honest, pure. If, as Nietzsche said, all the gods are dead, then man must become mature enough to assume the role. Yossarian's decision that life must pre-empt all other considerations is precisely this moral act of responsibility. In choosing life, Yossarian shows himself to be reflective, conscious, indeed free. All the others are slugs living in the swampy depths of self-deception; not bad men necessarily, they are simply unaware, and unaware they cannot be free.

When Yossarian strikes for freedom at the end of the novel (the fact that it is Sweden demonstrates Heller's concern with the good society made by good men), his act symbolizes more than defiance, certainly not cowardice. He has done his duty—Heller is careful to keep before us Yossarian's many missions (the word itself indicates a high calling). He has shown his responsibility to society at large, and has given his physical energy and his nervous sweat. Now he must seek a meaningful life, try to make order out of chaos. He must overcome nausea. In this respect, Sweden seems like Paradise: sane people, plenty of good sex, a benevolent government, jolly drunkenness. In Sweden, the individual seems to have a chance, what Yeats felt in part about his mythical Byzantium.

It is no more immoral for Yossarian to seek Sweden than for Yeats to have searched for Byzantium. Both places indeed are more a state of mind than a real place. We can be sure that when Yossarian reaches Sweden, he will be disappointed, even frustrated. Not all the tall, blonde women will capitulate, not all the people will be sane; the government will even expect him to work, and liquor will be expensive. Yet Sweden remains valid as an idea—one certainly has the right to seek it as an alternative to death. It may prove a false Eden, but man in his desperation may still desire Paradise. It is a mark of his humanity that he does.

There is, except for Sweden, really no community that Yossarian can join. An open character in a closed society, he must shun everyone to retain his identity: appear naked among the clothed, refuse to acquiesce to ill-motivated orders, avoid love while seeking sex, reject a mission that is no longer his. In virtually every situation, he is alone—his name, his racial origin, his integrity all indicate his isolation. Like an ancient hero rather than a modern *schlemiel,* he goes through his solitary ordeal, and the ordeal, as Heller presents it, is eminently worthwhile: to defy death in the name of reason and life.

A good deal of the humor of the novel derives from Yossarian's very openness in a society closed to authenticity and good faith. When an open character—responsive, sensitive, decent—throws himself upon a closed society— unresponsive, fixed, inflexible—very often the result can be tragic. What keeps Yossarian comic, however, is the fact that he never tries to change the society he scorns; he is quite willing to accept its absurdity if it will leave him alone. Never a revolutionary, rarely a rebel, unintentionally a hero, only occasionally a young Turk, Yossarian is more often a rank conformist. The only sanity he desires is his own, not the world's; the only joys he seeks are those he can himself generate; the only rewards he covets are the compensations, not of glory, but of full lips, breasts, and thighs. He is more Sancho than Don. The comedy of Yossarian is the comedy of a romantic, Rousseauistic natural man forced to do the dirty work of the world.

Yet this twentieth-century natural man is "with it," not against it. He is able to adapt to the forces that would otherwise destroy. He retains his naturalness (integrity, sexual balance, coolness) in situations that have frustrated and smashed men more rebellious and affirmative than he. What both impresses and dismays us is Yossarian's adaptability; his views do not cause rigidity, and without rigidity there can be only personal comedy. Tragedy is always "out there," involving those who try to fight the system or those who are trapped by a system they never understood (Clevinger, Nately, Snowden). Like Yossarian, Milo is of course comic because he *knows* about the system; he is the very fellow who masterminds systems.

The two extremes Yossarian must avoid include the avarice and egoism of Milo and the innocence and naïveté of Nately ("new-born") and Snowden (pure whiteness). As Heller presents the alternatives, a person must be in the know in all the particulars of life or else he cannot be true to himself. Only a fool walks in darkness. Yossarian is an honest man because Yossarian understands that the way to righteousness is through balance: he must assure his own survival without the help of others. Thus, Heller condemns both Nately and Milo; the latter obviously stands for a base, commercial acquisitiveness, while the former attempts to be Jesus Christ in a situation that calls for an instinctive sense of survival.

Those who have felt the tragic overtones of the novel often find it difficult to place its tragic center. Clearly, *Catch-22* is not simply a comic novel full of puns, highjinks, slapstick, witty dialogue, and satirical asides. It has these in abundance—perhaps, on occasion, in over-abundance—but its purpose and execution are fully serious, what we feel in Saul Bellow's work, to mention a contemporary American whom Heller comes closest to. At the center of the tragedy is Heller's awareness of a passing era, an era that perhaps never existed but one that might have if people and situations had gone differently. Heller's is the nostalgia of the idealist—such a writer's style is usually jazzed-up, satirical, somehow surrealistic—the idealist who can never accept that moral values have become insignificant or meaningless in human conduct. This heritage, what we find in Nathanael West, early Céline, and a whole host of similar writers, derives from the tragic undertones of Ecclesiastes with its monody against vanity, egoism, hypocrisy, folly—those qualities which have, unfortunately, become the shibboleths of the twentieth century.

Heller's recoil from these false qualities takes the form of his attack upon religion, the military, political forces, commercial values—as C. Wright Mills indicates, the whole power formation of a country successful in war and peace. What is left is the only true thing remaining for all men—sex: healthy, robust, joyful sex. Not love—Heller carefully draws the distinction—for love means entanglements and involvements that will eventually lead to phoniness. It is not so curious that love itself falls victim to a society in which true feeling had better stop at orgasm. Heller's non-treatment of love is of course indicative of his attitude, not of an inability: love is martyred amidst people whose every feeling is promiscuous. To expect more from them, even from Yossarian, is to accept their folly as truth.

The nightmarish scenes of *Catch-22* which convey its tragic sense culminate in the cosmic nightmare of Chapter XXXIX, "The Eternal City." Once glorious, Rome is now a "dilapidated shell," as though modern Goths and Vandals had destroyed everything in their path; or as if a modern God had visited his wrath upon it. The monuments are shattered, the streets contain surrealistic nightmares, the people seem the husks and shards of humanity. All values are overturned, all hopes and dreams made valueless; sanity itself becomes a meaningless term. Everything visible—an emblem of what lies beneath—is off balance, out of key. The center of western religion is godless. Here we have Heller's immoral world, a scene from Hieronymus Bosch's Hell, in which Aarfy can freely rape and kill while Yossarian is picked up for lacking a pass. Caught in such a dark world, Yossarian can only run toward the light. If he stays, he will—like Milo and the others—eat and sleep well at the expense even of those who share his ideals.

An early version of *Catch-22* was itself much more nightmarish in its development than the published book. Evidently strongly influenced by *Ulysses*, Heller had originally tried to make the narrative typically Joycean: that is, full of intermittent streams of consciousness and involutions of time. Further, he suggested the narrative through recurring symbols of devastation and doom, eliminating in several places orthodox plot structure. As a consequence, the reader who missed the significance of the symbols—and they were by no means clear, even peripherally—was lost in a surrealistic forest of words from which there was no escape. Added to the stream, the symbols, and the involutions of time was an impressionistic treatment of characters and events, a half-toned, half-tinted development that seemed neither to go forward nor to remain still.

For the final version, Heller retained in its entirety only
the first chapter of the original and then in part straight-
ened out both the narrative line and the character development. Words themselves became a kind of language
midway between evocation and denotation; at its worst,
the language overextends itself, but at its best it suits
Heller's zany, absurd world. So often misunderstood, his
language would not of course fit a rational theme—it is
itself an attempt to convey a world beyond the logic of the
word.

For Heller, the war is a perfect objective correlative, as it
was for Hemingway in *A Farewell to Arms*. Both, however,
are war novels only in limited ways. The war gave Heller,
even more than it did Hemingway, the community against
which Yossarian can operate. The military becomes an
entire society, looming so large that it casts its shadow on
the horizon and blocks out everything beyond. Such is the
nature of the curse, and it is this—the indefinable character
of what one is a part of—that Heller can exploit. The war
or the military (not the enemy) provides the conflict,
makes anything possible. The norm is no longer any
determinable quality: each action gives birth to a norm of
its own. Unlike the fixed roles that people assume in
civilian life, in war they hide behind masks (uniforms)
and redefine themselves, like the protean creatures in
Ovid's *Metamorphoses*. Here, Yossarian—the ancient Assyrian, the modern Armenian, but really a wandering New
York Jew—can give vent to his disgust and revulsion, and
through laughter show us that our better selves may still
turn up in Sweden.

NO FACE AND NO EXIT:
THE FICTION OF JAMES PURDY
AND J. P. DONLEAVY

Gerald Weales

IN "Mrs. Benson," one of the stories in James Purdy's
Children Is All, the titular heroine and her daughter sit in
an English tearoom in Paris talking casually "about people
they had both known in Philadelphia twenty-odd years
ago," an activity as impersonal as the yearly meeting that
has brought them together. The name of Mrs. Carlin
comes into the conversation, and Mrs. Benson, who "had
always been loath to 'tell,' to reminisce," recalls something
that once happened (or almost happened) between her
and the older woman. "But, Mrs. Carlin had already begun
to entertain her guests in one part of the house . . . and
to *live* herself in another! She had begun dividing up her
life in that way!" Mrs. Carlin, who must have thought she
saw something familiar in Mrs. Benson (having just been
deserted by her husband, Mrs. Benson assumed that "*she*
had never been too happy in her marriage, either"), asked
the younger woman to "the 'real' part of the house" and
later invited her to live there if she wanted to. Since in
Purdy's world, it is impossible for a person ever to get
beyond that part of the house where one receives guests,
Mrs. Benson had to refuse. Still, she did have a glimpse
into the living room, and it stays with her: "I don't know
why I treasure what Mrs. Carlin said to me . . . But it is
one of the few things that any other human being ever said
to me that I do hold on to." The story told, she lapses
again into the impersonality that keeps her and her daugh-

ter in one another's guest room, and the two women go out into Paris together and alone. Midway through her story, almost breaking it off, Mrs. Benson cries out, "Oh, it's all so *nothing!*" It is not only *something;* it is a *something* that pervades all of James Purdy's work.

The assumption is that all of us, in so far as Purdy really has the word on all of us, live in a house divided. For the most part the interior room, the "real" one, the one where we *live,* is sealed off from the ones in which we meet other people, talk to them, desire them, marry them, kill them, construct them in our own image. Once in a while we open the door ever so slightly and let someone look in, but what he sees there is a reflection. *"Mon semblable, mon frère,"* he cries and we say "Who, me?" and slam the door in his face. The need to open the door ("This here is an emergency phone call, Operator," shouts the desperate man in "Daddy Wolf") and the impossibility of being recognized is the subject of most of Purdy's work—the early short stories in *Color of Darkness* and the later ones in *Children Is All,* the novella *63: Dream Palace,* the play *Children Is All* and the two novels *Malcolm* and *The Nephew.*

Since the man in the interior room is so hard to get to, since he can be seen infrequently and then only obliquely, the suspicion begins to grow that he is not there at all. He becomes a kind of silly putty that assumes the shape of whatever it lies against. He becomes whatever another person, in a scramble to escape his own facelessness, wants him to be. Girard Girard in *Malcolm,* about to marry Laureen, explains that he is "entirely, entirely alone" and that he wants Malcolm "For my own—for Laureen's and my own." Since there is no chance of Laureen and Girard having the same "own," Girard is demanding that Malcolm be two things at once. Or rather, that he be the raw material out of which each of them can construct his own consolation. Most of us are failures as raw material since our acts—we are busy on our own consolation construction projects—make us break out of the neat and defining lines others have drawn around us. "I cannot go on being Mrs.

Klein," the woman insists in "Don't Call Me by My Right Name," although she is willing to go on being married to Mr. Klein; she cannot understand that, so far as he is concerned, that makes her Mrs. Klein. In many of the short stories and in *Children Is All* (in which Edna Cartwright's convict son comes home to be recognized and in which she can give him recognition only in act not in word), Purdy treats the struggle between conflicting needs. In the longer fiction, he provides leading characters who are little more than what others make of them. Malcolm describes himself, "I am, well, as they say, a cypher and a blank." Fenton Riddleway in *63: Dream Palace* may not be quite the *tabula rasa* that Malcolm is—he has a brother Claire to remind him of his West Virginia origins—but the other characters in the story use him as though he were Malcolm.

It is Cliff Mason in *The Nephew* who is the perfect Purdy hero. He never exists at all. We are introduced to him in the first chapter through a quarrel over the content of his letters between his Uncle Boyd and his Aunt Alma (brother and sister who live together and with whom Cliff lived before he went into the army); they cannot even agree on his handwriting:

> "He writes a good clear hand," Alma said, reading.
> "Just a bit childish," Boyd said, low . . .

In the second chapter a telegram (with "several misspellings") informs them that Cliff is missing in action. When, near the end of the novel, his death is confirmed, Alma explains: "There wasn't even enough left of him to ship home in his casket. There was nothing of our Cliff left." In this he is like Malcolm, who is buried in an elaborate ceremony, flawed only by the insistent rumor—spread by the coroner and the undertaker—that there is no corpse at all. Although the problem of whether Cliff is alive or dead nags at Alma through much of the book, his existence (or lack of it) is not altered by substituting the specific *dead* for the ambiguous *missing*. In describing Mrs. Barrington, "the old monarch," who through age (she is almost 90) and position has become a combination goddess, arbiter, sage and meddler to the neighborhood, Purdy says of her long-dead husband: "His actual death came like a mere corroboration to the public of the old suspicion that he had never existed at all."

The Nephew is the story of Alma's attempt to write a memorial of Cliff. "I'm writing down everything I can remember about him, you see," she tells a friend, who opens the record book and is confronted with blank pages. Insisting that she does have memories but that she cannot get Cliff clearly in mind, Alma sets out to discover him through people and through things. There are not many things and they are not much help. There is the formal photograph of Cliff, which "seemed almost retouched," which "made him look almost pretty in that pose," and there are the photographs that Vernon Miller took of him, which burn up before Alma and Boyd can do more than glance at them. There are Cliff's old clothes which Alma, "holding them as carefully as if she wished not to lose all the folds and creases Cliff had left behind in them," locks away in a chest; one is reminded of the "shrine" that Grainger makes of Russell's room in 63: *Dream Palace*. There are the papers and the *curriculum vitae* that Professor Mannheim has saved from Cliff's college days. There are his letters, but, as Alma says, "Cliff *doesn't* say too much in a letter." His uncommunicative letters are reminiscent of the record that the dying Malcolm makes of his "conversations," which is read only by Madame Girard, who no longer has occasion to mention Malcolm or his manuscript; and of the writings of Fenton Riddleway, who puts things down on paper so that he can understand them. Whether from lack of audience or lack of content, what these three young men write fails to declare them.

The people whom Alma consults are even less helpful than the things Cliff leaves behind him. She starts out imagining that she knew Cliff and discovers that everyone has a different Cliff. Boyd thinks he knew Cliff because of the night he found the young man, drunk, with four thousand dollars stuffed in his pockets and unable to explain where the money came from. It came from Vernon Miller, who thinks he knew Cliff, too. "Cliff was the loneliest boy I think I ever knew, outside of maybe me," says Vernon, and later, "Cliff maybe was unhappiness." Unable to break out of his own trap, as friend and servant and perhaps lover to Willard Baker, even after Mrs. Barrington has given him money to run away, Vernon passes the money on to Cliff, his way of making a vicarious escape. "He didn't know him from Adam," according to Willard. Professor Mannheim, it turns out, had confided in Cliff, told him about an affair he was having with a student (now his second wife) and had listened to Cliff's own troubles, which, of course, he dismissed; Mannheim thinks of him in terms of "how much he was expecting," but a foreigner and a radical, never accepted by the town he has lived in for years, Mannheim may have made of Cliff a reverse image of his own disappointment. "I don't think Cliff and he saw one another *at all*," says Boyd.

Alma never gets more than a few "sentence fragments" into her record book. In fact, she is in danger of losing rather than gaining from her research. Her Cliff, the young man who loved his old aunt and uncle and liked being with them, disappears, until Mrs. Barrington restores him. She does so, first, by giving Alma the memorial she wrote of her dead husband (also blank pages). She offers Alma the conventional comfort in the idea that it is her love for Cliff, not Cliff's for her that is important, but she goes beyond that to assure Alma that Cliff did really love her and Boyd. "You needn't believe me, of course. But I think you do, or will." The fine ambiguity of that last line (for in the end Alma and Boyd do accept that Cliff loved them) accounts for the presence of Clara Himbaugh in the novel. A Christian Scientist who wanders in and out of the action, making a conversion here, a suggestion there (the memorial is her idea), Clara represents fairly directly the need of everyone in the novel to find something which will confirm his own existence. "I guess Vernon is my Christian

Science maybe," says Willard. I guess Cliff is Alma's Christian Science maybe ("Cliff meant not just everything now but perhaps all there had ever been"), and to serve that purpose he needs only the existence that Alma gives him.

The Nephew, then, becomes the aunt's book. Alma learns a little about the way we invent the people around us (Mrs. Barrington's superiority, for instance, comes as much from Alma as from Mrs. Barrington), but fortunately not enough to keep her from finding her Cliff again. Boyd says, "We none of us, I'm afraid, know anybody or know one another." His words could be an epigraph not only for *The Nephew*, but for all of Purdy's work. In *Malcolm*, the hero sits on a golden bench in front of a luxury hotel (trailing clouds of glory, do we come), waiting for his father who has died and/or disappeared. Toward the end of the novel, Malcolm says, "Maybe my father never existed." Enticed into the world by Professor Cox (cocks launch us all into the world), Malcolm passes from character to character, each of whom lives in his own fantasy world and wants to acquire Malcolm the malleable as comfort and confirmation. "What did I buy you for, kiddy?" asks Melba, shortly before Malcolm dies. In *63: Dream Palace*, Fenton Riddleway wanders through a city in which lost souls seem to be trying to make contact with and trying to avoid one another. Grainger's mansion is specifically compared to the ALL NIGHT THEATER Fenton visits and implicitly to the park where Parkhearst picks him up. Parkhearst, Grainger, Bruno—all want to acquire him. "Why are we dead anyhow?" asks Parkhearst. "Is it because of our losing the people we loved or because the people we found were damned?" The short stories deal mostly with a moment in which someone recognizes a friend, a lover, a child as a stranger ("Color of Darkness," "Why Can't They Tell You Why?") or with a moment in which such close strangers indulge each other's masquerade ("Encore," "Goodnight Sweetheart").

For all of its persistence of theme, Purdy's work is not so much of a piece as this discussion suggests. He ranges from the dusty macabre of *63: Dream Palace* to the grotesque and sometimes funny comedy of *Malcolm* to the deceptive matter-of-factness of *The Nephew*. There is great range, too, in quality. His stories often appear to be slices, slabs cut out of something not quite perceivable. Ordinarily, he arrests his characters at a moment when drunkenness, uncontrollable garrulity, fear, some strong emotion brings a revelation which is, usually, oblique, suggestive, amorphous. The longer fiction—except for *The Nephew*—seems like a string of such moments. "Texture is all," Madame Girard says in *Malcolm*, "substance nothing." Her sentence might be a description of most of Purdy's work. At his weakest, his texture is only mannerism and his revelations become banal or vaguely "poetic" in the ugly sense of the word. When he is more effective, his arrested moments become vivid enough to suggest substance or to hide its absence. When he is better still—when Malcolm, running from the dead Gus, drops and breaks the testimonial shaving mug that Madame Rosita has awarded him for his sexual performance—the moment becomes a vehicle that carries us directly into some kind of truth. At his best, texture and substance become one. So far, that has happened only in *The Nephew*.

ii

Where James Purdy's hero has no face at all, except the one reflected in the eyes of others, the hero of J. P. Donleavy's novels has a multitude of faces, disguises that he slips into to protect himself from an unfriendly world. "Do you want me to be recognized? Do you?" wails Sebastian Dangerfield in *The Ginger Man*, in a scene in which he cannot find his sun glasses and in which, typically, he blames his wife for the loss. The hero of *A Singular Man*, who is called George Smith (that name is a disguise in itself), is another Sebastian, but one rich enough to enlarge his sun glasses, to have one-way glass in his limousine.

There is much about Sebastian Dangerfield that is familiar, conventional. He looks a great deal like both

Kingsley Amis's Jim Dixon and John Osborne's Jimmy Porter. Like Lucky Jim, he has developed a repertoire of defensive gestures—faces he makes, sounds he uses to keep from speaking words. "Eeeee and eeeee and eak." His favorite—*beep*—is also used extensively by George Smith. Sebastian's gestures tend to become small plays, fantasy productions in which he enacts the lead, always a commanding role whether he is the captain seeing that the lifeboats are properly lowered or the aristocrat keeping the common people in their place. If it were not for the last brief chapter, Sebastian's walk in the gray London morning and his recollection of the dream horses running out to death, *The Ginger Man* might be said to end like *Lucky Jim* or John Wain's *Hurry On Down*. Sebastian has—through no effort of his own—received money and a reconciliation with one of his loving ladies. But being Sebastian ("I do not trust this acute joy. Misery is my forte"), he can find no real comfort in his luck.

It is here that he suggests Jimmy Porter. Like Jimmy, he is awash with self-pity, convinced that everyone—even those closest to him—are part of a plot to destroy him. "I came down the stairs with my usual innocence and pain right smack into her silence which is the sign that she has a weapon." His one defense is the power of abuse. Like Jimmy, he strikes out blindly—an angry child—wanting really to hurt those around him. Thus he can drive his wife and child away, presume on Chris until she throws him out, victimize Miss Frost and Mary, feeling all the while that they have joined the "others" in an attempt to make a sacrifice of him—one with stature of course: "I set sail / On this crucifixion Friday." The similarity between Sebastian and Jimmy Porter is most obvious in the play version of *The Ginger Man*, a kind of skeleton of the novel with a little of the old dialogue still on the bones. In the novel, Sebastian is saved from being Jimmy by a greater degree of self-consciousness (he is, after all, the narrator). The self-pity is presumably real enough, but Sebastian is also aware of it as a useful device—to seduce Miss Frost or to get money out of O'Keefe. The pain is apparently genuine, but it is mocked a little. "I would say you had the odd bit of angst around the eyes," MacDoon tells Sebastian. In one other disconcerting way, *The Ginger Man* suggests *Look Back in Anger*—in the author's ambiguous attitude toward his hero. I suspect Donleavy of taking Sebastian at his own evaluation, of assuming a kind of virtue, a sensitivity in him and his company of outsiders (Percy Clocklan, MacDoon, Tony Malarkey, O'Keefe) which I cannot find in them. This may be unfair to Donleavy for surely George Smith in *A Singular Man* invents his own persecution or shares it with the other characters (and with us). In any case, Sebastian, as saint, is possible only if we accept that he makes his own arrows.

The introduction of Amis and Osborne into a discussion of Donleavy is misleading as well as helpful. It does indicate the likenesses among them, the way in which Donleavy is part of a literary pattern—an English rather than an American one. But he is a variation within that pattern. *The Ginger Man* is its own book and a more ambitious one than Amis's novel or Osborne's play. For one thing, all the references needed for Sebastian are provided within the novel. There are two important images—two girls whom Sebastian recalls—which can stand as definitions of Sebastian and the novel. One is the girl who picked him up in Baltimore when he was a sailor. Her attitude toward society ("it's contrary to everything I believe, I mean the frivolous, sophisticated life of society people"), her attempt to accept and reject at the same time suggests Sebastian, who wants all the comforts of a materialistic success and none of the trouble of trying to acquire them. He sees the degree that he cannot bring himself to earn as the philosopher's stone providing riches, position, power; and O'Keefe with his imaginary Daimler, his invented car and fancy clothes, his confusion of money with sex, echoes Sebastian's fantasy of wealth. The other girl is the one who comes bursting out of the restaurant kitchen, throwing plates and "yelling that she would commit murder, that she couldn't stand it any more in this hot hole." Marion tells Sebastian, "You were yelling a few nights ago, how do I get out of this." The girl's broken plates, like everything animate and inanimate that Sebastian breaks, provide no real weapon. "But she calmed down and they gave her five minutes off to be getting this rebellion out of her head." If a third image is needed, one that takes Sebastian beyond his trap and his attraction to it, there is the huge man who lies down in the center of the street in Dublin, stopping all traffic; Sebastian, seeing this, dances for joy. In A Singular Man, Shirl, George's wife, tells him that he will never stop traffic, not even by dying.

The suggestion throughout The Ginger Man is that what Sebastian really wants is death; "I need help and a polite period of rest, of sleep, of peace." The word peace echoes through the novel like a cry for help. "Once at college, I thought I'm dying," George Smith reminds himself in A Singular Man. "And tried to run. From the terrible loneliness." These words might stand as a description of The Ginger Man. Any temporary peace that Sebastian finds (with a woman usually) is deceptive. He continues to run, like those horses he recalls at the end of the book: "And I said they are running out to death which is with some soul and their eyes are mad and teeth out."

George Smith, a singular man who sometimes wishes he were plural, is an extension of Sebastian Dangerfield. He has the money that Sebastian lacks, but he is even more harried. The world is a plot against him; he is continually nagged by letters, phone calls, spies, casual vituperation, all of which, one assumes, is a reflection of his own suspicion. He has to tell himself, "don't let them get in close, keep them at arm's length, stop smiling kindly." The small satisfactions of life fail him; his coffee-making alarm clock spills coffee on his pillow and a coffee maker in a doughnut shop, where he stops for consolation, threatens to explode. An applause machine that he builds to play "When I'm lonely, sometimes, and feel powerless," breaks down "And thirty five thousand voices went hee hee." He reaches for and backs away from friendship and love. Sex seems to be a consolation, but, going into Her Majesty's apartment, he sees an imaginary sign above the door, "Dear Sir, we invite you to dance with joy, before we make you hobble with affliction." Even the mausoleum he is building for himself, his final shelter, is suspect; when the space salesman shows him around the cemetery, the sample mausoleum explodes.

Compared to *The Ginger Man*, *A Singular Man* is an extremely neat presentation of the hero consenting to the trap of his society. For all of its incidental invention, however, it is a repetitive and finally rather dull book. *The Ginger Man* shows some of the same tendencies, but, in it, the style has not yet become mannered. The rhetoric, hovering between bathos and mockery, is suitable to Sebastian. The stylistic device—and a very clever one—which allows sudden shifts from first to third person within a paragraph suggests that Sebastian speaks as himself and then steps back to see himself, that he is always both sufferer and observer. The interplay between Sebastian's reality and his fantasies give a richness to the novel which is diluted only by the recognition that, in fact or in fancy, he is a somewhat tiresome man to spend much time with. *A Singular Man* tries to go a step beyond *The Ginger Man*. George Smith's only reality is mythic. Like the hero of the Donleavy play *Fairy Tales in New York*, he is a fantasy figure in a fantasy setting, suggesting some satirical truths about our society. Yet, like Sebastian, he wears disguises, invents situations, plays many parts; unlike Sebastian, he never touches ground. The implications are fascinating—the relationship between the fantasies society imposes and the ones we invent to escape from it—but the book is not. Its style defeats it. It is not simply that some devices (the shift in person, the verse-like tags) seem merely hangovers from the earlier book. The second novel's chief stylistic innovation is self-defeating. Except for the dialogue, the book is written almost entirely in sentence fragments, as though it had been dictated by Mr. Jingle. Although Donleavy may intend these fragments to tell us something about George Smith or about his society,

the fragmentation becomes a surface annoyance and serves
finally to reinforce the impression that we are being given
the same thing over and over.

> *There was a man*
> *Who made a boat*
> *To sail away*
> *And it sank.*

INTRODUCING JAMES BALDWIN

Kay Boyle

ON A NUMBER of other occasions, in introducing my friend and fellow-writer, James Baldwin, I have begun by saying that it is not an easy thing to do. Tonight I find it particularly difficult. So much fury has been expressed, so much horror taken place in our country in the past weeks that it seems to me there is no time left for the making of introductions. In fact, James Baldwin long ago made his own introduction when he said that at the root of the American Negro problem is the necessity of the American white man to find a way of living with the Negro in order to be able to live with himself. As Baldwin spoke words such as these in San Francisco recently, fellow-citizens of his and ours in another part of the United States were being downed by firehoses and set on by police-dogs, because they had marched quietly and passively in Southern streets. This, and other outrages to other human beings, is what Baldwin refers to when he says the time has come to recognize that the framework in which we operate weighs too heavily on us to be borne, and indeed may be about to kill us.

Edmund Wilson has pointed out that in writing and speaking about what it means to be a Negro, Baldwin is merely writing and speaking about what it means to be a man. Baldwin himself has stated that the artist's struggle for integrity must be considered as a kind of metaphor for the struggle which is universal and daily in the lives of all human beings on the face of the globe to become and remain human beings. The largeness of purpose and gentleness of intention which Baldwin voices have brought a new climate, a new element, a new season, to our country in our time. That season, that climate, that element which are James Baldwin, they are now in the foreground of America's awareness. There is no way now that anyone can fail to recognize them, and to endure them, and to contend with them. They cannot be dismissed. It may even be that crops will have to be planted differently out of a consideration of this new season, or that quite new crops will have to be found which will flourish in the new climate, and that all the old fences and defences will be levelled by the fury of that new element. In his essays, his novels, his short stories, Baldwin has levelled the ground so that we may start anew.

Baldwin's first novel is *Go Tell It on the Mountain*, a powerful and lyrical work which prepared the way for the essays that followed, among them the great essay published in the *New Yorker* magazine, entitled "Letter from a Region in My Mind." Of Baldwin's first novel, a critic recently wrote that it seemed to have come into existence "within a vast area of freedom." This is, I think, peculiarly true of all Baldwin's work. That "vast area of freedom" is like a door flung wide on every page.

Baldwin's second novel is *Giovanni's Room*, his third published in 1961, *Another Country*. Between *Giovanni's Room* and *Another Country*, two collections of essays were published: *Notes of a Native Son* in 1955, and *Nobody Knows My Name* in 1961. "The Letter from a Region in My Mind" is, I believe, one of the great statements of our century. This "Letter," and Baldwin's "Letter to My Nephew," have appeared in book form under the title *The Fire Next Time*.

It was pointed out in the pages of the *New Republic* that the "Letter from a Region in My Mind" made its appearance flanked by some of the most extravagant and shocking advertising in America. Baldwin's words—such words, for instance, as those concerning the American Negro's past: a past of "rope, fire, torture, castration, infanticide, rape; death and humiliation; fear by day and night, fear as deep as the marrow of the bone; doubt that he was worthy of life, since everyone around him denied it; sorrow for his women; for his kinfolk, for his children, who needed his protection, and whom he could not protect" — words such as these were printed in the *New Yorker* side by side with ads of an Empress Chinchilla coat at thirteen hundred dollars, plus tax, and of a diamond clip and bracelet for eighteen thousand five hundred dollars, tax included. In these terrifying contrasts we are again made aware that Baldwin's prose, his voice, have evoked a spiritual climate which is now present in real and vigorous opposition to the material climate of our country. His work, his voice, define and articulate the hopes of those who cannot write, who cannot speak. A great part of his achievement is that he is the eloquence of the silent throughout our land. For the man of genius in all ages is he who, like an Aeolian harp, catches the sound of the longings and hopes of men who cannot give them shape or sound.

"Although we do not wholly believe it yet," James Baldwin once said, "the interior life is a real life, and the intangible dreams of people have a tangible effect upon the world." Baldwin's intangible dreams are real enough now to shatter our sleep for us. But the breadth of his vision and the tenacity of his belief in man offer us, if we can but accept it, a far better national reality than any we have ever known. It is this vision and this belief that illuminate his work.

Ladies and gentlemen, Mr. James Baldwin.

JAMES BALDWIN'S OTHER COUNTRY

Robert F. Sayre

JAMES BALDWIN has been exceptional among modern American writers by being both a novelist and also a very compelling popular essayist. To this we might add his almost equally artful performances—*opera* also—as a lecturer, panelist, and magazine and television interviewee. The third activity is much more than an adjustment to the modern fact that there is often more money to be made from a personal appearance than from a well-paid short story. Mr. Baldwin has become a kind of prophet, a man who has been able to give a public issue all its deeper moral, historical, and personal significance. For this reason, he appears as the one contemporary writer who is most beset with a vision, his vision being the great urgency and revolutionary implications of the race issue. It is a vision, despite the seeming narrowness of the starting point, because Baldwin has shown how the issue itself is connected with nearly every area of American life and belief. Ideas change. An experience can be told and forgotten. But a vision, such as Baldwin's, mercilessly grows and deepens, and it has affected, in some way, almost everything he has written. Certainly one mark of his achievement, whether as novelist, essayist, or propagandist, is that whatever deeper comprehension of the race issue Americans now possess has been in some way shaped by him. And this is to have shaped their comprehension of themselves as well.

i

Mr. Baldwin's reputation as prophet is based primarily on his three volumes of essays—*Notes of a Native Son* (1955), *Nobody Knows My Name* (1961), and *The Fire Next Time* (1963). They are remarkable books, and many critics have suggested that he is greater as an essayist than a novelist. The first question to ask, however, is the relationship between the essays and the novels, and I think we may be able to get at it by noting some of the qualities of the essays. They are by no means uniformly good.

The two most striking features of these works have been the re-introduction of personal experience into what has become a mainly impersonal form and, secondly, the presentation of a great deal of hatred and despair in a very elegant, graceful style. This is abundantly demonstrated in his "Letter from a Region in My Mind," which, to everybody's surprise, was first published in *the* magazine with the strictest reputation for impersonal, polished urbanity. Baldwin remained *New-Yorker* in manner, but he brought in subjects before taboo in those pages, while portraying himself with a sincerity unseen in its dandified regular contributors. Invisibly connected to this tough sincerity and delicate elegance is a quality of exact distance from his subject, whether himself, books, his society, or whatever. One of the reasons Baldwin can handle violence so smoothly is that he seems to know the emotions and hidden prejudices of his audience so well. In the *New Yorker* "Letter" and in other fine pieces such as "Notes of a Native Son" he now evokes, now balances, and now hushes the response of his audience so that it provides the energy while he fingers the keys. This is the real source of Baldwin's power—his finesse and his control of his audience—and, as he has been the first to admit, the need for power, in many realms, has been a matter of life and death. But we should stop to see that none of these qualities have been conspicuous in modern essays; they are the abilities of novelists (and of *story tellers*, generally) and of very fine orators.

The major defect in Baldwin's essays, on the other hand, is a dishonest intimacy and an elaborate, pointless self-consciousness. These are, of course, classic pitfalls of autobiography, and Baldwin is an extensive autobiographer. They are also among the most common deformities of this age, as can perhaps be illustrated by the elderly Robert Frost's public image as what someone once called "the only living Robert Frost in captivity." Such a "personality," based on the popular idea that his poems were the work of some Yankee wood-chopper, exploited the mass need for a quick and easy sensation of intimacy. Frost's pose seldom entered his work, but Baldwin on occasion performs in print as "the only living American Negro in captivity." In his best essays he very carefully frames his own moral experience inside and around other, more external materials in the most exciting combinations. In his worst he self-consciously parades inside the familiar cage which our culture has gratuitously provided him. The temptations simply to play the roles of being Negro are many; this is in one obscure way a revenge, and it is also a protection. But the roles alone, since they are insured— though only temporarily—by public innocence and gullibility and by the indulgence paid any celebrity, never by themselves make real moral challenges. The challenge depends on there also being public, impersonal material. In "The Black Boy Looks at the White Boy," a disingenuous chronicle of private spats with Norman Mailer, he comes out doing press-agentry for himself as "Negro author," clever stuff better buried in the magazine he wrote it for. It is neither very intimate nor very important —just gossip—and Baldwin's real consciousness is so much deeper. The only way down, though, is by indirection. To find the real subjective material, and its fuller significance, good autobiographers have always had to keep returning to exterior events, and Baldwin is no exception. In time he may be able to do this entirely in his autobiographical essays, also serving the enormous need in our society for ways of re-investing public issues with human meaning. But there has been little convention for this in contemporary essays, and his problems have been indicative.

ii

Practically every periodical that has published one of Baldwin's essays has identified him, in one way or another, as "a novelist." His first six books have come out in the order of one novel and then a collection of essays. This suggests, I think, the superior rank which is tacitly given novels and novelists. But I cite this status not because I automatically acknowledge it in Baldwin's work, but because it indicates one nearly certain reality in his biography: in his need for status as well as identity, it was very convenient to be known as a novelist. In some quarters, also, it was probably better to be a "novelist" than a "Negro," and in others a "Negro novelist" than a "white novelist." Such are the irrationalities.

A more essential consequence of writing fiction, however, is that it gave Baldwin a liberal education, a hard one and an unorthodox one, but perhaps a better one than he could have had anywhere else. Graduating from New York's De Witt Clinton High School in 1942, he says he spent ten years on *Go Tell It on the Mountain* (1953), the time many of his contemporaries have spent in colleges and graduate schools. In the same period he also worked on other books, worked as a socialist, reviewed books on the race problem, held many temporary jobs, and expatriated himself in Europe; but the discipline of novelist might be called his dominant instruction. It seems to have turned out a humanistic and liberating program. If it is true that the novel, as an art, remains the only form capable of embracing all the contradictions and variety of the modern adventure, it also seems true, in Baldwin's case, that the writing of novels has been the only way of looking at modern life with sufficient freedom, accuracy, distance, and care. This also meant equally fresh ways of looking at himself. It should be said, of course, that these are not necessarily valid standards for ultimate judgment of Baldwin's fiction, but they are an important viewpoint —important because when his fiction is good it does give the sense of liberation. This, in the end, is what art should do (so long as we are talking about the liberation which comes from seeing things clearly), and the rest of Baldwin's many struggles have depended on his giving himself and us this liberating vision.

From a narrowly literary point of view, *Go Tell It on the Mountain* is surely Baldwin's best book. It is economical, as *Another Country* is not; and the use of background and of dialogue is consistently good, whereas in *Giovanni's Room* the background is sometimes just theatrical and in *Another Country* there are pages of people endlessly mixing drinks and babbling bland inanities. Its subject is the religious conversion of a Negro boy on the morning after his fourteenth birthday. The boy, though tender and sensitive, is otherwise rather ordinary, and to give the experience greater weight Baldwin has done an excellent job of placing it against the setting of his family's fundamentalist church, their Harlem tenement, and the dark, complicated memories of John Grimes's parents and aunt. The novel is obviously heavy with autobiography, perhaps a truer autobiography than the author's "nonfiction." The father, to give one example, proves in time to be John's step-father, which was the actual relationship of James to David Baldwin, despite the portrait in "Notes of a Native Son." This is a far more thorough exploration of family tensions than in the author's essays. *Go Tell It on the Mountain* approaches John's conversion not only from a social and religious standpoint but in terms also of his needs for personal power. His real plight is that he is oppressed by his environment, afraid of the changes taking place in his body, and terrified of his overbearing step-father, who has control of the weapons of religion and salvation. The alternatives in Harlem, as his mother says (and as Baldwin has repeated in "Letter from a Region in My Mind"), are the church or the jail, just as various types of conformity or rebellion have seemed the only alternatives in a great deal of modern America. John sees his younger brother cut up from a knife fight and knows that overt rebellion is not for him. On the other hand, since the father is a deacon in their "Temple of the Fire Baptized," conversion appears a humiliating submission. What reviewers first thought was an irresolution in the book, however, may be its key: John's action is as tactically political as religious, a semiconscious discovery of how to outmaneuver the father within the father's faith. As John prostrates himself in confession, the father is immobile, caught "staring, struck rigid as a pillar in the temple."

The most common structural device in *Go Tell It on the Mountain* is the flashback, a natural recourse for Baldwin. In all his work the source of self-knowledge is always a new compound of the present and the past. To understand one is to understand the other and thus to become aware of one's illusions. This, in turn, is a fundamental basis of power, and leads also to becoming aware of the illusions held by one's culture. The interpolated recollections of John's elders, although they contain some of Baldwin's subtlest insights into the interconnections of religion, race, and power, do not bring these elders freedom. They seem locked in the patterns of their self-deceptions, and an unsure but promising change from the dilemmas of Negro fundamentalism and Negro inferiority comes only to John. He has had new necessities compelling a change, and he also realizes, obliquely, that in facing himself at the crisis of conversion, "I was down in the valley," really alone for the first time; "I was by myself down there." The important ingredients in Baldwin's later, more secular "conversions" are some relatively external conditions which force examination of the past, the two together bringing on a loneliness and self-reliance. In this sense the experience of John Grimes is but a prelude to *Giovanni's Room* and *Another Country*. The more mature characters of these books tangle with much more elaborate knots of guilt and history. An experience of homosexuality, for instance, is intimated to lie ahead of John; the protagonist of the next book is forced to look back on a very complicated affair he has concluded.

Giovanni's Room (1956) has many faults. Beginning with the very first lines ("I stand at the window of this great house in the south of France as night falls, the night which is leading me to the most terrible morning of my life"), the story labors with melodrama and self-pity. It is both unnecessary and unrealistic to jam all the narrator's self-examination into one short night, particularly such a fateful one. But the work is, as Norman Mailer has said, a "brave" book. Baldwin was willing to say things about homosexuality which can have pleased neither the custom's apologists nor its attackers. In doing so he may have risked some imprudent disclosures or inferences about himself. And he attempted to write using only white characters, perhaps partially for disguise, partially for experiment, and partially for thematic clarification. The underlying emotions are much clearer in terms of a sort of average blond-haired Anglo-Saxon. This boy, a middle-class American student in Paris named David, has had an affair with an Italian bartender named Giovanni. Ever since a night in bed with a childhood friend, David has protected an illusion of Protestant purity, and when he deserted Giovanni to return to his American fiancée, he repaired this false kind of innocence. Giovanni, however, was left friendless and jobless and was forced to return to his disgusting French patron. Rather than debase himself to the old monster, Giovanni killed him.

Baldwin frames this story in David's reminiscences on the eve of Giovanni's execution for murder. Where once he would not face his past and his inherited morality, he is now burdened with responsibility for Giovanni's death and must re-examine everything. "There are so many ways of being despicable it quite makes one's head spin," a grim old Belgian has told him. "But the way to be really despicable is to be contemptuous of other people's pain." What saves the book is the seriousness of Baldwin's moral insights. David does not appear to have been wrong in rejecting homosexuality (it is to his greater shame, in fact, that he has not given it up completely), but he was bitterly wrong in his manner of quitting Giovanni. Perfect and ideal homosexuality is the ageless and airless, kind of green, underwater chamber in which Giovanni and David make their love. This, actually, is innocent, as timelessly innocent as Giovanni (Baldwin's Donatello), but it is *Giovanni's* room, not David's, and David's aggressive, time-bound American instincts leave him suffocated in it. His symbol is the wind, and it is right and necessary that he move, change, and ultimately be free. In Baldwin's tough scheme, however, there is no freedom in simply running and keeping secrets from himself. His false sense of innocence, his denials of love, and his dissociation from life have been so great that only Giovanni's death has brought him back to consciousness and a real conscience. Here are the paradoxes of salvation in Baldwin: shame is usable if it provokes honest self-consciousness; death is purifying to the living if the loss is honored in a new conscience.

iii

These paradoxes are essential to *Another Country* (1962). As a projection of Baldwin's vision, it is definitely his most valuable book, but to understand it we must trace the various characters' inner allegiances to the memory of Rufus Scott, the jazz drummer who commits suicide in the opening of the book. None of his friends had then been able to help him, and he was overpowered by his own hatred and frustration. His younger sister Ida had been desperate to get in touch with him but had been left behind in his abandonment of his old-fashioned Harlem family. A red-headed southern renegade (Eric) had had affairs with him but then, in his own confusion, had gone to Europe. Later Rufus had slapped and beaten a simple southern girl friend into insanity, while Vivaldo Moore, a big, clumsy, unpublished writer from Brooklyn, was unable to help either of them. There was a latent sexual love between Rufus and Vivaldo which Vivaldo would not acknowledge.

The terrific impediments to awakened sensibility are clear in one of Baldwin's many stunning insights about contemporary New York City:

And the summer came, the New York summer, which is like no summer anywhere. The heat and the noise began their destruction of nerves and sanity and private lives and love affairs. The air was full of baseball scores and bad news and treacly songs; and the streets and the bars were full of hostile people, made more hostile by the heat . . . It was a city without oases, run entirely, insofar, at least, as human perception could tell, for money; and its citizens seemed to have lost entirely any sense of their right to renew themselves.

The greatest sources of renewal, Baldwin reminds us, are love and death, but the people in *Another Country* run from them. The paragraph above concludes:

Whoever, in New York, attempted to cling to this right [of renewal], lived in New York in exile—in exile from the life around him; and this, paradoxically, had the effect of placing him in perpetual danger of being forever banished from any real sense of himself.

All the characters are scrambling to win some status and power, but the more they attempt to learn about themselves and the more they penetrate their lingering connections with the dead Rufus, the more alien New York seems. It appears as a hovering number of hostile policemen and elevator men, a meretricious television producer, an unintelligent popular author, cries in the street, and the jungle quiet of Central Park at night. At the same time, this vivid image of the City and the isolation of his characters permits Baldwin to be equally precise in describing them, bringing in data about their lives which would otherwise be best-seller sensationalism. In the midst of his loneliness Vivaldo joins some old friends in smoking pot, and the passage is one of the mildest, loveliest things Baldwin has written. Scenes from Eric's life in southern France with his street boy have a dry, Mediterranean glitter not the least bit sordid. It is through Yves that Eric has overcome his anxieties about his relations with Rufus and won a sense of himself. Eric recognizes, by the way, that one of the social consequences of his homosexuality was the loss of any "honor" as the word is defined by his sick, mechanical age, thereby forcing him to seek his own more fundamental definitions. He passes his strength to

Vivaldo and the other characters, just as new energies and loyalties also come from Rufus' sister Ida. She and Vivaldo must work out Rufus' relation to their inter-racial romance, which is at moments both combustible and comic.

We should note that the title "Another Country" is lively with irony, for the novel presents a world as we know it but as it has not before been put in fiction to be seen, "other" by its ominous distance from what it ought to be and from real human needs, and then "other" as some private land where a handful of people have honored and renewed themselves. This tension epitomizes the book's role in Baldwin's vision. It does not cry out with the so bold and explicit warnings of "Letter from a Region in My Mind," but the prophet's tones there are really based in *Another Country.* An analogy is the way the self-reliance of "Civil Disobedience" is founded on the renewal and independence of vision Thoreau established at Walden. Baldwin had to discover his "distant land"—to use Thoreau's term—from which to see the essential unreality of New York. In this respect this third novel might be called the greatest of his liberal educations, just as it is the most informative for his audience. It is only from the distant land of *Another Country* that he can criticize the false land both toughly and compassionately, and the simultaneous violent content and delicate style in other work depends on this distance. The fiction also took him out of himself, enabling him to realize impersonal correlatives in other lives for the violence and confusion he knows to be in his own. And it gave him knowledge of the deeper sources and broader meanings of racial conflict such as study of race alone could never supply. Love and death are the real subjects of *Another Country,* neither of them "in the infantile American sense," to use one of Baldwin's phrases, but in the profound ways that they are also the subjects of a poem like *The Waste Land.* As a sensitive author, Vivaldo, for example, had to be willing to be a kind of Tiresias, aware of both male and female feelings and compassionate towards his own "drowned god," Rufus, who threw himself off the George Washington

Bridge. But he was afraid, afraid of this unknown and this beckoning darkness. On this basis Baldwin can say in the "Letter":

> And I submit, then, that the racial tensions that menace Americans today have little to do with real antipathy—on the contrary, indeed—and are involved only symbolically with color. These tensions are rooted in the very same depths as those from which love springs, or murder. The white man's unadmitted—and apparently, to him, unspeakable—private fears and longings are projected onto the Negro.

But this presents Baldwin with another one of his conundrums. It has been the thesis of this appraisal that his novels have been his "other country," one uncommonly valuable to him as a way of developing his talent, while his nonfiction has broadcast his prophecy and his reports. But the prophecy must also react upon the novels and the work as a whole, working its effect on their nature and structure. The less the problems which initiated some of the essays have to do with symptoms and appearances, the more, then, both essays and novels must expose the "unadmitted . . . fears and longings"—both white and Negro, after all, human ones. Baldwin has further pointed out in the fascinating essay "Stranger in the Village" that the race issue engages forms and symbols of blackness and whiteness which lie at the very origins of Western Civilization, like its Dionysos and Apollo, its Devil and its God. There can be no isolating of such unnamed elements of our life and no new ethical forms and language for our civilization without there being equally enormous changes in our literature and our literary forms. So far Baldwin himself has, I think, accomplished more house cleaning and rebuilding in the essay than in the novel. He has learned the art of the novel but taught the art of the essay. It could be, therefore, that his most suitable form might turn out to be the "letter," the flexible, honestly personal kind of essay he has been patiently improving through most of his career. Such "letters" seem peculiarly appropriate for his kind of distance and his continuing journey, for Baldwin is a pilgrim. Whether he can keep this distance without his fictional other countries remains to be seen. He has a big job, and the challenge to his art is every bit as great as the challenge of his material, which is a very serious challenge indeed.

THE FICTION OF HERBERT GOLD

Harry T. Moore

A TELEVISION PRODUCER once said to Herbert Gold, "I don't think you understand what we want. We want happy stories about happy people with happy problems." Gold in his fiction often displays a fine sense of comedy, but his characters don't have happy problems. Even at his poorest—and there are times when his people and situations don't rise above the commonplace—Herbert Gold never serves up the fake hopes and wistful outcomes of the popular-entertainment serial. If he calls one of his novels *The Optimist*, his intent is ironical.

And if he plays rather freely with irony, he can also be nostalgic, as in *Therefore Be Bold* and in such short stories as "The Heart of the Artichoke." But he lacks sentimentalism, that condition whose bedazzled victim simply expects too much of life. Gold's latest novel is called *Salt*: beyond certain symbolic and leitmotiv uses of the title-word in that particular book, the idea it suggests covers a good part of his writing, which is so often strong-tasting and somewhat acrid.

Another feature of his work which is always noticeable is his use of language. Herbert Gold is a neat stylist, sometimes too neat. He can upon occasion master words, use them to bring out exactly what he needs to say about people and incidents; but he often slips too easily into rhetoric. He has a sensitivity for the nuances of speech and can frequently catch the precise accent, rhythm, and tone of dialogue and dialect. But here too he can slip, simply by making the characters themselves speak a little too brightly, as for example in *Salt*. On the other hand, in *The Man Who Was Not With It*, Gold's use of carnival idiom is exactly in key. He shows its tricks of insincerity, an important part of the story, but also displays its force in expressing the deepest feelings of the people who speak it.

In a specific consideration of Gold's fiction, perhaps the best place to begin is with the collection of short stories he brought out in 1960, after he had published four novels. This collection, *Love and Like*, is in one sense a summary of Gold's career, even extending beyond that volume and into his fifth and sixth novels. Fortunately it contains much of Herbert Gold at his best, and can therefore indicate why he is worth talking about here. Similarly, his book of essays, *The Age of Happy Problems* (1962), helps toward a fuller understanding of Gold's fiction.

The gem among the *Love and Like* stories is "The Heart of the Artichoke," of which Gold has written that it "was personally crucial because it gave me a sense that I was now my own man. I had written other stories and a first novel, *Birth of a Hero*, but with this story I felt that I had discovered myself as a writer in some conclusive way." He has also said of this product of 1951, "by writing it I learned to be a writer. I had a sense of mastering my experience. Not just examining, not just using, but *riding* my world, with full sense of my faculties in the open air . . . After writing a heavily influenced, heavily constructed first novel—to prove I could learn from others—I was ready to throw a rock at the Henry James hive, a rock even at the great juicy Dostoyevsky swarm, and secrete my own gathered sweets into my own homemade jug."

The story, tender without being sentimental, is the first-person narrative of Daniel Berman, a Jewish grocer's son in Cleveland. It concerns his conflicts with his parents and his pubescent fixation upon a girl he meets at school. The blonde little Pattie Donahue has "aquarium eyes, profoundly green, profoundly empty, and a mouth like a two-cent Bull's Eye candy, and pale transparent fingers busy as fins"—which anticipates the imagery and symbolism taken from marine life in some of the later work. In the "Artichoke" story these devices are at least right for the ruefully humorous evocation of the ecstasies and miseries of a twelve-year-old boy's vision of an unattainable girl. Daniel Berman knows he is "no Culver Academy athlete calling for Pattie Donahue in his uniform at Christmastime"—Daniel, who has to work in his father's store, is what Pattie, not with contempt but with realism, calls a grocery boy. Daniel at the end of the story engages his father in a physical struggle whose meaning he realizes only with the passing of the years, when he writes the experience down.

Daniel Berman and his strikingly portrayed family appear in other stories in *Love and Like*, one of them ("Aristotle and the Hired Thugs") a brisk tale of the father's adventures in bargaining with truck farmers in the Cleveland marketplace during the depression. But most of the stories, including the one that gives the book its title, are about a young man who in the accumulation of experience becomes almost mythically representative. He is the lower-bourgeois intellectual of the junior-executive, assistant-professor generation, and maybe he is, under different names, various phases of Daniel Berman grown up.

In the *Love and Like* stories, under those different names but carrying a single temperament, he has wife troubles, visits France or Haiti on grants, tangles with his girl students, and wistfully thinks of the child or children taken from him by divorce. He earnestly confronts a gallery of richly assorted characters, including several versions of the embittered wife, a retired French colonel of fascist persuasion, an attractive but treacherous Finnish girl of the hipster faith, a pathetic husband of the "other woman," and some robust Haitians. They and others help to make these stories in their totality a crowded and lively chronicle of a young American's wide range of experience.

Here and there a failure appears, such as "Susannah at the Beach." With echoes of the Apocrypha, this allegory of innocence tells of a girl who accidentally rips her bathing suit open while diving and then, after jeers from a coarse lakeside beach crowd, swims out toward the horizon and probable suicide, for which her motivation is as flimsy as her easily shredded beachwear. Gold also includes a story about a messiah, one Jim Curtis (note the initials), who at thirty-three enters upon his ministry. Although more imaginatively credible than the "Susannah" episode, this story again indicates that the heavily symbolic and the transcendental have their dangers for such writers as Herbert Gold, who work most effectively in the tangible but, when they try to soar, all too often get caught in skytraps.

But in the stories about little Daniel Berman and the various young men whom I have designated as representative, Gold avoids both the mood sketch and the tricky ending. He shows that he can dramatically develop his people and project his scene in a narrative which, although complete in its limited space, often suggests the massiveness of a novel. Gold has noted that there is a difference between short stories (really just "a peek") and novels, which have a larger mission ("to explore possibility"). Yet the stories, in accumulation—except for the two I have called failures—have somewhat the effect of a novel and its "possibility." This is one of the main reasons why *Love and Like* is more than just another collection of stories and may be used to help give perspective to Herbert Gold's entire career so far.

The same year as his "Artichoke" story, 1951, he brought out his first novel, *Birth of a Hero*, a quite different kind of work, the book he referred to as being somewhat derivative and deliberately formal. This is one of his rare fictional efforts in which stylistic effects are muted. Reuben Flair, a middle-aged lawyer, has never realized his potential; when a good-looking neighbor, Lydia Fortiner, who passes for a widow, states that Flair is really a hero, Mrs. Flair says, "He's my husband. Why should he be a hero?" Flair has a love affair with Lydia, in itself unheroic, though it is the first time he has really been in love. There is a comic complication when Lydia's brother, Larry, turns up and camps on the Flairs. A mockery of the heroic, he fascinates them, in their different ways, with his rapid-fire and sometimes shocking anecdotes of his life as a drifter. But the situation can't last, for Larry finally reveals that he is really Lydia's husband. But he can't go on, either, and takes poison. The Flairs resume their marriage, with Reuben apparently becoming a better husband and father, heroic in rather unheroic and everyday activities. As a first novel, it is unusually mature. Reread today, it seems less exciting than when it first came out, and seemed so "promising." Nevertheless, the reader can still admire the author's grasp of character and at times his inventiveness. Ultimately, however, the story is an exploration of the commonplace which doesn't quite transfigure the commonplace.

The next book, *The Prospect Before Us* (1954), is considerably flashier. And it is in many ways a good story; not the traditional let-down of a young man's second novel. Once again avoiding autobiographical elements such as those which predominate in the short stories, Gold deals with a type of man quite different from a young writer just turning thirty. This is an immigrant hotel owner in Cleveland's honky-tonk district. He is fairly successful until confronted with a problem when the "Association" that is fighting racial discrimination moves an attractive Negro girl into the hotel of which Harry Bowers is so proud. The guests make threats and then begin to move out; Harry Bowers stands firm against them and the rival association of businessmen which threatens him. Even the official representatives of the community, the police, mistreat him. The girl, Claire Farren, is isolated from her own people as she lives on in the almost-deserted hotel. Harry too is cut off, and he is drawn erotically to Claire.

But what of the hotel, which has become a liability? Harry's rootless and disaffected roomclerk, Jake, insinuates to him that the building could be burned down for its insurance. Harry slowly yields to this idea and involves his weak brother in the plot. On the night of the fire, Harry mistakenly believes that Claire is in the building, and when he rushes in to rescue her he goes to his villain's and hero's death. This is melodrama rather than anything that might be said to resemble the tragic, and it is a resolving of the story which, along with the often-too-rhetorical language of the style, reduces the value of the book. For there is much in it that is expertly done, particularly the technical details of hotel operation; the author has made himself thoroughly familiar with the milieu and its properties.

Yet there is always that intrusive rhetoric: "The eyes of Jake roamed the dogdays morning sky with a conman's monkeyshine tricks of gaze, doomed to flesh but yearning away from it, asking faith and please-believe-me." In another passage of description and motive, the author writes of Jake: "He giggled and teased, and wiggle-waggled his chin and his Bailey Brothers pants behind, and pleaded across the counter to Harry: Hurry up and love me quick, somebody." Of course much of this may be excused as the work of a young writer groping toward expressional skill.

The most striking episode in the novel doesn't take place at Harry's Green Glade Hotel, but rather in Nancy's notch house, which is the opposite of Harry Bowers' place, even to the point of its being in the good part of the city rather than in the skid-row section. At Nancy's, sexual acts are performed before a small group of spectators. One girl who is watching runs out to vomit. Harry Bowers, who doesn't vomit and stays to watch, sees a mingling of black and white (Negro man, white girl) that underscores his relation with Claire. And the very name of the proprietor, Nancy, suggests another parallel: the implicit homosexuality of Jake and the unconscious homosexuality of Harry's brother, Morris. Indeed, the book is excellently plotted, marred somewhat by the ending (Jake dies in the fire also) and considerably by its extravagant idiom, of which examples have been given.

Gold's next novel, *The Man Who Was Not With It*, came out in 1956 and, because I consider it his best, will save discussion of it for later, meanwhile dealing with *The Optimist, Therefore Be Bold,* and *Salt.* Burr Fuller, the center of attention in *The Optimist* (1959), is one of today's schizoid Americans who at mid-life find themselves split between an urge to make slow but steady progress and a compulsion to keep speeding frantically ahead. This kind of American futility has so often been presented that it can now be taken as a basis for serious literature only when the treatment of it sounds new depths. *The Optimist* doesn't do that; it is mostly a skillful reflection of surfaces.

The first part of the story is by far the more successful in its treatment of even such overworked themes as campus life and the second world war. The University of Michigan phase of Burr's youthful experience has some sardonic bits of anthropological value: fraternity life and campus eroticism. In describing Burr's army years, Gold's gift of realistic observation is given full play. In his use of dialogue here he shows that he has an eager and expert ear for regional varieties of speech, and among his characters in that first part of the book he includes some out-of-the-way personalities of the kind that appeared so zestfully in his first three novels.

After the war, there is a ten-year hiatus in the story, 1946–56, and from this point on the narrative never quite picks up again as it takes Burr through the later stages of an unhappy marriage. He is a successful lawyer in Detroit who decides to run for Congress; outwardly he seems to be a man of principle but inwardly he is tricky. His former campus sweetheart, now his wife and the mother of his two children, is hungry for barbituates and the psychoanalyst's couch. Burr in the sweep of his political campaign takes on an attractive young mistress, and the complications which result make the evasive optimist aware of the jagged division in his nature. But this last part of the book, with its suburban agonizings and all too sketchily presented picture of politics, fails to fulfill the promise of the first part. These later sections fail to bring to the hackneyed themes the freshness they need.

Little can be said about Gold's next novel, *Therefore Be*

Bold (1960), except that it is charming. It is also unambitious and indeed hardly seems to be a novel at all, but rather a memoir of what it was like to be adolescent in Cleveland in the 1930s. Daniel Berman reappears, along with some of his friends, including the attractive Pattie Donahue, with her fin-like hands; Pattie plays a very small part here, and a brief epilogue reveals that she later became a social worker. Most of the book is a joyous, youthful romp; Dan Berman is interested in the verse-writing Eva Masters, who has an antisemitic father. In portraying her family, Herbert Gold once again draws upon the marine imagery through which he often sees people: "The Masters home was a house of crabs. They obscurely swarmed; they moved sideways over each other, claws everywhere." But Dan evades their claws, and he isn't taken by the finny hands of Pattie Donahue, but rather by the harpist's fingers of Lucille Lake, whom he will ultimately marry. This book, which took its author more than ten years to write its less than two hundred and fifty pages, is an attempt to see life through the hot-eyed innocence of youth. The vision may not be deep, but the picture of adolescent, depression-era morals is vital and attractive.

Salt (1963) is highly ambitious and, except for a surprisingly strong conclusion, seems to me somewhat of a failure, at least in not realizing all the ambitions it implicitly announces. It is the story of two men and a woman. Peter Hatten, a young Wall Street broker, plays girls as he plays the market, and in order to keep in shape practices juggling, a tricky pastime. The other leading male character is Peter's friend, Daniel Shaper, who appeared in the story "Love and Like" as the young man with a broken marriage who had gone to revisit his native Cleveland and exercise his right to see his children occasionally. He might well be Daniel Berman grown up and living in New York, working for a successful semi-intellectual magazine. The girl in *Salt* is Barbara Jones, up from the South. Peter has known her first and becomes weary of her; Dan becomes serious about her. Peter can't go on telling her he loves her—even the most strenuous juggling is easier—but Dan is essentially a family man, despite the unfortunate experience of his first marriage.

Salt is, among other things, an attempt at a full picture of New York life, or rather of the part of it where young Wall Streeters and Madison Avenuers play. Some of the characters are makers of pornographic films, but they are only comic background figures whose activities are a symbolic commentary on Peter's Casanova-like adventures. For Peter's love life is extensive and is devoutly described —Herbert Gold is the sharpest girl-watcher among American novelists. Peter knows a varied gallery of girls, and as Mr. Gold graphically shows him putting them through their paces, the book becomes among other things a Baedeker of the sex lives of young Americans living in Manhattan. Peter can't help going back to Barbara once, even after she has seriously become Dan's girl; so Dan beats up the juggler-athlete in a ferocious sidewalk fight. After this display, he has an even harder fight to win back Barbara, who has returned to her home in Virginia. "Peter's smart," she tells Dan, "he believes love is impossible. He tried his best to teach us. He did his best to convince us." But Dan, who believes in love, breaks through the barriers Barbara has put up. He offers marriage, but not in New York. Dan, whose thoughts and phrasing sometimes come from the Bible, tells Barbara she is the salt of the earth. This is in contrast to one of Peter's fantasies about himself in which the salt of the sea is his element and he is a quick fish swimming above "the monumental excrescences of tiny shellfish"; and in another of his fantasies he thinks of a continuous poker game, which he knows is crooked—and yet "he felt himself yearning to swim in it." Barbara and Dan are of a different substance and outlook; it is only after Dan's proposal that she tells him she is expecting his child.

The ending, as I noted before, has strength, with Dan accepting Barbara's lapse—she doesn't want to be "forgiven," so he merely "accepts." Unfortunately, however, the author, in attempting to show the falsity of New York existence, is too often too slick. The people he introduces are mostly fringe types of journalism, television, and show business, and far too epigrammatically clever. Some of their behavior reflects the results of the author's shrewd observation, but their speech is always sprinkled with verbal gold dust; the people talk like characters put forth by Scott Fitzgerald before he matured. That this level of New York social existence is glittering and brittle, the reader would hardly dispute, but the total effect of its representation here is one of a high artificiality, in which the dialogue makes the purposeful artificiality of the characters into something not always believable. That is, if one may use the expression, they are often just too artificially artificial. In these passages the author is of course trying for satire, and while he occasionally succeeds —once again, through the actions rather than the speech of his people—the satire is not sharply enough fanged to bite very deep.

Salt nevertheless shows Herbert Gold as still a writer of more than promise. Not long after completing it, he went to Haiti, the setting of some of his short stories, to work on what will apparently be a different kind of novel. He is still ambitiously trying. And while we wait for this further work, we have *The Man Who Was Not With It* as evidence of what Gold can accomplish when he brings together his varied gifts—observation, comedy, and ear for dialogue. And the moral implications usually found in Gold's fiction are all emphatically present in this book.

The novel tells the story of Bud Williams' two sojourns with a smalltime carnival, and of his return home between the two. Motherless, he had run away from the father he didn't like, but even in the life of the "Wide World and Tuscaloosa Too Shows" he hadn't found security and had become a dope addict. Then, forceful interference by the carnie's barker, Grack (Gracchus), cures him. Bud goes back home to Pittsburgh and an unsuccessful visit with his father; then heads south to pick up the show again. Relationships change; the small daughter of Pauline, the fortune teller, has budded: "She was a female already, and

I knew I had been away for many months. She turned red at the sight of me. At last someone meant welcome home." Grack, the substitute father, is no longer there; Bud marries Joy Deland, Pauline's daughter, in one of the carnival tents, with a small-town Southern minister presiding. That night, Bud finds a thief trying to open the carnival owner's safe and says, "Hello, Grack. Did you know I got married tonight?" Bud and Joy drive north for their honeymoon, aiming for Niagara Falls and the border of Canada, the native country of "Frenchie" Grack, who goes with them from motel to motel. Joy is pregnant. A stop in Cleveland includes a visit to Nancy's notch house, which Gold had written about earlier in *The Prospect Before Us*. Calamities abound: Joy loses her child, and Bud loses his desperate fight to cure Grack of the drug addiction into which he has sunk; he fights to help him, in the phrasing of this milieu, kick the habit. Grack winds up in the arms of the police, and Bud and Joy settle in Pittsburgh, friends now of Bud's father, and have a son, whom Bud's father wants brought up "to be with it." But even for people who have, in carnie lingo, become squares, this isn't easy.

The Man Who Was Not With It—in the few years of its paperback existence rather wildly called *The Wild Life*—is a book to which synopsis can't do justice. It can merely indicate some of the main trends of the story. Herbert Gold has marvelously captured carnival life, with its lures for marks and its fights with rubes, all the excitement and tinsel and struggle. Grack is the most successful of the author's vitalistic characters, and to hear him giving his pitch on the midway, with his "lookee" and his "hee hee hee" and "ho ho ho," is to be in the gusty atmosphere of the fairgrounds. In having Bud tell the story in carnie slang, Gold makes full use of his own ability to handle colorful idiom. It crackles. But the language isn't flashed just for its own sake; it is organic. Through it, the author is able to present nuances of character and investigate the depths of his particular kind of people in a way which would have been less intimate with straight language. Herbert Gold's tendency toward the bizarre in style exactly matches the subject matter in this book.

Let me say once again that the whole novel needs to be read for its story to be appreciated. And it is a good story, one of a redemption or partial redemption, and of a failing attempt at redemption. To use this last word is to oversimplify, something which Herbert Gold avoids doing in this story. But the word is a kind of semaphore to indicate partially what happens in the novel. And such matters, involving important changes in character, are never simple, as Bud carefully suggests at the end of the book. Commenting on his father's wish to have his grandson brought up "to be with it," Bud concludes: "Joy and I had other ideas. We will not—and cannot—pull our son out of the way of our own hard times. They go on. There's a good and with it way to be not with it, too."

A number of good novels came out of America in the 1950s. *The Man Who Was Not With It* ranks among the best of them. It is reassuring to know that Herbert Gold, who is in his early forties, is still trying, despite some recent rather harsh, or at least unappreciative, criticisms of his work. He has the potential. And he has not succumbed to the temptation that besets so many of our authors: to write about happy problems.

HARVEY SWADOS:
PRIVATE STORIES AND PUBLIC FICTION

Charles Shapiro

> There ought to be, behind the door of every happy, con-
> tented man, someone standing with a hammer, continually
> reminding him with a tap that there are unhappy people.
> Anton Chekhov—epigraph to A Radical's America by
> Harvey Swados.

WE HAVE BECOME a bit too sophisticated of late, afraid of
not only commitment but a point of view. This seems to
be especially true of our novelists. If pressed on this point
they could offer, in their defense, the past fictional
foolishness of too many writers of our recent past who
sacrificed their art, which they possibly never really possessed, for a political position they never completely
understood. And certainly muckraking and fiction seemed
to suffer when brought together, for art demands much
more of the creator than the knowledge of present evils
and possible solutions.

Critics have, for quite a while, announced the death of
the novel of social criticism. For one sample:

> No wonder . . . the novel of social criticism is dying, as
> was demonstrated some time ago. And not only because in
> our fluid, diversified society the writer has no traditional
> base from which to view the human comedy. It is dying
> chiefly because the writer has ceased to believe that the so-
> cial world can reveal the direction of man's soul. "For the
> advanced writer of our time, the self is his supreme, even

sole, referrent," as Diana Trilling so well explains in her essay on Mailer. The serious writer whose faith in exterior reality is shaken, if not wholly shattered, who questions even the concept of "inner" man (now no longer immune to social conditioning) is turning increasingly to the inmost self, examining it both in relation to the higher levels of being which it controls and the outside world by which it is set in motion.[1]

It has not always been so. Charles Dickens, for one glorious example, could make his outrage an inherent part of his craft, using his Gradgrinds and Pecksniffs to entertain as well as shock. He did more than present his society to us; he exposed it and made us sorrow for an England gone wrong in so many heartbreaking ways. The problems inherent in creating polemical fiction, or better still, fiction which does take serious note of how society can work on our lives, has been brilliantly discussed by Irving Howe. He notes that, at its best, "the political novel generates such intense heat that the ideas it appropriates are melted into its movement, are fused with the emotions of its characters." [2]

In the past few years in America we have had few effective novels which incorporate a steady, critical point of view. The Negro novelists, of course, are the chief exception, for they have been forced, since birth, to confront what many of us can ignore. And Jewish novelists often have the same concerns; yet as assimilation speeds up, as the Jew moves to the center of American life, his fiction chronicles much more than his oppression. Harvey Swados, in an essay on "Certain Jewish Writers," cites as an example of the new Jewish "hero" Philip Roth's athlete, Ronald Patimkin, "who hangs his jockstrap from the shower faucet while he sings the latest pop tunes, and is so completely the self-satisfied muscle-bound numskull that notions of Jewish alienation are entirely 'foreign' to him." [3]

As we know from Harvey Swados' essays, he is a man with strong ideas about American life; what is too often forgotten is that he is also a fine writer of fiction, and one of the few whose concerns are meaningfully incorporated into his novels and short stories. In his introduction to the collection of essays, A *Radical's America*, Swados has defined himself in terms of four crucial actualities which helped form his identity. Much like the puzzle we played as children, connecting dots until we got an outline, these four items help us to understand the work of a talented, versatile writer.

First of all: "I am a novelist." And, as a novelist, Swados hasn't been afraid to take chances, exploring the life of the American factoryworker as well as the tribulations of artists and businessmen.

Secondly: "I am a middle-class man of the mid-century, born and brought up in a middle-sized American city . . ." He is, as he clearly understands, very much middle-class "in temper and outlook." And he freely admits that certain areas of American life are foreign to him: the rich, the migrant workers, cafe society.

Swados' third point of reference is that he is a Jew, though in conversation he acknowledges that this aspect of contemporary American literary life has been over-played. What is important to him, as we have already noted, is the realization of the American Jew's march from a marginal position in society towards its center.

Finally, he describes himself as a socialist (and note the small letter "s"). Recent events have strengthened this faith. "If anyone is leading us to socialism it's the Negro. The young are being driven by the economic logic of the situation."

Swados, commenting on the problems of writing in the 1950's, admitted he feels torn between "playing the oracle . . . and playing the traditional game of telling private stories about private people. Both, however, are equally important to me, and I continue to hope that at my best, one will imply the other." [4] In his best work this is just what happens. Consider how Swados opens his remarkable first novel, *Out Went The Candle* (Viking, 1955):

For some Americans the Second World War began as a breeze from the sea, with the first heady scent of a flowering of business, a proliferation of prime contracts, subcontracts, and cost-plus bonanzas bringing to their dilated nostrils the odor of wealth beyond their wildest imaginings. For some it began as a nameless terror, a fearful vision of separation and disruption, of death by drowning and explosion, of endless deaths yet to come. For some it began as a thrilled voice interrupting the Sunday-afternoon broadcast of the Philharmonic, bringing new hope of a bright new world, of peace and freedom arising from the necessary destruction. For some it began as a serpentine line, before the recruiting station, of boys anxious to escape from the prison of the dead past. For some it began as an annoyance.

Thus, firmly and effectively, the story is set in its place, in a specific social and political context, and, as we get to know the protagonists, we come to realize just how much they are a part of the America of the forties. Their personal adventures are played out against the background of an America adjusting to war and readjusting to peace. Values are re-examined against what history has done. We see this occurring in the second paragraph of the novel as we are introduced to one of the key characters, a young man who is forever judging himself against the moral failures of those he admires:

For Joe Burley of New Jersey the war began in 1943 with a summons from his draft board. A dangling man, angry at Hitler but afraid to fight, in love with the life of action but living quietly at home with his widowed mother, dreaming his nights away with fantasies of fame as a foreign correspondent but spending his days as a reporter for a provincial newspaper, covering henhouse fires and Rotary Club luncheons, he was driven to make a move—like a dilatory chess player prodded on by an impatient opponent—by the chairman of his draft board. Mr. Humpel, the patriotic butcher, perhaps remembering a plate-glass window that Joe had broken with a baseball ten years before, ruled that reporters were expendable and placed Joe in IA, thereby forcing him to make a choice. So his new life in a world at war began, and so did the chain of circumstances that were not only to make a soldier of him, not only to make a foreign correspondent of him (thereby fulfilling his dreams), but, most important, were to lift in that one short summer the curtain separating him from love, from involvement, and from a knowledge of those audacious few to whom war meant not death but life, not a contracting but a broadening of their horizons.

As a sensitive novelist, Swados must begin with concern for his characters; for, as he realizes, if we are to become interested in what society does to them, they, in turn, must be worth our caring. His central figure, Herman Felton, schemer, war profiteer, family man, uses the energies left over from his wheeling-dealing to shape the lives of his children. His girl, Betsy, his son, Morrow, both love and reject their father, and in their fury they seem bent on self-destruction. Joe Burley, the observer of the frightening family tensions, moves into their lives and becomes, in a positive sense, a third child of Herman's and Felton thus becomes a shabby, contemporary King Lear who must learn, too late, what he should always have known.

Out Went The Candle is Swados' best novel, and Felton is certainly his finest creation. We see him as explained by his children, as he might appear to casual observers, and, most interestingly of all, in his revealing letters to his daughter, strange cries of pain, love, arrogance, and confusion:

Here in Wash. its a big thing if you get appointments with right men—if they keep them your a regular hero— everybody wants to know how do you do it—look dumb and keep your powder dry is my motto—its a shame how everybody including yours truly is taking uncle Sam for a buggy ride, but what are you going to do—its the kind of world where as they say the devil "take the hindemost"—if you don't take care of your family who will. . . . Daddy does not want to be a nag, but be cautious with Mr. Burley and other gentiles like Mr. Taylor? he wants to see Scharf— dont know why—dont take advantage, boys looking for fun before they go to fight Hitler—all the world wants fun but price is too high—now my pride is only in you.

I charge you—for you—and I know you want to be that *mensch* that is real true-blue and the only worth while kind —You have that opportunity at present Love

Dad

In one remarkable chapter, devoted to Herman Felton's day, we get to know this unhappy man. "Toothbrush in hand, Herman Felton raised the lid of the ebony toilet seat and recoiled in dismay. Floating in the clear water, a red and luscious mouth was looking up at him, lips parted sensually. He bent forward, peered down into the bowl, and saw a folded sheet of toilet paper bearing the imprint of someone's lips—Clara's? Betsy's? The price you pay for living with two women." Herman recalls the morning he blundered into Betsy's bedroom and observed her naked, beautiful body; he remembers the look she shot at him, "pride, anger, voluptuousness, recklessness, and worst of all a calculating recognition of what she had seen in his face."

The business day is tedious and frantic. For lunch Felton goes to a vegetarian restaurant where food is perpetually disguised as something better.

> All around him people were eating, and Herman found himself wondering how they could live like this, stuffing, gorging, shoveling food into their mouths as if they were eating their last meal; as if everything was going to disappear at two o'clock and they had to cram down as much as they could before then; as if they didn't have a thought, a vision, an ideal, except gluttony. It was enough to make you hate everybody, Herman thought, stabbing at the cutlet with his fork, because they were worse than animals really, when you considered that animals could never know any better. But how do I know, he thought, that they have no visions? Am I unfair?

The pressures on Felton, Freudian as well as political, become almost unbearable. His business and his family seem ruined, and, over and over, he places the blame, not on himself, not on America, but on world conditions, or, more specifically, on Hitler. "The force that they were struggling against was greater than any of them. He called it Hitler, and people laughed at him for it behind his back; he knew it. He knew too that Hitler would crash into the dust; it was ordained; but by that time it would be too late for himself and his family."

Swados is especially adept at short, incisive descriptions of people, a talent which is best exploited in *On The Line*. What is even a rarer talent is his ability at catching the spirit of a particular place in a particular time. Thus the Felton family is seen as rooted in contemporary, urban America, and, as the novel progresses, we begin to understand how their haunted lives, in many ways, tells us about ours. While *Out Went The Candle* is a powerful work, it suffers, at times, from ever shifting points of view, for often the transitions are rough. Unfortunately Swados has also seen fit to lace his tale with a number of super-obvious coincidences. And, most troublesome of all, the Lear equals Felton equation becomes too much of a literary cryptogram, a gimmick rather than an artistic device.

Swados' second work is equally ambitious, a depiction of factory life, a work that can be uneasily placed in a fictional no-man's-land between the category of "novel" and that of "a collection of short stories." At times, of course, a group of stories blend together to become, in essence, a novel: Joyce's *Dubliners*, in its progression from "The Sisters" to "The Dead," builds up to a convincing, yet kaleidoscopic portrait of a city in spiritual decay; and Sherwood Anderson's *Winesburg, Ohio* creates, tale by tale, a frightening picture of small town Americans, essentially decent folk estranged from one another. *On The Line* (Atlantic-Little, Brown, 1957) is in this tradition, chronicling separate adventures of workers on an automobile assembly line and adding up to an evocation of this aspect of American life which has been neglected by writers. The stories are connected, not only by theme, but in more prosaic ways: a number of characters reappear in the tales, and several stories are directly connected in plot as well as action.

Swados, in a number of important articles, has shown his understanding for the problems of the industrial laborer; and in *On The Line* he extends this compassion. Not since Upton Sinclair's *The Jungle* have we had such a direct, steady look at the workers' world, one of hard dullness, continual pressures, and very little satisfaction. (Having worked, for a brief but too long period on an assembly line, I would like to offer testimony to how well Swados has caught the essential spirit of this life, to how well he has served as both reporter and creator.)

Swados has chosen to dramatize a steady tension between the dehumanizing effect of the line and the dreams of the workers who try, at first, to preserve their private enthusiasms—one man plans to be a professional singer, another worker wishes for a new car, a third wants his son's love—as the assembly belt rolls on. The factory must destroy the individuality of each man, and as this cruel process is exposed, we come to accept the line as well as despair of it. The little tragedies, placed together, become a damning indictment.

While the worker has been neglected in American letters, the same cannot be said of the artist, the musician or the writer. The commercialization and corruption of these men has become almost a fictional stereotype, and Swados, in turning his attention to this part of our lives is caught up by the inevitable cliches of this overly discussed problem. *False Coin,* as Ihab Hassan puts it, probes "the subtle pressures which, with the best of human and scientific intentions, subordinate the quality of individual excellence to the popular needs of mass communication." [5] This very contemporary problem has been handled to much better effect by Swados in such short stories as "The Dancer" and "The Man in the Toolhouse." *False Coin* (Atlantic-Little, Brown, 1959) is set at Harmony farm, a vast, complicated daydream come alive which is, in the words of its director, "A massive attempt to heal the crazy split between mass culture and art, between lowbrow and highbrow, not by asking the artist to water down his work, or by force-feeding the general public with abstract art, but by undoing the barriers that separate the two."

This noble end is to be accomplished by herding together an assortment of writers, composers and sociologists in order to have them produce a work of art with a basic theme that can be translated into an opera, movie,

T.V. film, radio program, comic book, and God knows what else. Almost at once there is trouble. Compromises have to be made, and the inevitable Congressional investigating committee arrives on the unhappy scene. The conscience of the project is, oddly enough, a sound engineer, a man in his fifties who loves music and, existing on the periphery of the arts, demands an unwavering devotion to the integrity of the creative mind. He is horrified by a world "compounded of low compromises and lower betrayals, all, all committed in the name of the higher virtues."

There is a good deal of wit to this novel and the message is undeniable; unfortunately the characters seem, too often, to exist as mere pieces in a political game, reciting their lines while remaining lifeless. As cartoons they have their say, but this reduces a novel to what it should never be, a framework for little speeches on big issues.

Swados' latest novel, *The Will* (World, 1963), is, in some ways, reminiscent of *Out Went The Candle*; a family in torment is at the center of the work, and there are steady allusions to a literary masterpiece, in this case *The Brothers Karamazov*. Three sons, paralleling the three brothers in Dostoevsky's novel, are involved in a fight for a large inheritance. The time is the present, the place urban America, and, as in Swados' first novel, contemporary events bear down hard on the private drama. One brother, a counterpart to Aloyosha, has been a recluse and is temporarily reentering the active struggle. "Ray said to himself. It was not so much that you had to learn mistrust when you went out into the world, as that you had to teach yourself a prudence, a holding back." A family friend, Dr. Solomon Stark, observes the contest, offering appropriate, psychologically oriented comments about the contestants. He is placed there to remind us that there is more to the family misery than can be seen in legal or political terms.

References to *The Brothers Karamazov* abound, enough to offer hours of pleasure to the *PMLA* boys, but the horror of the suffering is more akin to, say, Saltykov-

Schedrin's *The Golovlovs*. While the Swados book is a noble and often successful experiment, none of the characters are as well realized as Herman Felton, and not one is as successful as several of the figures who featured in Swados' shorter fictional pieces. What is splendid in *The Will* is the intelligence behind the narration and the quality of the structure. One reviewer has referred to it as a "symphonic" novel; and Hilton Kramer, in the most perceptive discussion of *The Will* to date, gets quickly to the heart of this disturbing book: ". . . in essence, a novel about the hoarding of wealth and aspiration by which the immigrant generation in this country hoped to provide its sons with a privileged place in the mainstream of American society, and the tragic, life-denying compromise which that ambition bequeathed to the very lives it has intended to benefit." [6]

A good deal of Swados' most effective work appears in his stories, a genre in which he takes chances and more often than not succeeds in making art out of his severe social criticism. While he failed, in *False Coin*, to effectively depict the artist as he is spoiled by American life, this important theme does succeed in "The Man in the Toolhouse" and "The Dancer" (*Nights in the Gardens of Brooklyn*, London: Rupert Hart-Davis, 1962), two stories which are strikingly different in concept. "The Dancer" involves Peter Chifley of Elyria, Ohio, a naive, good-hearted country boy who, while in service in Japan, falls in love with the old Fred Astaire-Ginger Rogers dance films. After watching *Top Hat*, "he was overcome with a breathless bouyancy, and he began to dance at once." Two military policemen immediately assume he is drunk.

On discharge Peter tries to realize his potentialities as a dancer; but, one by one, he is exposed to the various elements of American culture which can distort and misuse his real talent. The business, artsy-craftsy, homosexual, political special-pleaders all work on Chifley. Finally, inevitably, he climbs on the ledge of a high building. "Then he opened his arms and dove slowly through space, his hair streaming back in the summer sky, his eyes flashing silver tears, as the stone curtain of the sidewalk rose triumphantly on his final dance."

"The Man in the Toolhouse," avoiding the grotesqueries of "The Dancer," is a straight, almost reportorial account of how the passion of a man's life, a book he labors on for years and under unbelievably hard conditions, is refurbished into a best-seller. The writer must face the consequences of his deceit. The stories vary, from an especially incisive study of a bloodless scholar to a tale of a lonely, frightened man at sea. Best of all is the title story, a loving, fictional remembrance of what post-war New York City was for young people in love, with their city, their lives, and their possibilities. History changes all this. "And like everything else I endured in those passionate years, it will remain until the end of my days embedded in the very core of my being, an internal capital, aflame with romance and infected with disillusion."

As a reporter Swados is aware of the dangers in failing to note the new tensions of a changing society. In a recent article on the U.A.W.[7] he compares the spirit of the great organizational drive of the C.I.O. automobile workers with what he finds today. "I found . . . that it is impossible in the sixties to make the kind of generalization that used to come so easily." Keenly aware of the social realities of today, Swados, as a splendid and imaginative creative artist is well equipped to transform these realities into fiction, a fiction that will give the lie to all who so patronizingly announce that the novel of social criticism is dying.

JOHN HAWKES:
THE SMILE SLASHED BY A RAZOR

S. K. Oberbeck

ASTONISHING SYMPATHY, satanic humor, cold detachment: these playful postures best describe the experimental fiction of John Hawkes, who "finds both wit and blackness in the pit." Ten years ago, Hawkes still had what critics of faint praise and damnation called "a tense following." *The New Yorker*, taking note in 1949 of *The Cannibal*, observed that Hawkes "writes like no one else at all." Only slightly less daring, *The Saturday Review* dubbed the book "an extraordinary work of fiction." Another publication mumbled something about "troubling nightmares" and rolled over, one presumes, with a few grains of Seconal to try to forget about John Hawkes. But his writing leaves an indelible mark in the mind, a cloven hoofprint stamped in brass.

His later novels, *The Owl, The Goose on the Grave, The Beetle Leg,* and *The Lime Twig*—in addition to his first novella, "Charivari"—got passing notice of the same undernourished consistency from consumer news and literary magazines. For Hawkes has never been treated by popular publications to the largesse granted such authors as Salinger, Mailer, Bellow, Roth and Malamud. This is a pity since he writes with deeper talent and conviction than any of these.

Time seems neither to mellow nor sophisticate the average reader of experimental fiction; time does, however, mellow and sophisticate an author to a point where he can elbow his way (he has to, it seems) into the front ranks of the publicity patch. Bemused very slightly over his following, and quite unexcited over the lack of a nice, personal tidbit about him in *Esquire*, Hawkes has changed his prose very little and continues to maintain his basic impulse and energy. He has developed, as Albert Guerard predicted in 1949, a tendency toward the more realistic form of extended fiction. The development of his capacities, seen in passing from "Charivari" to his recent *Second Skin*, will astonish most of his readers.

Leslie Feidler wrote an introduction to *The Lime Twig* as if he were discovering Hawkes to the common market, but he made many lucid comments about his reactions to the book. He saw the author as a rebel writing in an age of literary recapitulation, when traditional novels are rewritten in a number of inventive ways. Certainly it is true that Hawkes happens to be a rebel in the present spectrum of modern literature. It could hardly be otherwise. And certainly it is gratifying to read his highly original and difficult prose in this period when too much of our fiction seems smoothly tailored for a specific market, or audience. Perhaps it is much to his credit that Hawkes would seem out of place, really *too* disturbing, in *The New Yorker*, *Esquire*, *Playboy* or *Atlantic Monthly*—no matter how nearly acceptable his flamboyant grotesque and vision of terror.

While it is true that Hawkes writes like, sounds like, no one else at all, it is equally true that his fiction "shares a birthmark," as he puts it, with a body of writing that might arbitrarily be represented by authors such as Faulkner, Kafka, Conrad, Lautréamont, Djuna Barnes, Flannery O'Connor, Nathanael West and Kraft-Ebbing. His pure creative energy, mordant and mundane, has the effortless sting and bite of these authors and their names come readily to mind when one discusses Hawkes.

But to talk of his fiction merely by relating it to another body of writing is to dismiss his consistent and truly original talents. For, obviously, Hawkes tailors his fiction to no standard but his own, "the satiric writer, running maliciously at the head of the mob and creating the shape of his meaningful psychic paradox as he goes." He is unafraid to step out into the thin, cold air of what he calls "a climate of pure and immoral *creation*." His fictions are totally refined abstractions, clear enigmas poised in brilliant rhetoric, evoking the inexorable, unhurried and deliberate touch of terror.

The richness of his prose resists neat critical summation, for his is a disturbingly resonant and precise language, expression urged from an intense clash with our deepest obsessions and everywhere rewarded with what Guerard calls the author's "demonic sympathy." This sympathy, Guerard observes, enters "into the saved and the damned alike." All characters bask in its cruelty, all events are tinged by its love, for to understand everything is to ridicule everything—or to sympathize with everything. In this posture is a curious banality, and many of Hawkes's readers find it difficult to separate sympathy from ridicule in his fiction. They are much the same. When Thick beats Margaret Banks in *The Lime Twig*, one feels a quickening in the prose, a tensing of cadences, almost a rhetorical sense of jubilation: Here is something about which one can write! I thought of Flaubert as I read that deliciously horrible passage, how he dwelled with an almost similar delight on the slow death by poison of Emma Bovary. The excessive detail, clinical authenticity, long, lingering view, full of love and hate, at Emma expiring . . . Surely Flaubert enjoyed getting rid of Emma finally. He almost dances on her empty coffin, though he was said to remark, "Emma Bovary, c'est moi!" The novelist too must be able to satisfy his frustrations violently.

Hawkes also finds a mixture of pity and exhilaration in such violence, in the objective evidence of what he calls "the terrifying similarity between the unconscious desires of the solitary man and the disruptive needs of the visible world." Surely his pity for Margaret is tinged with pride in the fine job he was doing, through Thick, on her. In each of his novels, Hawkes grimly uncovers both the "unconscious desires" and the "disruptive needs," making them objective in a particularly creative way.

In both his conception and his language, one feels a tremendous compression, the sense of suffocation Flannery O'Connor said she experienced reading *The Lime Twig*. To borrow from Camus' *The Rebel*, one might say that Hawkes writes in such a way that "the malady experienced by a single man becomes the mass plague." When, again in *The Rebel*, Camus discusses Lautréamont, he remarks,

> We find in Lautréamont this refusal to recognize rational consciousness, this return to the elementary which is one of the marks of a civilization in revolt against itself. It is no longer a question of recognizing appearances, by making a determined and conscious effort, but of no longer existing at all on the conscious level.

This remark applies its insight perfectly to Hawkes's fiction. One sees clearly his refusal to recognize, or abide, the rational consciousness in his fondness for withholding narrative information and in his habit of shuffling ordered events in time. He throws the map-hungry reader delicious bits of abusive, brilliant detail and will for pages toss out the false scents that send readers stumbling past his true authorial intentions like a shipwreck chasing his own footprints. His rigid consistency of tone and language leaves readers panting, breathless and dismayed.

He celebrates the game in which we are all imprisoned by our wishes to be free of rational consciousness. His comic treatment of violence, extreme detachment and crackling satire—thoughtful horrors driven through tangles of complex distortions—all combine to unsettle his reader, making him dependent on the author as a guide in this contrary and confusing landscape. Like Faulkner, Hawkes can gracefully subjugate his reader, and in this delightful violation of a reader's conventional trust is a measure of perverse satisfaction such as a Faulkner or a Flaubert must have enjoyed. How sad that many readers are unable to partake in the perverse pleasures which the novelist invites them to share.

But these considerations lead us away from the heart of the fiction, Hawkes's own heart of darkness. It seems wise to mention, however, that Hawkes's techniques and craftsmanship have earned him different tags and rubrics — "antinovelist," "anti-realist," even, as one professor squeezed out, "a master of controlled incoherence." Like the effulgent "isms" of modern art, such labels take us only into the safety of speculation over literary schools.

Hawkes has, however, been lumped in with the French school of "anti-novelists," represented by Robbe-Grillet, Sarraute, Butor, Simon, Sapota, Duras, etc. Such references are spurious. The French authors, whose revolt is ostentatious and sentimental, are not anti-realists but intensified realists, minute regimentationists, pragmatic, seamless. Their revolt has roots in sociological, not literary, problems. They seem like children who reduce disobedience to the most superficial contrary acts of sulking behavior. Their distortions are so inconsistent, so haphazard, vibrant details and nuances of character rarely come across. And their revolt is doggedly stubborn and dull, all quite the opposite of Hawkes's.

His matchless disrespect for our habitual reading expectations has quite different an effect from that we experience by looking at a piece of bread from many angles for many pages. The difference is playfulness, humor, richness. The best method of expressing Hawkes's richness of language and conception would be to quote for pages. But anyone who has savored the indignant, haughty language of *The Owl* or *The Cannibal*, in which the author constantly undercuts Zizendorf's delightful pomposity, will understand Hawkes's ability to assume a voice and maintain it from cover to cover. The common rhythms of lower-class England are reproduced in *The Lime Twig* with a comic lilt that goes deeper than mere authenticity. The same is true of *The Beetle Leg*, with its dead twang of parody.

A similar depth and sensitivity breathes life into Hawkes's purely creative settings, landscapes with no real counterpart in the conscious world. They are so skillful a mixture of the real and the imagined that readers can barely notice any separations. In *The Cannibal*, the landscape was a suggestion of post-war Germany in ruins, a lifeless legacy of holocaust, decay and dry copulation. It was a mythical, medieval kingdom cleft high in the Italian mountains in *The Owl*, a timeless landscape so barren that walls fell away from the proclamations pasted upon them. In *The Goose on the Grave*, Italy was again the setting, Italy stumbling through war, and in *The Beetle Leg*, vivid glimpses of the rutted American West with its corroded jail, roaming motorcyclists and suspicious ghosts of people moving over the useless dam in which a body is entombed.

The setting of *The Lime Twig* is also packed with significant detail, but the more easily followed narrative has been supported by a more realistic background — though the infernal steam bath, with its imps sloshing cold water from buckets, is a purely imaginative vision of Hell. In *Second Skin*, the modern setting shuttles between a curiously prehistoric Maine coast and the primitive, langorous pleasures of a tropical island that might be in the West Indies chain. Yet as various as these settings may appear, each possesses the particular kind of timeless violence that Hawkes injects into all his locations: "He brought back creation to the shores of the primeval seas where morality, as well as every other problem, loses all meaning," as Camus says of Lautréamont's Maldoror. The same is true of Hawkes, elemental and immoral.

The way in which readers experience a Hawkes narrative is equally elemental. Flannery O'Connor has said that one "suffers [*The Lime Twig*] like a dream." This is true of each of Hawkes's novels. His narratives move with the pace and color of a dream. Something in the dream reassures us; something either draws us on or repels us. Attraction or repulsion: these two violent reactions become suddenly mixed in the narrative as Hawkes writes it. A frustration, a tension, is created in which the reader finds it impossible to judge events and react as he would in consciousness. When Jacopo beats Edouard in the outdoor lavatory in *The Goose on the Grave*, the beating becomes a nightmarish dance, as if two figures were for a moment fatigued boxers, or marathon dancers, holding each other up in a dark, empty stadium.

Lucid colors of the dream are there: "It was true, his eyes did flash, and at one of the more painful blows—it grazed his eyelids—he took heart because he loved color." In this episode of pathetic comedy, the reader learns of Jacopo's presence in the lavatory just as Edouard does; a fragmentary shadow, glint of an ear-ring, odor of Jacopo's breath, a sinister figure heaving through the empty air that for a moment separates them. Silently, with agonizing slowness and deliberate hesitation, the narrative blossoms into a recognition of the fact that Jacopo is beating Edouard, for reasons unknown.

In each of Hawkes's "dreams" is this aspect of hallucination—a blank figure swimming into consciousness, still dream-like in its threat, materializing so indistinctly, we do not know whether to stand or bolt. The dream—what Hawkes calls "the nightly inner schism between the rational and the absurd"—carries in it our obsessions, what we hope and fear. Characters in *The Lime Twig* succumb to a mixture of what they hope for and fear, and readers who try to judge their deaths—Margaret mashed under Thick's rubber billy, Michael pulverized by the race horses, Hencher crushed by the ghostly, white stallion—are faced by the same frustration occasioned by the mixture of attraction and repulsion. Neither saved nor damned, Hawkes's characters are only human, figures to be given life by the author's malice or pity.

If we "suffer" the fiction as a dream, it can be argued, I think, that what we suffer most is the aftermath of the dream, the jarring recapitulation in consciousness, the cold creak of terror that does not disappear with opened eyes. For most of what we dream, we try to rationalize away. Hawkes does not. For him, the dream is the deeper reality; for the terror of experience, not ideas, is the only reality for the gothic writer. His aim is to make the dream a reality on paper without sacrificing its unconscious aspect of terror and indistinctness. What we feel moves us more than what we can prove.

The intense nightmare of *The Cannibal* or "Charivari" is steps away from the haunting narrative of *Second Skin* or *The Owl*, however. The insanity and corruption of characters in *The Beetle Leg,* though no less fierce, are less apparent than in *The Lime Twig,* in which the gangsters' calculated violence seems wittingly natural, easy, full of grace. Yet whatever the degree of terror, one can expect from Hawkes a fixed quantity, a spectrum across which the novelist slides his narrative like a scientist revving up the juice in electrodes in his patient's skull.

Obviously, the effect the aftermath of the dream has on a reader depends on his personal insight and taste. Many readers absolutely wallow in the apparent grotesque of Hawkes's loving sacrifices—the chicken's head torn off, the female hostage slowly beaten to death, the dreamer trampled under flailing hooves, the child bitten by a rattlesnake and left virtually alone to die, the blind Pipistrello smashed and thrown from a cliff by a capricious boulder. The list could continue for pages. Projections of such naked horrors, made so platable by the "demonic sympathy" and elegant detachment and diction, thrill readers abstractly, move them to admire Hawkes's subtle craftsmanship. But, says Hawkes, "mere malice is nothing in itself, of course, and the product of extreme fictive detachment is extreme fictive sympathy."

These same readers savored the coupling of a cow and an idiot in Faulkner's "The Hamlet," or the dwarf taking into his mouth his injured fighting cock's head in "The Day of the Locust." They cheered, perhaps, Maldoror's razor-slashed smile and the ingenious machine that serves up absurd retribution in "The Penal Colony." I suppose the unflinching gaze at purely creative horrors is what makes readers respond with admiration. Certainly, for pure, inventive evil and violence, one would search far to surpass Hawkes's slow description of the Duke cutting up his prey, a child, in *The Cannibal,* or his delicate narration of the brutal knifing of Fernando in *Second Skin.* But Hawkes's novels possess a deeper, less obvious violence, that which is undeclared and potential, like anxiety that hasn't yet the referent of a specific fear.

Extreme repugnance is the other extreme in reactions to Hawkes. A reader looks up from the episode in *The Beetle*

Leg in which Luke hooks a bloated foetus—"God's naked child"—floating in the river, a flaccid bag of unformed guts, and threatens to be sick on the floor: A common reaction to the less palatable horrors of Mr. Hawkes. And surely, both the delight and the revulsion, macabre enjoyment or frank disgust, are entirely compatible with the author's intentions. In each sacrifice is a challenge to the reader to enter into the spirit of the saved and the damned alike. The banality of revulsion, in such a case, is a saving grace.

Sacrifices abound in *The Cannibal*, for example, where readers find their sympathies challenged in astonishing ways. First of all, Germany itself has been sacrificed in a cannibal feast of pride and violence. The "institution" has no function; for the living inhabitants, less lively than the ghosts of this landscape, simply prey on each other in a larger, undeclared institution. Freedom is a worthless caprice. Morality has been bombed out and one man devours his fellow without a hint of rational remorse or disgust.

In this atmosphere, murder and suicide, love and violence lose the distinction of differences. Only primeval urges reign and every question of morality is a dead issue. None of this is explained by the wars, which occur vaguely, a plane which happens to drop into the street killing Stella's mother, the American agent, Leevey, on his motorcycle. It is not history that concerns Hawkes but only its effects that fill the skull of a single character. He shrinks the world, as Guerard suggested, into the skull of one man or woman; the "mass plague" becomes the single experience. The same compression is evident in *The Owl*, in which the fascism of tyrants from antiquity to the present is reflected in the hangman's control over his ironclad monarchy, Sasso Fetore. He controls marriage, death—life.

And in these "worlds" where everything is subject to control and sacrifice, everything is subject to terror. In such a condition, anxiety balloons, and the distinction between what one hopes for and fears, once more, becomes almost pathologically similar. The distorted merging of past and present in *The Cannibal* helps produce this disturbance. Finally a reader must accept it and allow himself to be increasingly led by the hand through these curious landscapes that grow less absurd the longer he inhabits them. By mixing time and conceiving from a viewpoint of extreme distortion, Hawkes forces upon us a fiction to be felt rather than talked about intellectually. He gives power to his voice and surely shares in the might enjoyed by characters such as the hangman, Cap Leech, Zizendorf, Larry.

In *Second Skin,* the roving, amorphous band of wicked potential that were dogs in *The Cannibal* has become a trio of hard-nosed Maine fishermen. The inhuman motor-cycles of *The Beetle Leg* Red Devils become hot-rod automobiles. Undeclared evil, potential violence—these are Hawkes's concerns as he describes the masterful Kissin' Bandits of Company C, AWOL soldiers who descend on the narrator, Skipper, and his daughter after their bus is wrecked in the desert. They hold the father and daughter at gun-point, strip off their uniforms—but leave on helmets—and steal kisses from Cassandra. One expects them to rape her on the spot, and it is a delightful irony that moved Hawkes to create such a humorous violation of Skipper's affection for his daughter.

His humor is similar in the scene during which Skipper, in Maine, is lured from a dance out into the snow and pelted by the fishermen and the sadistic Miranda with snowballs. Fat, a wheezing kind of Walter Mitty, Skipper is blessed with a preciosity and sentimentality. Sexless, withdrawn, neither father nor lover, he guards his daughter with a pathetic kind of loyalty and passion. The fishermen, Bub, Jomo and Red take turns at Cassandra, while the candor of their evil fills Skipper with a paralyzing horror.

They threaten him with a conscienceless wit and single-ness of purpose he cannot possess. In Skipper, Hawkes has articulated much of the indistinct estrangement that kept his readers so distant from Il Gufo. Skipper seems to be Hencher in a naval uniform. Of course, as Larry and his mob went scot free in *The Lime Twig*, the fishermen go scot free in *Second Skin*. Those who come by evil naturally go unpunished in Hawkes's world, where society's "disruptive needs" cannot be reconciled with society's morality. The disruptive needs create their own morality—or the lack of it—and this is the nightmare to be faced which looms constantly in Hawkes's novels. The dogs, the Red Devils, the fishermen in their infernal hot-rod, the rolling boulder that crushes Pipistrello, the phallus-God of Larry and his mob—these are the obsessions, bestial puzzles, portents of malice and indifference, that haunt the fiction of John Hawkes. They are brilliant fictional images of our unmanageable existence, the events and personalities we can never tame to our wishes. They roam in these ruined landscapes and lives with a particular abandon, untamable and enviable, as well as frightful and pitiable.

The mixture of pity and exhilaration in the human condition is recreated with chilling authenticity by Hawkes, who, speaking about the writing of Djuna Barnes, neatly described his own: "Surely there is unpardonable distinction in this kind of writing, a certain incorrigible assumption of a prophetic role in reverse, when the most baffling of unsympathetic attitudes is turned upon the grudges, guilts and renunciations harbored in the tangled seepage of our earliest recollections and originations."

Certainly, Hawkes's laughter is Maldoror's laughter of a mouth slashed by a razor. His is a search into the pit that stops at no amount of terrifying discovery. He is into everything and if there is confusion and blackness in his truth, then it is up to us to find out why, to discover with him both the wit and the blackness in which we all unconsciously partake. His disturbances are those that start cracks creeping out in every human spirit, and perhaps the acceptance of such disturbances will save the spirit from crumbling completely. Admitting everything, rejecting nothing, Hawkes writes from a viewpoint held by few American authors.

In *The Beetle Leg*, the Red Devils, black centaurs in the night, careen through the dead town and streak off into the darkness on their motorcycles. In wonderment, a young boy exclaims, "They had jewels all over them."

"We don't want to hear about it," replies Luke Lampson.

I believe that states the purpose for which John Hawkes writes.

JOHN UPDIKE AND
WILLIAM STYRON:
THE BURDEN OF TALENT

William Van O'Connor

REVIEWERS REFER TO William Styron as "incredibly gifted," "amazingly talented," and to John Updike as "without peer among his contemporaries," or as "endowed with a feeling for language that recalls only the greatest English stylists." Each is used to high praise. And each undoubtedly has had his eye on the golden ring, for either could turn out to be the foremost novelist of his generation. At present, Updike would seem to have the greater promise. Styron simply has no subject; he has enormous talent in search of a subject. Updike has sensitivity and a kind of genius for words, and sometimes they serve only trivialities. His poems, for example, are clever as all hell, but don't amount to much, thus far. Yet he has written one novel, *The Centaur*, which shows that he has a mature sense of humor, of fatuousness, of asininity—and of magnificence. He knows what the fundamental questions are.

i

Faulkner, like Hawthorne, was fascinated by the evil done in the name of righteousness; thus *Light in August*. He was also fascinated by the need to live intensely so that one could willingly be dead a long time; thus *As I Lay Dying*. Hemingway, like Hardy and Conrad, looked out at the world of accident, the forces of decay and irrationality in which the sensitive human being finds himself caught, and he formulated a code of conduct; thus *The Sun Also Rises* and *A Farewell to Arms*. Fitzgerald dreamed a dream of success, of money, and the graces money buys, and he discovered that the dream had another side, that money can destroy conscience, magnanimity, sympathy, love; thus *The Great Gatsby* and *Tender Is the Night*. One must, none the less, confess to an uneasy feeling about all three—each could make a real ass of himself, in or out of print.

These are the big names of the past generation. They know how to formulate fundamental questions. We still have writers who ask such questions. There is J. F. Powers, who, in *Morte D'Urban*, pursues an ancient quarry, man's desire to achieve the pure act of success. Father Urban, intelligent, knowing, moral, saves a deer from drowning, and thereby loses a patron who would provide thousands of dollars for enterprises dear to his heart. When he is in a position, as superior of his order, to rectify all the things so painfully and inefficiently wrong in his eyes, he is struck in the head by the Bishop's golfball, he begins to decline, and soon is beyond caring. Malory's dreams of perfection are, in a sense, reduced to Malory's own story, a man arrested for breaking and entering, and possibly for actions worse than that. Flannery O'Connor's range is less than Powers', but she treats subjects that would be meaningful in any generation. These two writers are immediately recognizable as having a subject, a focus, a sustained point of view, and a theme that is capable of enlargement. This is also true of Bernard Malamud. One knows that such novelists, the question of their ultimate position aside, could continue to grow.

There are also writers like Herbert Gold, or Leslie Fiedler, also talented, who use their gifts to titillate, to show off, to do finger exercises. Jack Kerouac is a kind of teen-ager Whitman, down the open road, looking for Henry Miller and a truck load of brown-bellied girls, working on a California ranch; they pick some sex-symbol fruit, and have a hell of a wild time on the black earth. Salinger seems reduced to picking his sensitive nose in front of the three sided mirror, with members of the Glass family with great sensitivity, in attendance. Carson Mc-Cullers and Truman Capote continue to create oversized ugly hirsute females, who are tormented by waxed midgets. A bizarre tale finds its own way, with a little clever assistance here and there. Norman Mailer, it now appears, never had it as a novelist; he has always wanted to be a pundit, setting everyone straight. James Purdy, on the other hand, has a distinct talent; the question, however, is whether his subject is complex enough to develop or whether he sees enough in it; he may be reduced to finding less and less rewarding situations. And so we go.

ii

Styron started out with great promise, with *Lie Down in Darkness*, and with *The Long March*. With *Set This House Afire* the acclaim continued, but with growing reservations. Updike has written three novels, *The Poorhouse Fair*, *Rabbit, Run* and *The Centaur*, and the acclaim continues. Of the two Styron is the more florid, the more rhetorical, in the Southern way, and Updike is more neatly clever, with language, with asides, in the *New Yorker* way. He also shows greater promise—he grows.

Updike's *The Poorhouse Fair* is a narrow-gauge story, quietly yet effectively done. The story concerns a county poorhouse, its inmates, its prefect, and visitors to the annual Fair. The building housing the inmates is a decayed Victorian mansion. In the cupola, three or four stories high, Conner, the rationalistic, ambitious, idealistic homosexual prefect has his office. He sees himself as a scientifically minded director of his elderly, sickly, and indigent charges. Because he envisions future and better positions with the federal government, he wants to be successful as prefect. Therefore he attempts to institutionalize the lives of the inmates. For example, he puts name tags on chairs, claiming this gives each individual his or her chair. The inmates know better—it gives each of them a tag or number; they resent his busy work.

The entire action takes place on the day of the Fair.

During the afternoon there is rain. Conner joins the inmates, wanting to show them his charity and chumminess. They resist him, and as the rain continues their resentment, like the humidity, increases. Finally the rain stops. Outside, as Conner is bent over, one of the inmates, Gregg, slightly intoxicated, throws a stone at him. The others also pelt him. Trying not to display wrath or lose his dignity, Conner walks off.

Gregg, dour, obscene and mean-spirited, resents being seventy—and makes Conner, whom he constantly curses, the symbol of everything that offends him. He is typical of most of his fellows, except for Hook, a ninety-year-old ex-school teacher, who has salvaged a few aphorisms and a sense of day by day well-being from his experiences. If the book has a "hero" it is Hook. "He stood motionless, half in moonlight, groping after the fitful shadow of the advice he must impart to Conner, as a bond between them and a testament to endure his dying in the world. What was it?"

Updike's elderly indigents have few comforts, and mostly don't even want those. They want to be themselves, unorganized, experiencing the days or years left to them. Being poor, they have few illusions about their eminence or significance in the social order. The visitors to the Fair seek power, sexual encounters, and money. These three—power, sex, money—compose their dream of the world and their roles in it. There is symbolic cat, with a broken leg and crushed face—it had been hit on the highway—which Conner orders destroyed. Despite its suffering, the cat had simply "asked" to be let alone. The elderly poor, externally broken, also ask to be let alone. They have only their integrity—but that is more than Conner and most of the visitors have.

iii

E. M. Forster said that one of the advantages of fiction over life is that in fiction life is made to take on formal patterns, themes are tested dramatically by the opposition of characters who represent a point of view or way of life; for example, the Schlegel sisters and the Wilcoxes work out Forster's dialectic. Many, perhaps most encounters in life, have an air of meaninglessness, or even fatuousness, because there is no one theme under examination, and the participants have not agreed on the need for, or the nature of, a dialectic. Emotions, feelings, moods carry us through the day. Each of us has his dream, and, walking in a world of fortuitous events, does his best to live it. Forster implies the fictional Schlegel sisters and the Wilcoxes are more stable than we are.

John Updike's characters in *Rabbit, Run* can hardly be said to be participants in a dialectic. Mostly they *feel*. This in a passage in *Rabbit, Run* describing the feelings of Rabbit Angstrom after he has made love with Ruth, whom he had met that evening for the first time:

> . . . The more awake he gets the more depressed he is. From deep in the pillow he stares at the horizontal strip of stained-glass church window that shows under the window shade. Its childish brightness seems the one kind of comfort left to him.
>
> Light from behind the closed bathroom door tints the air in the bedroom. The splashing sounds are like the sounds his parents would make when as a child Rabbit would waken to realize they had come upstairs, that the whole house would soon be dark, and the sight of morning would be his next sensation. He is asleep when like a faun in moonlight Ruth, washed, creeps back to his side, holding a glass of water.

Like the protagonist in *Catcher in the Rye*, whom he resembles, Rabbit *runs*. Coming home from work—he demonstrates Magi-Peelers—he stops to play basketball in an alley. Characteristically, he is not concerned with the reactions of the kids to his intruding himself. He likes to show off his skill, and remembers frequently that in his first high-school game he made twenty-three points. He finds his wife Janice, swollen in pregnancy, sitting behind a locked door, watching the Mousketeers on T.V. and drinking an Old Fashioned. She has many anxieties, and he no longer finds her pretty. She asks for a cigarette. He says he has given them up. She asks whether he thinks he's a saint. A quarrel develops. He goes out, to pick up their son who is at his grandparents, Rabbit's own parents. Disgust and frustration have been building in him. From outside his parents' house he sees the boy, his parents, and his sister—

> His mother's glasses glitter as she leans in from her place at the table with a spoon of smoking beans at the end of her fat curved arm. Her face shows more of the worry she must be feeling about why nobody comes for the boy. . . . His father, fresh from work, . . . The new teeth he got last year have changed his face, collapsed it a fraction of an inch. Miriam, dolled up in gold and set for Friday night, picks at her food indifferently.

Not seeming to have come to a decision, Rabbit takes off down the street. He finds his car, bought from his father-in-law, for $1000, a real bargain, because old man Springer didn't want the embarrassment of a son-in-law driving around in a '36 Buick. Rabbit drives off, out of town, from highway to highway, experiencing the twilight, mountains, fear over being pursued, exhilaration, eating a juicy hamburger, then hours later he parks in front of the apartment of Mr. Tothers, who had been his basketball coach. In the morning he catches Tothers coming out. Tothers, half-homosexual, defeated, and full of sententiousness, lets him sleep in his warm, unmade bed. That evening they go out with two tarts, and Rabbit goes home with one, Ruth, who needs $15 to pay the rent. On it goes, with Rabbit *running*.

Rabbit is given plenty of canned Advice: "Learn to understand your talents!" "The *sacredness* of achievement." "That's a harsh thing to say of any human soul." "This tragedy, terrible as it is, has at last united you in a sacred way." Tothers and Eccles, the Episcopal minister, say these and other things to Rabbit, who remains impervious to such appeals. At the end, after he has unintentionally contributed to his son's death—Janice in an alcoholic stupor, has allowed the child to drown—Rabbit is still *experiencing*, still *feeling*. "His hands lift of their own and he feels the wind on his ears even before his heels, hitting heavily on the pavement at first but with an effortless gathering out of a kind of sweet panic growing higher and quicker and quieter, he runs. Ah: runs. Runs."

Presumably, Updike is not saying that Rabbit Angstrom is following the only honest course in rejecting the sententious platitude offered him. The novel catches many little ironies—Rabbit's notion that he is praising his coach when he is praising himself, or the minister's wanting a glass of water while consoling Mrs. Springer, and many others, Human motives and actions show a welter of inconsistencies. But there are certain consistencies: Eccles is something of an ass, but he does help certain people; Ruth, the prostitute, is quite capable of loyalty and devotion, and, in her own way, maintains her self-respect. Janice is terribly weak, but she wants to make a go of her marriage. Tothers is a dirty old man, physically and mentally, but he'd prefer not to be, and his advice is on the side of the angels. The novel seems not to be saying that man's moral gestures are all fraudulent. It could even be saying, with Auden, *Love your crooked neighbor with your crooked heart.*

Structurally, and stylistically, *Rabbit, Run* is skillfully handled. The action is in the present tense—Rabbit *feels*, Rabbit *sees*, Rabbit *touches* . . . Sometimes he remembers but he does not reflect. Updike explores physical details with great sensitivity. A woman's round pink bottom after a steaming shower, the faint sickish odor of a recently slept-in bed, a child's dismay in biting cherry-covered chocolate, and a thousand other touches. Updike also has a fine sense of metaphor.

Rabbit, Run is about life in its dingier aspects. The people are little people. No weighty theme is explored. In lieu of that, there are acutely observed scenes, insights into character, and a sense of awe at the mystery of human sensibilities—all in an everyday world of Magi-Peelers, T.V., cars, gas stations, cheap restaurants, and furniture bought on a credit plan. John O'Hara has been praised for catching lower middle-class life in a small Pennsylvania town, Gibbsville. Updike does it much better.

In *The Centaur*, his latest novel, he gives promise of becoming a writer of considerable stature. He appears to be very knowledgeable, and it is hard to know, in reading *The Centaur*, how much he is concerned with guiding the tale or in showing us the tale as it *found* him. Mr. Updike, of course, is not the first novelist to reach out knowingly to the Greek myths for analogies, for characters, and stories. *Ulysses* is the great example. Robert Graves has spelled much of all this out in *The White Goddess*. "The Syrian Moon-goddess was also represented so, with a snake-head to remind the Devotee that she was Death in disguise, and a lion crouched watchfully at her feet. The poet is in love with the White Goddess, with Truth: his heart breaks with love and longing for her." He says "the theme . . . the one grand theme . . . is the life, death, and resurrection of the spirit, of the Year." Recently Miss Caroline Gordon, studying *The Young Lovell*, *Parade's End*, and *The Good Soldier*, all representative of the best of Ford's novels, show that he too was in pursuit of the goddess, following her in fascination, as he followed his own death.

The ancient tales have another advantage; they lift us over the accidents of the affluent world in which, willy-nilly, and fatuously, we find ourselves. Joyce and Eliot sought other civilizations to set a norm against which to see their own and to take its measure. Presumably Updike's *The Centaur* is an effort to get away from Shillington, Penn., or, better, to stay there and yet be able to view it from a distant time and place.

By and large, *The Centaur* is successful. *Rabbit, Run* presents a humanity that is pitiful, yet hardly pitiable; it is the foreground of a Breughel scene—with no redemptive lights in the distant valley or on a nearby river; there is no effort to justify or to redeem. *The Centaur* in a series of Breughel scenes, more heightened. Zimmerman, the principal of the high school, is a bottom pincher, and carries on an affair with a female member of the school board: in the summer, they "do it" outside, but in the winter they "do it" in his office. Pimply adolescents show each other pornographic pictures, for example, of the position vulgarly known as 69, etc. One protagonist, G. W. Caldwell, a high-school teacher, is the Centaur; he suffers from mucinous colitis. A middle-aged hitchhiker talks in this fashion to Caldwell and his fifteen-year-old son:

> "Buddy, that's horse poop," the hitchhiker said, lurching into intimacy. "Just keep the burgers thin's all the bastards run these suckin' joints give a dick about. Give 'em grease and spare the meat; if I had one of those bastards gimme the word I had a hundred. The great god Dollar's the only one they're looking out for. Christ I wouldn't drink the nigger piss they call coffee."

And there are many similar scenes and characters.

Caldwell, the high-school teacher, was the son of a minister; he has experienced poverty, the Depression; put himself, with some distinction, through a small college; and he supports his family, not well but as well as he can manage. Teaching and coaching are drudgery, and he is in constant fear of being dismissed. He is not a good disciplinarian, but he is a good teacher, and students depend on him and love him. Constantly he deprecates himself, as an ironic stance to minimize opposition, but also out of humility and kindness. The narrator, his son, is, when he writes the book, an artist in New York, a nice, decent human being, but no great shakes as an artist. He knows his father struggled to keep going, day after petty day, to give him, "the kid," a better chance, and he asks, "Was it worth it?" The reader answers for him, "Yes, it was worth it!" and he agrees that Caldwell's legend should be as follows:

> But it was still needful that a life should be given to expiate that ancient sin,—the theft of fire. It happened that Chiron, noblest of all the Centaurs (who are half horses and half men), was wandering the world in agony from a wound that he had received by strange mischance. For, at

a certain wedding-feast among the Lapithae of Thessaly, one of the turbulent Centaurs had attempted to steal away the bride. A fierce struggle followed, and in the general confusion, Chiron, blameless as he was, had been wounded by a poisoned arrow. Ever tormented with the hurt and never to be healed, the immortal Centaur longed for death, and begged that he might be accepted as an atonement for Prometheus. The gods heard his prayer and took away his pain and his immortality. He died like any wearied man, and Zeus set him as a shining archer among the stars.
—Old Greek Folk Stories Told Anew,
by Josephine Preston Peabody, 1897

Updike doesn't hesitate to intrude the legendary names —Zeus, Hermes, Poseidon, Medusa, Daedalus, *et al.* He even includes a mythological index for clues. Perhaps this is in part awkward, and infelicitous. Awkward and infelicitous or not, it enables Updike to see G. W. Caldwell against ancient stories, to compare his strength and weakness with the strength and weakness of the gods, his love with their loves—their mutual pursuit of the White Goddess. In his way, Caldwell deserves the place Zeus reserved for him as a shining archer among the stars.

iv

Lie Down in Darkness is written in the convention now known as the Southern novel; it would be a very different novel from what it is if Faulkner had not written *The Sound and the Fury* and other novels. It is set in Virginia. One of Quentin Compson's memories is of being on a train going south, and passing through Virginia. "He [an old Negro, with a mule] stood there beside the gaunt rabbit of a mule, the two of them shabby and motionless and unimpatient. The train swung around the curve, the engine puffing with short heavy blasts. Then the train started to move. I leaned out the window, into the cold air, looking back." Quentin says he then knew he was in the South, home. On the second page of *Lie Down in Darkness* there is this:

Now the sun is up and you can see the mist lifting off the fields and in the middle of the fields the solitary cabins with their slim threads of smoke winding out of plastered chimneys and the faint glint of fire through an open door, at a crossing, the sudden, swift tableau of Negro and his hay-wagon and a lop-eared mule: the Negro with his mouth agape, exposing pink gums, staring at the speeding train until the smoke obscures him, too, from view, and the one dark-brown hand held cataleptic in the air.

The dramatis personae is Faulknerian too. Peyton Loftis, spoiled by her father, is something of a bitch. She commits suicide, and the arrival of her coffin in Port Warwick is the occasion for the lives of the various characters, some of them following the casket to the cemetery, to be examined (in structure the action is not unlike *As I Lay Dying*). There are Milton Loftis and his wife, Helen. Loftis is a combination of Jason Compson III, father of the Quentin who commits suicide, and Horace Benbow. He drinks a great deal, and he has an affair with a married woman named Dolly, who is reminiscent of Belle, with whom Benbow has his affair. Helen, pious and self-righteous, is rather like Mrs. Compson, except that she is a good hater, and occasionally has flashes of insight into her own nature. Maudie, the sister of Peyton, is the incubus in the family, and might suggest the burden that Benjy is.

If the novel has a center, it is in Helen and Milton Loftis. On her wedding day, the troubled and distraught Peyton says to her mother:

> You know, I suspect you've always hated me for one thing or another, but lately I've become a symbol to you you couldn't stand. Do you think I'm stupid or something, that I haven't got you figured out? You hate men, you hated Daddy for years, and the sad thing is that he hasn't known it. And the terrible thing is that you hate yourself so much that you just don't hate men or Daddy but you hate everything, animal, vegetable and mineral. Especially you hate me. Because I've become that symbol.

Peyton adds that her mother would like her to marry some boy from town who works in the shipyards, so Peyton could live in a little bungalow. "You'd have your claws in me then. I'd be obeying your precious code of Christian morality, which is phony anyway. But it's not the way. I'm free and you can't stand it." Loftis loves Peyton, almost incestuously, and his tenderness and affection for her lead him into deeper and deeper bouts of drunkenness, during which he usually makes an ass of himself. Between them, Helen and Loftis contribute to Peyton's despair and death.

The scenes preceding her death described in the penultimate chapter, are reminiscent of Quentin Compson's death in Cambridge. Here is one:

> He's soft and tender, I thought, is my Harry and how does it go: bind him with cowslips and bring him home. But it's decreed that I shall never find him. When I was a little girl I had the earache and Bunny [her father] held my legs and Mr. Lewis, up the street, held my arms and Dr. Holcomb stuck a thing in my ear to puncture it: I'd scream out loud it hurt so, and she said poor Peyton, poor little Peyton, but did it really hurt so much, did you have to scream: then she and Bunny got in an argument: I went to sleep then with a fever. I dreamed of a fat woman sitting down on me and then of a little boy in a field picking a violet. "Here you are young lady. You just take these and then go straight to a doctor. Hear me?" "Yes," I said. . . . "Thank you," I said. "Thank you very much. Which way is Cornelia Street?"

Like Quentin, she has become obsessed with time, and as she goes about, feverishly, out of her head, she carries a clock. And like Quentin, she is a victim of her family's sickness.

The Negroes, believing Christians, are stable. This is one scene:

> . . . A band began to play, brassy, jubilant—and a big bass drum.
> "Happy am I!" the crowd was singing.
> *Thump*
> "In my Redeemer!"
> "Happy am I!"
> "I am so happy!"
> *Thump*

"Those Negroes," Mr. Casper said, "are having some kind of revival or something. We'll have to detour down that road." Like Dilsuy they are a kind of chorus back of the action of the sick and troubled Loftis family. Helen Loftis is a faithful communicant, and despises Milton because he doesn't go to church. She sometimes takes her worries, and troubled hatreds—it troubles her that she hates her daughter Peyton—to the Reverend Carey Carr, who, except for Hightower, is close to Faulkner's views of ministers, rigid, narrow-minded and rather stupid. Religion, in *Lie Down in Darkness*, and as in *The Sound and the Fury*, once gave man his reason for enduring, for laboring, and for loving. The religion of Helen's father, a colonel in the cavalry, is almost empty. He would, she thought as she saw him in church, singing vigorously, destroy the devil after he finished destroying the huns. Peyton and her father have not even that kind of faith. The generations have no message to pass along to their successors. Loftis' father (sounding like an optimistic Jason III) says "I do not intend to presume upon your good judgment, a faculty which I believe you possess in abundance inherited not from me but from your sainted mother, so as you go out into the world I can only admonish you with the words of the Scotchman, videlicet, keep your chin up and your kilts down and let the wind blow." He also spoiled his son, partly by sending him to the University when he was seventeen. By the end of his first year he was already a sot. During World War I Loftis managed to stay on Governor's Island, where he met Helen. The story of the Loftis family, as Peyton interprets it for her first lover, is this. "I am sick," she says, "of hearing about my father's generation as the lost generation. They weren't lost. They were losing us." Like *The Sound and the Fury* and many another novel, *Lie Down in Darkness* is concerned with the failure of Christianity, or with the inability of two generations, or more, to credit its validity.

In structure, *Lie Down in Darkness* is in the impressionist tradition of *The Secret Agent, Lord Jim, The*

Sound and the Fury, Absalom, Absalom! or *The Wild Palms*. Present action is in the foreground, and shades off into earlier scenes, events, and memories. Chronology exists only in terms of the present impressions of a character. There are flashbacks, and the story winds on, in circular fashion, or forward and back, until the theme, and even the whole subject, stands still, and the novel is over, static and understandable, because then, at last, shadow, comment, image, and memory have merged into one unified and comprehensible action.

Skillfully constructed and beautifully written, *Lie Down in Darkness* remains pastiche. It demonstrates the impact of Faulkner's work on a gifted younger writer. Understandably, Styron, in *The Long March*, and *Set This House Afire*, tried to get away from the conventions of the Southern novel. *The Long March*, an extended short story, not a novel, is, for Styron, tautly written. As with his other work, it is a pleasure to read; it is excellently paced and exciting. But on the morning after, one wonders what it adds up to. Random House put it into the Modern Library, then dropped it—and the moral would seem to be that the reading public didn't believe it was that *kind* of a book.

Set This House Afire again exhibits Styron's control of language. This is a description of a square in Rome, where the narrator is sitting, drinking a glass of beer:

> For a while after this the square was deserted. Once a cat loped across my gaze with squint-eyed piratical look and a suave grin. Bent on who knows what unholy mission, he cruised up over the fountain steps, a yellow blur, and plunged dauntless into the shadows. Then all was serene and decorous once more, the heavens clear, starry, the air aromatic with blossoms, the fountains leaking slow trickling notes of water, like memorandum. I sat until the bell struck again, when the waiter came near, insinuating with a yawn the lateness of the hour.

The control almost threatens to flow over into self-parody, and perhaps it does. The story itself goes on and on, and the reader, half hypnotized by the sentences, only slowly realizes that little of any significance is going on. Perhaps Styron felt this too, and hoped that more pages, more descriptions, and more clever dialogue would transmogrify themselves into a self-contained and meaningful novel.

The narrator is from Port Warwick, Virginia, the setting for most of *Lie Down in Darkness*. For a part of the novel, he takes us on a tour of the town, noting the changes, and letting his father, while driving in a perilous manner, carry on about Eisenhower, cellophane, the disintegration of morals, and so on, none of which has any relevance to the main action, which is set in Italy. The narrator has been working there, in a government job. Why Italy? Apparently because of the scenery, and the full-bosomed, round-bottomed peasant girls, who are described in masterly detail.

At a poorish private school in Virginia, the narrator had known a boy named Mason Flagg (what a name!), the son of a successful Hollywood producer, who is now trying to be a gentleman in Virginia, and an alcoholic mother, named Wendy. Mason has been thrown out of a number of schools, because, despite an I.Q., he says, of 156, he rarely studies and his sexual mores are out of keeping with those allowed by the authorities. He is kicked out of one school because he gets a feeble-minded thirteen-year-old drunk and then seduces her. When the girl's father comes to the Flagg estate to protest, Mr. Flagg runs him off, saying he'll have a check sent to salve the man's hurt feelings. Through this sort of thing, young Mason moves with an air of ennui, and bravado.

When next we meet Mason Flagg, he is in New York, carrying on in his fashion, taking part in sexual orgies, and yet giving promise, so we are told but not shown, of great talent for writing plays. Our next encounter is in Italy, where he is cavorting with a Hollywood group that is making a movie. Rosemary, a nympho, suffers his sadistic abuse for the sometimes privilege of sleeping with him. Mason Flagg is a thorough-going s.o.b., and delights in causing an alcoholic painter, Cass Kinsolving (these names!), to degrade himself by reciting stories on the level of "Dan McGrew." When he is in a drunken state, Cass has no shame, and willingly, even eagerly, suffers the humiliation in exchange for a bottle. His good wife Polly and his many children suffer all this because, well, at bottom he's a good Joe, and besides they love him.

Cass is said to be a talented painter, and we learn about his sojourn in Paris, and the months in Italy. There are two juicy Italian girls, one of whom, Francesca, is in love with Cass. Sometimes she poses, in the nude, for him, but because she is so lovely, so innocent, so seductive, he resists going to bed with her. (Sometimes the logic of these things gets a bit confused.) Anyway, she steals food from the Mason kitchen for her dying father. Nasty old Mason forces her into a bedroom and deflowers her. When he tries to rape her a second time, she lets him have it, you know where, with her knee. Later Francesca is raped again, by a local looney, who also beats her brutally, so that she will die. Cass chooses to believe that Mason was again the villain, and thus he has two good reasons for murdering his erstwhile chum. Mason Flagg must die, and die he does, under the heavy stone that Cass uses to open his skull, and let the whitish brains drip.

We learn much of all this when the narrator, Peter Leverett, visits good old Cass at his home in Charleston, S. C. They have a number of fine bull sessions, recalling livelier days in Italy. Cass is off the sauce, and painting well. He's regenerated, and highly affirmative about things: "The one thing I did know was that to choose between them was simply to choose being, not for the sake of being, or even the love of being, much less the desire to be forever—but in the hope of being what I could be for a time. This would be ecstasy. God knows it would."

One has to conclude, simply, that it is a shame that someone as gifted and talented as William Styron has no subject, and falls back on rhetoric. Dreiser, as we all know, had an awful time with the English sentence, but he managed because he had something he wanted to say. Styron is about as gifted a stylist as anyone now writing, but apparently has nothing important to say. Updike, on the other hand, has a subject. His second novel was better than his first, and his third was better than the second. If the gods continue to favor him he should have a magnificent future.

RECHY AND GOVER

Terry Southern

RECHY AND GOVER form an interesting juxtaposition, because the only thing they would seem to have in common,
aside from their youth and their use of the first-person
narrative, is a creativeness that is undeniably genuine and
is perhaps unique to each. Broadly speaking, Rechy's work
may be said to belong to the self-revelatory school of
Romantic Agony, while Gover's, less readily classified, is so
remarkably disciplined that, at its most imaginatively
developed, it is entirely devoid of sentiment. In other
words, one is attempting to relate opposites; yet each is
totally contemporary, in both content and technique, and
comparison is invited—if only as opportunity for considering ideal representations of two current literary extremes in America.

Romantic Agony, in the great tradition of Rimbaud and
Baudelaire, may be likened to the manic-depressive syn-
drome in abnormal psychology; in order to be genuine, the
human emotional range has got to be traversed completely,
from elation to anguish. Each "yea" must be matched by
an equally strong "nay"; otherwise it is mere eccentricity,
in terms of psychology—or, in terms of literature, simply
pap. Until recently, with the American publication of
Miller's *Tropics*, Romantic Agony had not had a fair shake
in this country, doubtless because its negative aspects were
inherently so offensive to a puritanical culture, and its
authors, for whatever reason, were so lax in insisting upon
them. In any case, it is apparent that our strongest

romantic writers—Whitman, Wolfe, Sandburg—had the "nay" edited right out of them; and whether this occurred in their own cradles or on the publisher's desk, would seem irrelevant, the salient fact being that for many years this sort of emasculated romanticism was taken very seriously indeed, reaching its intolerable nadir only with the extreme abuses practiced by William Saroyan. With the American acceptance of Henry Miller's *Tropics* however, we have wiped the slate clean, because this is the *summum bonum*, though somewhat dated now, of Romantic Agony, balancing every ecstatic ejaculation or mystic transcendence with a howl of sheer pain or disgust. John Rechy's work is solidly, even aggressively, in this tradition; if it seems to be "cooler," that is simply a matter of current fashion, the crucial thing being its strict adherence to the basic mandate of its school: *"Feel everything and leave nothing unsaid."* Naturally this often leads to an embarrassing amount of overstatement, subjectivity, and a complete lack of craftsmanship—sometimes all in the same breath, as, for example, when the narrator of *City of Night* refers to the death of his father: "And throughout the days that followed—and will follow forever—I will discover him in my memories, and hopelessly—through the infinite miles that separate life from death—try to understand his torture: in searching out the shape of my own."

The phrase "in searching out the shape of my own" is the single carefully literary construction in the paragraph, and is one of the very few in the entire book. The rest is, à la Wolfe and Kerouac, straight off the top of the head—but this is, of course, the real strength of such work: the relentless, almost schizoid integrity of self-revelation, the absence of conscious artifice. Even during extremes of self-indulgence, when giving himself over wholly to his infatuation with the styles of other writers (principally Wolfe and Genet) it seems to be done quite without guile. The real probability is that those things which are generally thought of as literary faults and weaknesses, when they occur in first-person narratives have the subliminal effect of suggesting the *honesty* of the narrator, which is undoubtedly the greatest asset one can bring to that form. For example, there is the sharpest difference in credibility between the first-person narrative of a Henry Miller story and that of a Somerset Maugham story. We immediately assume that one is "autobiographical" and that the other is "fictional." This is strictly a matter of *style*, quite aside from what either may *purport* to be, and the crucial factor is that Miller's narrator will shock, disgust, meander, and bore you to tears, whereas Maugham's is extremely careful not to. What lends Miller's narration credence then is our conditioned knowledge that it is only in *real life* that story-tellers shock, disgust, meander, and bore—not in literature, authors are too artful for that. So Miller's narrator emerges as a real person, and Maugham's as an imaginary one. The quality of *credibility* is of first importance to a book like *City of Night*, because we are being taken into an unfamiliar world, that of the male-prostitute, and we need to feel that we are being told the truth about it. When, for example, the narrator relates his first meeting with Miss Destiny, "a youngman possibly 20 but quite possibly 18 and very probably 25," and describes him ("her") as having turned his eyes "alternately coyly and coldly at Chuck then me seductively: all of which you will recognize as the queen's technique to make you feel like such an irresistible so masculine so sexual so swinging stud, and queens can do it better than most real girls, queens being Uninhibited," then the reader *does*, in fact, want to "recognize this as the queen's technique." The notion of a homosexual being able to flirt more effectively "than most real girls" is something that has never been stated except on the most ludicrously subjective level; the explanation though ("queens being Uninhibited"—complete even to emphazing the secret *x*-factor by capitalizing it) strikes one immediately as truth. It is the kind of truth however which can only obtain after the narrator has convinced us that he has *nothing to gain or lose* by telling it. And then we believe it absolutely, and in so doing we receive an insight (or a very satisfactory illusion of one) into a world of which we may otherwise be ignorant throughout our lives. Such convincing glimpses of a reality other than our own are extremely rare and are to be cherished; they are what give literature of the romantics its worth.

Robert Gover, of course, works the other side of the street. Very few books have been written with such extraordinary care as *One Hundred Dollar Misunderstanding*. It is probably the most successful presentation of two distinct points of view since *The Sound and the Fury*. And somewhat like Faulkner, but very much unlike Rechy, Gover is at great pains to keep his own feelings well out of it. If we do recognize where his sympathy lies, it would seem to be in the nature of the tale itself—after all, who *wouldn't* empathize more with a fourteen-year-old Negro prostitute than with one of our typically Babbitt college sophomores? The fact is, of course, that this novel is the most devastating indictment of American middle-class mentality written in many years. "They all sittin roun some ol table an lookin an talkin like somebody dyin. They jes a-sittin roun talkin sad," is about as abruptly definitive as it is possible to be. Here Kitten (the fourteen-year-old Negro prostitute) is describing one of our in-depth television panels on global affairs, but the words are certainly more comprehensive than that; they seem to embrace every bit of pious hard-sell that infests our social and political existence. The notion that pulling a long face and mouthing a lot of patriotic, hygienic, God-loving, anti-communist, regular guy, chamber-of-commerce gobbledygook is the same as "being serious" is surely the curse peculiar to our time and place. Gover takes this dream apart, cliché by cliché—and without seeming to care; and therein lies his craft and subtle art. In other words, if Rechy is singing Wagner, Gover is whistling Bach. *City of Night* tells us, in a sustained and melodic scream, what is wrong with our world and how to cure it ("love and understanding"). Gover suggests, almost musingly, that there is no possibility of either; and any such tantalizing glimmer is immediately doused. At the very moment when one might expect our young Babbitt, J. C. Holland, to drop on his knees in gratitude to the girl for a degree of enlightenment, he will say something like: "I mean she was incapable of profound feelings. She was quite obviously a shallow woman who lived a tremendously fast life, and being a professional lady, what harm could I do her?" This inherent wrongness and eternal cross-purpose of things is the thesis developed even more elaborately, though less effectively, in his second novel, *The Maniac Responsible*. This is a book however, which, despite its monumental ambition (to prove that under conducive circumstances, *anyone* is capable of murder), is so crippled by allowing event to dominate character and so flagrantly derivative (of Faulkner) in style, that it was almost bound to fail.

> What I do not understand is why, in the name of infinite orderliness, should there be this madness to mate madness. Why must I crave the lovely form and motion of her and despise the reflection of us in her, the babbling of the company policy you fools dish up to support a bargaining point? And it is a bargaining point, because if my less succeeds, I'll have my fill of filling her and be gone from her in less than a month, satisfied. But I cannot allow her holding off to suppress me, nor repress me, or she will end up my master.

Etc., etc. One cannot read this sort of thing page after page without beginning to doubt the very existence of the character, nor indeed without becoming completely distracted from the story at hand and simply waiting for Gavin Stevens to pop out from behind that mask. It is all well and good for Rechy to imitate Wolfe, because the world he laments (and praises) is weird and engaging enough to make anything believable—that is to say, the *events* in *City of Night* are so outlandish that character is automatically subordinate to them, and moreover is automatically acceptable after the initial disarming honesty is laid down. In *The Maniac Responsible* however, the events, despite their sensational implications, are commonplace. To give creative credence to the commonplace—that is, to *experience* it, rather than be aware of merely *reading* it—the voice behind must be *personal*, not *literary*. Had Gover written this book in the first person, it might well have been a masterpiece. For his third novel, not yet published, he has returned to the format of choice, the first-person narrative and the same two characters. Young Holland has now "completed his education," has a $10,000-a-year job (which his father got him) and is "investigating" a $2,000 social-aid fund which he suspects of being in some way subversive. The idea of his being paid $10,000 to investigate $2,000 is dead on, and would seem to hold great promise indeed. Kitten, naturally, turns up during the course of the investigation. One may hope this is the second of many sequels—perhaps in the end Kitten and J. C. will begin to understand and accept one another, or, more likely, the reader may begin to understand and accept himself, which, in Gover's own words ("I'm concerned with addressing and pleasing readers who want to own what's inside their own skins") is, after all, the idea.

Hoffman—Saul Bellow's Fiction

1. Isaac Bashevis Singer, *Gimpel the Fool and Other Stories* (New York: Noonday Press, 1957), p. 14.

2. "A Discipline of Nobility: Saul Bellow's Fiction," reprinted from the *Kenyon Review*, 24 (Spring, 1962), 203–26, in *Recent American Fiction: Some Critical Views*, ed. Joseph Waldmeir (Boston: Houghton Mifflin, 1963), pp. 121–38. This is the best study of Bellow's work I have so far discovered.

3. *The Myth of Sisyphus*, tr. Justin O'Brien (New York: Knopf, 1955), pp. 124–38.

4. *Recent American Fiction*, p. 134

5. "Distractions of a Fiction Writer," in *The Living Novel: A Symposium*, ed. Granville Hicks (New York: Macmillan, 1957), pp. 14–15.

6. For a discussion of the last two terms, see G. J. Goldberg's essay on *The Adventures of Augie March* in *Critique*, 3 (Summer, 1960), p. 20.

7. *Dangling Man* (London, John Lehmann, 1946). Originally published, New York, Vanguard Press, 1944.

8. See Chester Eisinger, *Fiction of the Forties* (Chicago: University of Chicago Press, 1963), p. 346: Joseph "cannot reconcile his two worlds, and he cannot exist as a whole man with dignity in the real world." Like other statements, this one comes under the classification of what Eisinger calls a "useful oversimplification"; I fail to see why an over-simplification is useful. In any case, in Eisinger's book, Bellow is made again and again to serve a reductive meaning and purpose.

9. "Bellow's Dangling Men," *Critique*, 3 (Summer, 1961), p. 5.

10. *The Victim* (New York: Vanguard Press, 1947).

11. Eisinger (p. 350) says that "Schlossberg is in the novel to represent the concept of humanity that Bellow generally advances in his work and to provide a scale against which we may measure Asa's failure, as he himself does." This may be true in a limited sense, but it ignores the fact that Asa's world is much more fully represented than Schlossberg's, that we know very little about Schlossberg and therefore have to take Asa's word for him. It is a foreshortened judgment, like several in Eisinger's treatment of Bellow.

12. Goldberg, p. 18.

13. *The Adventures of Augie March* (New York: Viking, 1953).

14. See his statement in *The Living Novel*, p. 15.

15. *Henderson the Rain King* (New York: Viking, 1959).

16. He concludes by bringing a Persian child back with him to America.

17. *Seize the Day* (New York: Viking, 1956).

18. This essay is unfortunately written before Bellow's new novel, *Herzog* (due for publication in the fall of 1964) is available. I much regret not being in a position to comment upon it.

Webb—World of Jack Kerouac

1. *The Town and the City* includes both worlds. The "beat" works, in order of publication are: *On the Road* (New York: The Viking Press, 1957); *The Subterraneans* (New York: Grove Press, Inc., 1958); *The Dharma Bums* (New York: The Viking Press, Inc., 1958); *Tristessa* (New York: Avon Book Division—The Hearst Corp., 1960); and *Excerpts from Visions of Cody* (New York: New Directions, 1960). The "Lowell" works, in order of publication, are: *Doctor Sax* (New York: Grove Press, Inc., 1959); *Maggie Cassidy* (New York: Avon Book Division—The Hearst Corp., 1959); and *Visions of Gerard* (New York: Farrar, Straus and Cudahy, 1963). *Big Sur* (New York: Farrar, Straus and Cudahy, 1962), which is discussed briefly in the concluding paragraphs of this study, is in a separate category. References in the text are to these editions.

Other works by Kerouac are: *Mexico City Blues* (New York: Grove Press, Inc., 1959); *The Scripture of the Golden Eternity* (New York: Totem Press in association with Corinth

Books, 1960); *Lonesome Traveler* (New York: McGraw-Hill, 1960); *Pull My Daisy*, text ad-libbed by Jack Kerouac for the film by Robert Frank and Alfred Leslie (New York: Grove Press, Inc., 1961); and *Book of Dreams* (San Francisco: City Lights Books, 1961). I have been unable to locate any information regarding *Desolation Angels*, which is listed in Kerouac's last two books as being among his works.

2. Clellon Holmes, "This Is the Beat Generation," *New York Times Magazine*, Nov. 16, 1952, p. 10. See also Jack Kerouac, "The Origins of the Beat Generation," *Playboy*, VI (June, 1959), p. 32.

3. "This Is the Beat Generation."

4. The items referred to or quoted are *New World Writing: Seventh Mentor Selection* (New York, 1955), pp. 7–16 (two other sections of *On the Road* appeared in *Paris Review* in 1955 and in *New Directions 16* in 1957, but neither section uses the term "beat generation"); Malcolm Cowley, *The Literary Situation* (New York, 1955), p. 241; Lawrence Lipton, "Disaffiliation and the Art of Poverty," *Chicago Review*, X (Spring, 1956), 53–79; and Kenneth Rexroth, "San Francisco's Mature Bohemians," *Nation*, CLXXXIV (Feb. 23, 1957), 157–62, are representative of a number of articles; Richard Eberhart, "West Coast Rhythms," *New York Times Book Review*, Sept. 2, 1956, p. 7.

5. Rexroth's article, which appeared in May, is "Disengagement: the Art of the Beat Generation," *New World Writing #11* (New York, 1957), pp. 28–41. Ferlinghetti discusses his trial in "Horn on *Howl*," *Evergreen Review*, I, no. 4, pp. 145–58; a fairly complete transcript of the trial appears in J. W. Ehrlich (ed.), *Howl of the Censor* (San Carlos, California, 1961).

6. Typical anthologies are Gene Feldman and Max Gartenberg (eds.), *The Beat Generation and the Angry Young Men* (New York, 1958); Seymour Krim (ed.), *The Beats* (Greenwich, Conn., 1960); and Elias Wilentz (ed.), *The Beat Scene* (New York, 1960). The studies referred to are Francis J. Rigney and L. Douglas Smith, *The Real Bohemia: A Sociological and Psychological Study of the "Beats"* (New York, 1961), and Lawrence Lipton, *The Holy Barbarians* (New York, 1959). Kerouac spoke at the Brandeis University seminar at Hunter College in 1958; Corso, Gins-

berg, and Orlovsky performed at Columbia University in 1959.

7. The phrase is spoken in *Go*, p. 122, by the character who represents Kerouac. In "The Philosophy of the Beat Generation," *Esquire*, XLIX (Feb., 1958), 36, Holmes attributes a similar statement directly to Kerouac.

8. I use the names "Jack" and "Dean" to avoid confusion. Kerouac's protagonist is Peter Martin in *The Town and the City*, Sal Paradise in *On the Road*, Leo Percepied in *The Subterraneans*, Ray Smith in *The Dharma Bums*, and Jack Duluoz in all other works. Kerouac's hero, absent from *The Town and the City*, is Dean Moriarty in *On the Road*, Leroy in *The Subterraneans*, and Cody Pomeray in all other works. The two are Gene Pasternak and Hart Kennedy in *Go*. Kerouac discusses this matter in prefatory statements to *Excerpts from Visions of Cody* and *Big Sur* and matches up some of the characters in a dramatis personae in *Book of Dreams*.

9. Prefatory statement to *Excerpts from Visions of Cody*.

10. Warren Tallman, "Kerouac's Sound," *Evergreen Review*, Vol. IV, no. 11, p. 167.

11. For some other uses of the childhood image see *Dharma Bums*, pp. 58, 62, 97, 142, 151.

12. "Origins of the Beat Generation," p. 42.

13. *Ibid.*, p. 79.

14. *Ibid.*, p. 32. The list continues with more details from the movies, pulps, and comics.

15. *Ibid.*

16. See, for instance, *Maggie Cassidy*, pp. 13, 23–24.

17. Norman Podhoretz, "The Know-Nothing Bohemians," *Partisan Review*, XXV (Spring, 1958), 306, 318.

18. Paul O'Neil, "The Only Rebellion Around," *Life*, XLVII (Nov. 30, 1959), 125.

19. See "The White Negro," *Dissent*, IV (Spring, 1957), 276–93. Reprinted in *Advertisements for Myself* (New York, 1959), pp. 337–58.

20. *Advertisements for Myself*, p. 465; Podhoretz, p. 314.

21. The dedication to Jack Kerouac in *Howl and Other Poems* (San Francisco, 1956) lists "eleven books written in half the number of years (1951–1956) — *On the Road*, *Visions of Neal* [*Cody*], *Dr. Sax*, *Springtime Mary* [*Maggie Cassidy*], *The Subterraneans*, *San Francisco Blues*, *Some of*

the Dharmas [*The Dharma Bums*], *Book of Dreams, Wake Up, Mexico City Blues,* and *Visions of Gerard*" (published titles given in brackets are speculation). Thus, only *The Scripture of the Golden Eternity; Tristessa,* which may have been excised from *On the Road; Pull My Daisy,* which is not really a book; *Lonesome Traveler,* much of which probably belongs to the 1951–56 period; *Desolation Angels;* and *Big Sur* are post-1956. Indeed, two of the last group may be the *San Francisco Blues* and *Wake Up* mentioned by Ginsberg.

Shapiro—Harvey Swados

1. Nona Balakian and Charles Simmons (eds.), *The Creative Present* (New York: Doubleday, 1963), p. xiv.

2. Irving Howe, *Politics and the Novel* (New York: Horizon, 1957), p. 21.

3. Harvey Swados, *A Radical's America* (Boston: Atlantic-Little, Brown, 1962), p. 174.

4. In Herbert Gold (ed.), *Fiction of the Fifties* (New York: Doubleday, 1959), p. 27.

5. *Radical Innocence* (Princeton: Princeton U. Press, 1961), p. 134.

6. N. Y. *Herald-Tribune Book Week,* Nov. 3, 1963, p. 17.

7. "The U.A.W. and Walter Reuther: Over the Top or Over the Hill?" *Dissent,* Autumn, 1963, p. 321.